Learning Mambo :
A Step-by-Step Tutorial to
Building Your Website

A well-structured and example-rich tutorial to creating
websites using Mambo

Douglas Paterson

PUBLISHING

BIRMINGHAM - MUMBAI

Learning Mambo : A Step-by-Step Tutorial to Building Your Website

First published: December 2006

Production Reference: 1131206

Published by Packt Publishing Ltd.
32 Lincoln Road
Olton
Birmingham, B27 6PA, UK.

ISBN 1-904811-62-0

www.packtpub.com

Cover Image by www.visionwt.com

Golf course photographs courtesy of Dennis Collet
(http://www.flickr.com/photos/35925794@N00/)

Note that Zak Springs Golf Club and its employees are fictitious. Any similarity to any existing golf club or individual people, either living or dead, is a remarkable coincidence.

Credits

Author

Douglas Paterson

Reviewer

Jayme Cousins

Development Editor

Louay Fatoohi

Assistant Development Editor

Nikhil Bangera

Technical Editors

Rajlaxmi Nanda

Viraj Joshi

Editorial Manager

Dipali Chittar

Project Manager

Patricia Weir

Indexer

Bhushan Pangaonkar

Proofreader

Chris Smith

Layouts and Illustrations

Shantanu Zagade

Manjiri Nadkarni

Cover Designer

Shantanu Zagade

About the Author

Douglas Paterson is a full-time development editor and part-time author for Packt Publishing. He is a Doctor of Mathematics and has over five years' experience of working on programming books across a number of different subjects. When not playing Resident Evil, he is probably thinking about playing Resident Evil, or recommending other people play Resident Evil.

He lives in Birmingham, England with his girlfriend, and his unusually hairy dog, Zak.

Many thanks to Dennis Collet for the kind use of his outstanding golf course photographs from `http://www.flickr.com/photos/35925794@N00/`. Also thanks to Jayme, who fought through illness to review the chapters. For the record, I believe he was already ill before starting to read. Thanks also to everyone at Packt involved with the book, for putting up with my random schedule and seeing to it safely into print. Finally, I would like to acknowledge the co-operation of Otto Simplex and everyone at Zak Springs Golf Club. I do hope they manage to catch the strange, shambling creature haunting their back nine.

About the Reviewer

Jayme Cousins started creating commercial websites once released from University with a degree in Geography. His lives have included marketing super-niche software, the overnight preparation of online content for the city newspaper, printing road names on maps, painting houses, and teaching College tech courses to adults. He currently lives behind a keypad in London, Canada with his wife Heather. They enjoy matching technology with real-world applications and people.

Jayme now provides web development consulting and technical support through his business, In House Logic (`www.inhouselogic.com`).

Table of Contents

Preface

Mambo is a free tool to manage the content of dynamic websites. To be more specific, Mambo is an open-source content management system, written in the PHP scripting language which is probably the most popular and straightforward language for creating websites and web applications. Mambo allows you to create a powerful, dynamic website with minimum effort and programming knowledge.

As one of the most popular applications on the Internet, Mambo has grown into a complex, powerful tool with an impressive range of features, and a loyal community of supporters.

This book targets the 4.6 release of Mambo, and it'll take you through creating an example website. The book is packed with practical steps for you to learn how to build your own website, beginning with a discussion of the requirements for the example site. The site unfolds as you progress through the chapters, learning more about Mambo.

What This Book Covers

Chapter 1 introduces us to Mambo, and what it can do for us. The chapter concludes with a discussion of the Zak Springs Golf Club example site, including a list of the requirements for the site.

Chapter 2 takes you through installing Mambo on a local machine for development purposes.

In *Chapter 3*, we take our first look at the main elements of a Mambo site, meeting menus, modules, components, templates, and having a quick look at the arrangement of content on a Mambo site. We also take our first steps in the administration area, and are introduced to the important concepts of publishing and access restrictions, and the HTML editor that will be used to enter most of the content on our site. We conclude the chapter with some basic changes to the front page of the site.

We start our Zak Springs example site in *Chapter 4* by creating a fresh, empty installation of Mambo. Then we look at the fundamental configuration options available to our site, such as setting up the system to send mail. We also take a look at the Private Messages component in this chapter, which provides us with a quick test of our mail server setup.

Chapter 5 continues the theme of site configuration, by looking at module and component management. These are the main functional elements of your site, and in the chapter we look first at module management, choosing how and where, and on which pages to display them. We walk through the creation of simple RSS and HTML modules from the administration area. To get modules and components into your Mambo system there is a "Universal Installer", that allows you to effortlessly install any kind of Mambo add-on. In the chapter we download and install a third-party calendar add-on. We also have a look at managing media, whereby you can upload resources such as images or documents directly onto the Mambo server, to be used in your content.

Chapter 6 is about menus and templates. Without menus, visitors would have great difficulty in finding anything on your site. A menu is made up of menu items. Menu items point to pages on your site, and also define how the target page should be displayed. In the chapter we walk through creating menu items. We also consider the different types of menu items that are available, and the consequences of these choices for the target page. Templates control the look and feel of your site. A new look for your site can be selected by assigning a new template. We look at the basics of managing templates in this chapter, including how to apply different templates to different pages on the site, so that your site does not look "uniform".

Your site is created for people to visit, and in *Chapter 7*, we walk through the basics of managing user accounts. Visitors are able to create an account on your site, and in this chapter, we look at what this process involves, and also at some other ways in which user accounts can be created. Users can be put into groups, to which permissions can be assigned. Different types of administrators can be created, as well as different types of front-end users. We look at all this, and create some of these different user types for our Zak Springs site.

In *Chapter 8*, we finally come to content management in Mambo. The Content component is the main content engine of Mambo, and in this chapter, we look at the organization of content into sections and categories. After creating some of these, we proceed to enter content and examine the options available for entering and controlling the display of our content. We also see how to create menu items that point to our pieces of content, and examine the different views of content provided by the menus, which can display the content as a single item, or list items with a different layout and format.

You can create special users that can add, edit, or publish content from the front end of the site, and in *Chapter 9*, we look at this. We also look at the publishing workflow this involves, whereby notifications are sent to various administrators to advise them of content submission that requires their approval. The notification system is not entirely straightforward, and we take a careful look at the process, and suggest some solutions to produce a more usable system.

In *Chapter 10*, we explore some more of the standard components that come with Mambo, and install and walk through the use of some third-party components for adding discussion forums, event scheduling, and a gallery of images.

In *Chapter 11*, we look at the details of customizing a template to produce a new-looking site. We start with one of the standard Mambo templates, and make changes to the stylesheet and background images to gradually produce a different-looking set of pages.

In *Chapter 12*, we look at the steps required to deploy our local Mambo site to a remote web server. We also tackle setting file-system permissions for various operations of Mambo to function properly on the remote server. We conclude with a look at restricting access to your administration area using HTTP Authentication.

Appendix A has a walkthrough of installing the XAMPP package, which provides a working installation of PHP, MySQL, and Apache, ready configured for you to test your Mambo site on.

What You Need for This Book

To use this book, you will need the latest version of Mambo, which can be freely downloaded from `http://mamboxchange.com/frs/?group_id=5`. The steps to get Mambo up and running are detailed in Chapter 2.

To get Mambo running, you need a working Apache/MySQL/PHP (AMP) environment on your local machine. The detailed installation of the latest XAMPP package is covered in Appendix A.

Conventions

In this book, you will find a number of styles of text that distinguish between different kinds of information. Here are some examples of these styles, and an explanation of their meaning.

There are three styles for code. Code words in text are shown as follows: "Once you've copied that folder, rename it to `mambo`, and we're ready to go."

A block of code will be set as follows:

```
[default]
$mosConfig_host = 'localhost';
$mosConfig_user = 'mamboer';
$mosConfig_password = 'mamb071Passv0rd';
$mosConfig_db = 'mambo';
$mosConfig_dbprefix = 'mos_';
```

When we wish to draw your attention to a particular part of a code block, the relevant lines or items will be made bold:

```
[default]
AuthName "Restricted Area"
AuthType Basic
AuthUserFile /home/.htpasswds
Require valid-user
```

Any command-line input and output is written as follows:

```
htpasswd -c "c:\passwords\mypasswords" secretuser
```

New terms and **important words** are introduced in a bold-type font. Words that you see on the screen, in menus or dialog boxes for example, appear in our text like this: "Once you've entered your database details here, click the **Next** button to continue."

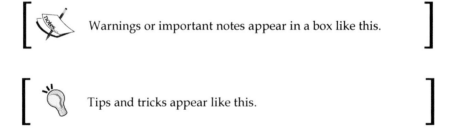

Warnings or important notes appear in a box like this.

Tips and tricks appear like this.

Reader Feedback

Feedback from our readers is always welcome. Let us know what you think about this book, what you liked, or may have disliked. Reader feedback is important for us to develop titles that you really get the most out of.

To send us general feedback, simply drop an email to feedback@packtpub.com, making sure to mention the book title in the subject of your message.

If there is a book that you need and would like to see us publish, please send us a note in the **SUGGEST A TITLE** form on www.packtpub.com or email suggest@ packtpub.com.

If there is a topic that you have expertise in and you are interested in either writing or contributing to a book, see our author guide on www.packtpub.com/authors.

Customer Support

Now that you are the proud owner of a Packt book, we have a number of things to help you to get the most from your purchase.

Downloading the Example Code for the Book

Visit http://www.packtpub.com/support, and select this book from the list of titles to download any example code or extra resources for this book. The files available for download will then be displayed.

The downloadable files contain instructions on how to use them.

Errata

Although we have taken every care to ensure the accuracy of our contents, mistakes do happen. If you find a mistake in one of our books—maybe a mistake in text or code—we would be grateful if you would report this to us. By doing this you can save other readers from frustration, and help to improve subsequent versions of this book. If you find any errata, report them by visiting http://www.packtpub.com/ support, selecting your book, clicking on the **Submit Errata** link, and entering the details of your errata. Once your errata have been verified, your submission will be accepted and the errata added to the list of existing errata. The existing errata can be viewed by selecting your title from http://www.packtpub.com/support.

Questions

You can contact us at questions@packtpub.com if you are having a problem with some aspect of the book, and we will do our best to address it.

1
An Introduction to Mambo

Mambo is a free tool to manage the content of dynamic websites. To be more specific, Mambo is an open-source content management system. While that sounds nice, it probably doesn't answer the basic question of what it can actually do for you.

Mambo allows you to create a dynamic website with minimum effort and programming knowledge. To get the most out of Mambo, a knowledge of web development will prove to be useful, but even then, Mambo is written in the PHP scripting language, which is probably the most popular and straightforward language for creating websites and web applications.

In this chapter, we will take our first look at Mambo, understand what it can do, find out where to go for further resources, and discuss the site we will create in this book.

What Mambo Can Do for You

Put simply, Mambo helps you create websites easily. It provides a back end, a control area if you like, from where you add content and information to the site, configure the way things look, and also create a front-end public view of your site.

Maybe you want to create a site about wine making, flowers, programming, zombie films, or even dinosaurs. Maybe you want to create a site to promote your business and your products. Whatever type of site you want to create, Mambo helps you to structure the site to hold information relevant to your visitors; be it news stories about a forthcoming zombie film, links to other zombie sites, or even a gallery of stills from zombie films.

The best bit is, you don't have to be an expert programmer to achieve all this. With only rudimentary knowledge of HTML, you can engineer a unique-looking Mambo website, packed with the information you want for your site and your visitors.

The Visitor Experience

The standard installation of Mambo provides many features for its visitors. Some of them are:

- Searchable content items (articles) organized into groups
- Ability of visitors to create an account on the site, and log in to their own personal area
- Ability of visitors to add comments about articles
- Straw polls
- A catalog of web links
- RSS syndication of your articles to share your content with other sites

That's just some of the features of the standard installation. With a couple of clicks, you can install new features on the site, such as:

- Discussion forums
- Galleries of images

Mambo can be customized and extended easily, and there is a huge range of third-party customizations and extensions to be found on the Internet. Any of these can add to the range of features your site provides.

The Management Experience

As a potential 'manager' of a Mambo site, as you read through the list of features above, you may think they sound rather attractive, but might also wonder how you will handle all of that.

Mambo provides a web-based management interface. You, as the manager of the site, visit the site and log in with a special super user, or site administrator, account. After this, from the comfort of your web browser, you run the show. You can:

- Add new information, edit, delete, or move existing pieces of information
- Control how the site will look
- Decide the features of the site
- Add media (documents, images, sounds) directly to the site
- Control what is displayed on the pages
- Control who is able to see what

In fact, you don't need to do all of this yourself. You can set up accounts for other people to take over the running of various parts of the site, maybe adding or checking content, or maybe just making sure everything runs smoothly.

The power and flexibility Mambo offers you to manage a complex website would be difficult to achieve without many, many hours of careful programming.

What Exactly is Mambo?

Mambo is a collection of PHP scripts that run on a web server, connect to a database, and display the retrieved data in a systematic way. In other words, Mambo is a data-driven PHP web application.

Mambo can be downloaded for free, and then installed to your local machine for testing and development. The files and the database can be uploaded to a web-hosting service, so that your site will be available to anyone on the Internet. There are even web-hosting services that offer Mambo installation at the click of a button.

Component-Based Architecture

Mambo is built around a 'core' set of functions, which perform mundane tasks such as selecting what part of the application the user should be shown, checking who the user is, and what they can do on the site. What makes Mambo exciting to the world is its support for components. These are extensions to the Mambo core, and provide the real functionality of your site. Mambo's support for managing content comes from the Content component, and there are components for displaying news feeds, discussion forums, and galleries among others. These extensions can be easily configured, and new extensions can be added to the system.

There is no shortage of third-party components on the Internet, and you can find a Mambo component for almost any imaginable purpose.

Templated Interface

The look of a Mambo site is controlled by a template. This is a collection of images, styles, and other resources, together with instructions that determine the layout of the page. A new template can be selected, and your site will be transformed immediately. In fact, you can even apply different templates to different parts of your site, so that your site can have different looks across different pages should you wish.

User and Permission Management

Mambo allows users to create their own account on the site, and takes care of boring details like making sure users can get a new password when they forget their current one. Pages on the site can be restricted so that only certain types of user get to see them, and also, certain users can be given certain permissions so that they can add or edit content themselves. Instead of you having to do everything yourself, you can set up other people to help with the running of the site.

Mambo as an Open-Source Content Management System

We used the expression 'open-source content management system' earlier in the chapter to describe Mambo. Let's take a closer a look at this term.

Open Source

Mambo is free, and it is also open source. After downloading Mambo, all the source code of the application is there in front of you. This means, if you are so inclined, you can dig around to see how it works, or check why something is not working as it should. Mambo is not a perfect application (what is?), and there will always be parts that do not work as they should. Since there are many people using Mambo on the Internet, the problem is usually spotted and the solution is posted on one of the Mambo forums.

Another advantage of having the source of the application (the code) available to you is that you can modify (hack!) it, or extend it in whichever way you choose.

Mambo is released under a license, the **GNU General Public License (GPL)**. The GPL bestows much freedom in the way that you can work with Mambo, but it also brings along some restrictions. The ins and outs of the GPL are pretty complex, and we aren't even going to attempt an in-depth discussion of the consequences of this. For more information about the GPL visit `http://en.wikipedia.org/wiki/GPL`.

The GPL should always be respected. The GPL is one of the cornerstones of the free software movement, which was set up to promote rights to use, modify, and redistribute computer programs. The upshot of the license is that Mambo will not be going away. Even if some future version of it were to become completely commercial, the existing code could be taken and modified to create a new version, also released with a GPL license.

Content Management System

We have spoken a lot about adding and editing 'information' on a website. A broader term for information here would be 'content'. To summarize our earlier discussions of Mambo, it allows you to manage the content of your site. In other words, it's a content management system.

According to Wikipedia, a **Content Management System (CMS)** is a 'system used to organize and facilitate collaborative creation of documents and other content' (`http://en.wikipedia.org/wiki/Content_management_system`).

Well, it is difficult to define content management system and avoid the words 'a system for managing content'!

You can think of a content management system as playing three roles:

- **Capturing** content
- **Maintaining** and **Organizing** content
- **Serving** content

Capturing the content is usually done by users entering data in forms in a web browser. This content is then stored in a database for later retrieval. Serving the content allows the right data to be selected, sorted, and ordered, and then displayed to the visitor in a coherent and consistent way.

Mambo achieves all of these. Users with special accounts can input content from either the administrative part of the site, or even the front end of the site. This content can be maintained and organized from the web-based administration interface by the site administrator. When a visitor requests a page from the site, Mambo will determine which content should be displayed and how it should be ordered. It then handles the output of the content, along with the rest of the page.

Getting Help in the Mambo Community

Mambo has a substantial user base. There is a large group of people who run Mambo sites, develop extensions to Mambo, and create visual customizations, among other activities. In addition to these people, there is also a team of developers that work on the Mambo code. All of this adds up to a vibrant community that pushes the product forward, helps to address the problems faced by people working with Mambo, and offers support and encouragement to users.

There are a number of sites dedicated to Mambo that contain a range of Mambo resources, such as add-ons, bug fixes and patches, tutorials, and so on. You will also find the option of paid support for Mambo, and since Mambo is such a popular and widespread application, it will not be difficult to find a PHP developer who has experience of working with Mambo.

Each of these sites is well worth a visit to see what they offer:

- `http://www.mamboserver.com`: This is the home of Mambo. This site is your first stop for news of the latest offerings from the Mambo community. Here you will also find links to the **Mambo Developers Network**, a list of Mambo developers worldwide, offering their products and services.

- `http://www.mamboxchange.com`: The MamboXChange. This is a recepticle for Mambo software that can be downloaded for free. In addition to being the home of a multitude of extensions for Mambo, it is also the place from where you will download the source of Mambo itself.

- `http://forum.mamboserver.com`: The Mambo forums. Here you will find many posts about problems encountered by Mambo users like yourself, along with tips and answers to solve the most common (and sometimes uncommon!) problems. If you find yourself with a problem, then the Mambo forums are a good bet to find a solution.

- `http://templates.mamboserver.com/`: This site provides a number of free Mambo templates you can download and use to give your site a different look.

Any of the Mambo sites will have links to other recommended Mambo sites. In addition to providing valuable resources and information, all these sites will give you a good idea of what it is possible to accomplish on a Mambo site.

Forks, the Mambo Foundation, and Joomla!

Mambo has had a rather chequered history in recent times. Mambo was originally created by an Australian company, Miro, `www.miro.com.au`, and an open-source version was released in 2002, under the name of "Mambo Open Source". Since then, Mambo has continued to be developed by a group of developers from around the world.

In August 2005, the Mambo Foundation was set up by Miro to govern the future direction of the product. The purpose of this foundation is "to provide support and protection for the development of the Mambo software system" (`www.mambo-foundation.org`).

However, following the setup of the Mambo Foundation, many of the core developers resigned from the project, and began to work on a new product based on the existing codebase of Mambo. In the world of open source, such a new venture is called a "fork". (Remember we said that the GPL means that the code can't go away? Well this is exactly the kind of thing that can happen!) The new product the developers began work on later became Joomla! (www.joomla.org). Both Mambo and Joomla! continue to develop, with the developers of each system having different views on the direction of the respective products.

Whatever the cause of the split, Mambo is still going strong, with the August 2006 release of version 4.6 being the first major new release in over two years.

Zak Springs Golf Club Website

We're going to create an example site, "Zak Springs Golf Club", as we move through the book. Rather than just arbitrarily adding features to an empty Mambo installation, we will see how the list of requirements described below translate into actual actions for configuring Mambo, and the kind of decisions that need to be made to complete the site.

Zak Springs Golf Club is a rather colorful client. Before we get started with Mambo itself, let's take a moment to understand the site we're going to build.

The Client

Zak Springs Golf Club is located near the Skull Mountains, and boasts two 18-hole golf courses, practice facilities, and extensive hospitality facilities. The Golf Club was recently bought by a mysterious businessman, Otto Simplex, who now runs the club as General Manager. The club had fallen into disrepair over the last 10 years, beset by a number of mysterious incidents and unfortunate accidents. The club was founded 12 years ago, built on land cheaply bought from the military, following the immediate and uncommented closure of the top-secret Nemesis Project. The history of the club is still evident today, since the tougher of the two courses is in fact called Nemesis. The other course is the Sinistra course. Both are now in excellent condition, and present a formidable challenge for even the lowest-handicap golfer.

The Club is looking to expand its membership, and welcome new members from a number of the large metropolises that skirt the Skull mountains.

The Club currently has no website, but Mr. Simplex views the site as key to recruiting new members to the club, and also providing a community for the members of the Club, many of whom live far from the club. In addition to securing new members, retaining the existing members is key to the growth of the Club, and Mr. Simplex feels that keeping the members remotely involved in the club, in addition to providing excellent service and facilities at the Club itself, will go some way to ensuring this.

The Club also has no dedicated IT support person, but the Assistant to the Club Secretary is regarded as the "go-to" person when there is a technical problem.

Staff

The senior staff of the Club are:

President

Otto Simplex

Administrative Staff

- General Manager: Marie Flame
- Club Secretary: Audrey Pores
- Assistant to the Club Secretary: Edgar Hooch
- Marketing Manager: Brad Visionary

Golf Staff

- Director of Golf and Club Professional: Neil Vortex
- Assistant Golf Professional: Dax Carew
- Head Green Keeper: Cuthbert Cutty Cuthbertson

Hospitality

- Executive Chef: Bunsen Honeydew
- Assistant Food and Beverage Manager: Betty Book
- Assistant Food and Beverage Manager: Chuck Spung
- Receptionist and Guest Relations: Mya Lop

Requirements

From detailed meetings with the clients, the following list of objectives and functionality of the site was arrived at. Note that none of these relate specifically to Mambo. Fitting these requirements into Mambo will be the challenge of the later chapters. It is entirely possible that not all of the requirements will be achievable within our first attempt at putting the site together.

Key Objectives of the Site

- Promote the club and its objectives
- Publish information to attract new players and members
- Provide online services to build community and retain members

General Functionality of the Site

- All content to be managed in-house without technical skills
- Intuitive and easy-to-use browser-based administration interface
- Multiple users with different permission levels and publication rights
- Consistent presentation for all content
- Site search facility
- Optimized for search-engine finding

Specific Functionality of the Site

- Categorized news publishing; course news, membership information, competition results
- Image gallery for showcasing holes on the courses
- Calendar for forthcoming competitions and other course events
- Discussion forum for members to interact
- Members-only areas
- Staff contacts
- Information on local accommodation and leisure partners
- Course scorecards
- Weblog for Club Professionals, offering equipment and game tips
- Weblog for Club President
- Newsletter
- Content for hospitality facilities
- Course rates
- Membership application forms, membership conditions, club rules
- Contact Details

Permissions and Privileges Required

- Administrative Staff to be able to publish and amend news items
- Hospitality staff to be able to publish and amend content for hospitality facilities
- Marketing Manager to be able to amend any content on the site
- Nominated member of Administrative Staff to have full control over site
- Ability to amend these permissions in future
- Club President to have full control over site

Curiously, that last requirement was added in handwriting by the president himself, and did not appear in any earlier document.

Might Have... One day

The Club President has an ambitious vision for the site. However, in the first version of the site, there are some things that we have postponed. Some of these include:

- E-commerce Features for the Professional's shop
- Online Handicap register
- Competition charts

This is a pretty extensive list of requirements to be going on with, so let's not hang around, since rumor has it that Otto Simplex is not a patient man.

Summary

This chapter has introduced Mambo. Mambo is an open-source content management system; you can also think of it as a free tool for managing the content of websites.

We looked at what Mambo offers in terms of a visitor experience, and also what this will mean for the person who is in charge of maintaining the site. Mambo has functionality to make site maintenance easy, and the site can be run from a web-based interface. We found out about the Mambo community, and where to go for help or further Mambo resources.

The chapter concluded with a quick description of Zak Springs Golf Club—the site we are going to create in this book.

We are ready to begin on this journey, so the next step is to actually get Mambo up and running.

2
Setting up the Development Environment

In this chapter we will cover how to install Mambo on a local machine running in an Apache/MySQL/PHP (AMP) environment. We will not cover the installation of AMP here; you can find a walkthrough of installing the XAMPP package in Appendix A. XAMPP is a free software package that includes PHP, MySQL, Apache, and much more, and is a quick way to get yourself a working AMP development environment.

Since in this chapter we are only dealing with creating a local installation for testing purposes, we shall postpone the coverage of how to deploy and set up Mambo on a remote web server until Chapter 11.

The steps to install and configure Mambo are simple:

1. Download and extract the Mambo files.
2. Copy the files to the web server root.
3. Step through the screens of the Mambo web installer.
4. Create another, less powerful database user to run the site under.
5. Remove the `installation` directory.
6. Test it out!

Let's get started.

Downloading Mambo

The latest version of Mambo can be downloaded from:

```
http://mamboxchange.com/frs/?group_id=5
```

There is a link to this page from the **Download Mambo** link on the homepage of the mambo website, www.mamboserver.com.

Mambo Lite and Complete

From version 4.6 of Mambo onwards, Mambo comes in two flavors, **Complete** and **Lite**. Mambo Complete is the full Mambo package, with all the standard components and templates already included. Mambo Lite is a cut-down version of the full Mambo package, intended for people who don't want all the features of Mambo straightaway. The Lite package lacks a number of the standard components and templates, but still has enough for you to run a functional Mambo site.

Importantly, Mambo Lite contains the **Content** component, which drives the content management functionality of Mambo, and is the main focus of this book. All the things included in Mambo Complete but not in Mambo Lite can be downloaded and installed from the MamboXchange site. So, you are not cutting yourself off from Mambo's full potential by installing the Lite version, but it does mean you will have to do some more work to get extra parts installed.

 In this book, we will work with the Complete package so that we can get a picture of everything that's available in standard Mambo.

If you choose to install and work with the Mambo Lite package, you will find that installation steps are identical.

You will find that you can download each package in a variety of compressed formats, like ZIP (.zip extension), GZIP (.tar.gz extension), etc. We will grab the ZIP file for the Complete package. It is a larger file than the GZIP version.

Extracting Mambo

Once you have downloaded Mambo, extract the contents of the Mambo ZIP archive to the hard drive.

If you don't have a tool for extracting the files, you can download an evaluation edition (or buy a full edition) of WinZip from www.winzip.com.

There are also free and powerful extracting tools such as 7-Zip (http://sourceforge.net/projects/sevenzip/) among others.

In the Mambo folder, you will find a number of subfolders; some of these include:

- components: Contains the PHP code for the components that will make up your Mambo site. Components are the essence of Mambo's operation. We will start looking at them once we've got Mambo installed!

- modules: Contains the PHP code for Mambo's modules. Modules are mini-functionality units and usually provide snippet views of components.

- mambots: Contains the PHP code for Mambo **mambots**. Mambots are "little" plugins that hook into various parts of the system, and perform various tasks like filtering or preparing output.

- language: Contains language files that allow the language of Mambo's interface to be changed.

- images: Contains images used in the display of the Mambo site. This is where images used in your pieces of content will go.

- templates: Contains the Mambo templates. The use of templates allows you to completely change the look of a Mambo site with a click of a button. Within each template folder is the CSS for that template, along with images used by it.

- includes: Contain the core code that powers Mambo.

- administrator: Contains code to power the administration area of your site.

Putting Mambo Files into the Web Server Root

In this book, we are going to use two installations of Mambo. The first will install the sample data, and will be accessed with the following URL, once we have installed Mambo:

```
http://localhost/mambo/
```

The second installation will be blank; it will have no sample data and we will work with this to create our example site, Zak Springs. This installation will be accessed via:

```
http://localhost/zaksprings/
```

For now, we'll concentrate on the first installation.

The first thing we need to do is to copy the folder containing the extracted Mambo files into our web server root directory (`\xampp\htdocs\` if you are using XAMPP). Once you've copied that folder, rename it to `mambo`, and we're ready to go.

> We will refer to the `mambo` folder in the web server root as the 'root of our Mambo installation'. Once the Zak Springs site is created, the `zaksprings` folder will contain its code and will be the root of that Mambo installation. The fact that we have two installations should not cause confusion.

Installing Mambo

Open up your web browser and navigate to `http://localhost/mambo/`. You should see the following screen:

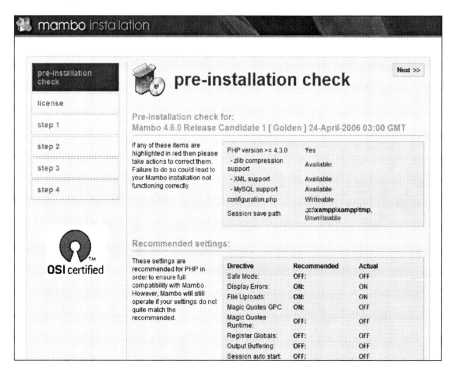

This first screen shows the status of a number of settings required to install Mambo. When a setting has a value that could prevent or compromise the Mambo installation, it is shown in red. If you scroll down the screen, you will see the write-access of the folders in the Mambo installation:

Directory and File Permissions:

In order for Mambo to function correctly it needs to be able to access or write to certain files or directories. If you see "Unwriteable" you need to change the permissions on the file or directory to allow Mambo to write to it.	administrator/backups/	Writeable
	administrator/components/	Writeable
	administrator/modules/	Writeable
	administrator/templates/	Writeable
	cache/	Writeable
	components/	Writeable
	images/	Writeable
	images/banners/	Writeable
	images/stories/	Writeable
	language/	Writeable
	mambots/	Writeable
	mambots/content/	Writeable
	mambots/editors/	Writeable
	mambots/editors-xtd/	Writeable
	mambots/search/	Writeable
	media/	Writeable
	modules/	Writeable
	templates/	Writeable

On your local machine, most of the settings in the **Directory and File Permissions** section will show as **Writeable**. This is not likely to be the same when you attempt to install Mambo on web-hosting server, since that will have different permissions. Some of Mambo's operations require write access to the filesystem, which means that PHP must have write permission to the filesystem. On a typical web server, PHP will have limited write access to the filesystem, but this is not a problem that we will likely experience on our local machines.

 Without distracting from the ongoing discussion, we will postpone the tackling of the write-access problem on the web server until Chapter 12, where we will discuss it in greater depth.

Everything looks fine on the pre-installation check, so go ahead and click the **Next** button. The next screen shows us the license agreement for Mambo. We have to check the box to accept the license agreement and click the **Next** button before we can continue:

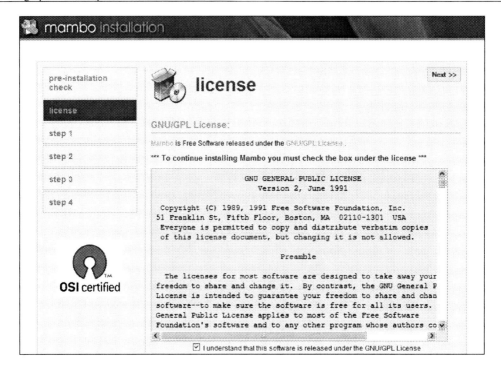

Database Setup

The third screen in the web installer is where we set up the details of our database.

We need to specify:

- The name of the server that the database is running on (usually **localhost** unless you know otherwise).

- A MySQL user account that will be used to access the database (usually **root** unless you know otherwise), and the password to go with this database user account. Many MySQL installations have the password left blank. If you don't know the password for the root account to MySQL, it's probably blank!

- The name of the database we want to create; by default it is **mambo**.

- A table prefix for all the tables in the database. This is something added to the front of the name of each table in the Mambo database, to make the table names a bit more unique. This means that the Mambo tables can live in a database along with another application (some web hosts may restrict the number of databases you are able to create) without the name of any table clashing with the name of a table from another application. We'll leave this at the default value of **mos_**.

There are three further options: **Drop Existing Tables, Backup Old Tables,** and **Install Sample Data. Drop Existing Tables** and **Backup Old Tables** are used if you are creating a new Mambo installation into a database that already has one. The third option, **Install Sample Data,** we will leave checked. This will install some sample information into our Mambo database, so that we've got things to look at as we take our first steps.

Once you've entered your database details here, click the **Next** button to continue. A dialog box will pop up checking if you've entered your settings correctly. If you think you have, click **OK**.

The next screen prompts you for the name of your Mambo site. This name will appear in the title of pages from the site, in the subject of emails sent from the site, and so on. We'll just enter **Mambo Site** for now. After entering the site name, click on **Next** to proceed.

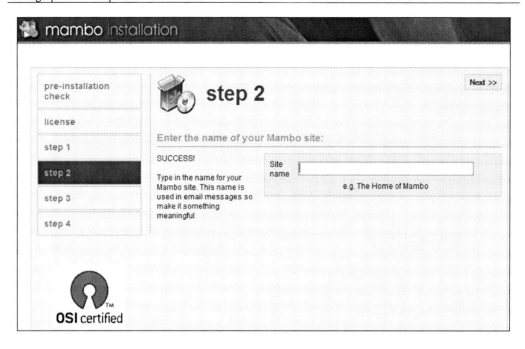

Site Details

The next step of the web installer is where you confirm the details of your site, and the details of a Super Administrator account. The Super Administrator is an account with ultimate power over your Mambo site, and will be used to do most of the configuration work on setting up the Mambo site.

The **URL** that will be used to access the site, and the **Path** on your machine to the Mambo installation are already provided for you.

You have to provide an email address for your Super Administrator account. Put your own email address into the **Your Email** field.

Next you have to provide a password for the Super Administrator account. The account is called **admin**, and it may be tempting to enter **admin** for the password. But bear in mind that you must remember to change it before you actually put your site live. One thing with Mambo is that the place for the administrators to log on is the same for virtually every Mambo site on the Internet, and if you've still got that Super Administrator account with the username of **admin** and the password of **admin**, then it won't take long before someone else has taken control of your site. It is, however, possible to change the name of this account later.

A random, strong, password is suggested for you. If you don't want to change that, make a note of it! If you do change the password, make a note of it!

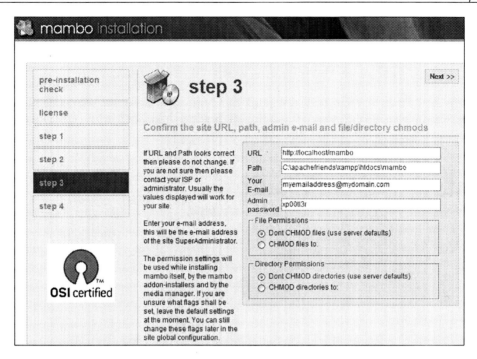

Once you've entered your email address and decided on the password, click **Next** to move on.

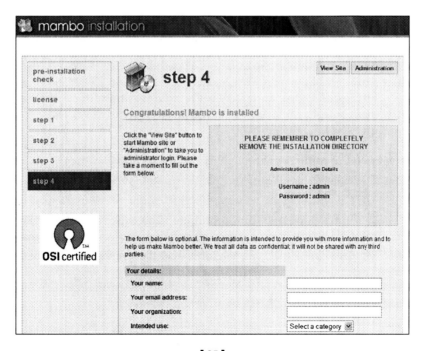

Your installation is complete. The name of the Super Administrator account and its password are displayed, along with a form for you to register your Mambo installation. This is not required, but will help to give the creators of Mambo a better idea of exactly what people are intending to do with the system.

You now have two choices: view the front end of the site from the **View Site** link, or have a roundabout way through the **Administration** link. We'll stick with the front end for now, so click the **View Site** link.

Testing the Installation

Finally, we are ready to start testing the installation.

Click the **View Site** link from the web installer, or enter the URL http://localhost/mambo/ into your browser. You should see the following screen:

Let's do as we're told, and delete the installation directory from our Mambo folder. In case there is some confusion with the term installation folder (after all, the Mambo folder is our installation), then look in the folder containing your Mambo files (in the root directory), and you will see that there is a folder called installation. This is the folder you will want to delete.

The reason you need to remove this folder is that it contains the pages for the installer we have just used. If somebody were to access these pages again, they could, in principle, reinstall your site!

If you want to reinstall Mambo at any point, you can simply copy the installation folder (it should still be where you extracted it to!) back into your working Mambo folder, delete the configuration.php file, and installation can begin again.

We'll soon see more about the significance of the configuration.php file. Instead of deleting the installation folder, you could rename it.

If you working on your live site, you should delete the `installation` folder rather than renaming it. If you rename it, someone could still access it and reinstall your site! Since we are working in a local development environment, this is not so much of a problem.

After deleting (or renaming) the `installation` folder, you should get your first taste of Mambo:

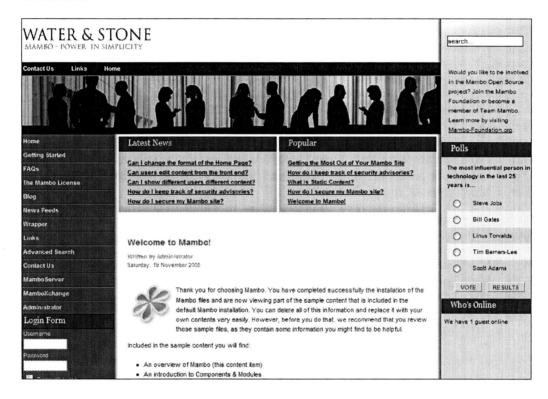

If this is what you see in your browser, then you can proceed further.

Creating a Database User

Now that things seem to be working fine, we will create a database user that can access *only* the Mambo database. This user is not a human, but will be used by Mambo to connect to the database while it performs its data-handling activities. The advantage of creating a database user is that it adds an extra level of security to our installation. Mambo will be able to work with data *only* in this database (in the

MySQL server), and no other. Also, Mambo will be restricted in the operations it can perform on the tables in this database. This will be useful in case our system is hacked by some outside evil.

The reason we did not do this before was that Mambo creates its own database, and creates tables in that. It requires a user account with a lot of privileges to do this kind of a thing. The `root` database account has the ultimate power, and can do this quite easily. Once the database is set up, the demands on the database in terms of creation are less, and so we do not really need this extra power on a regular basis. Thus we will switch to another user.

Also, we do it now so that we can assign privileges only to the Mambo database. Until the database is created, you can't really do that. Now that the database is created, it's an ideal time to switch to our less powerful, but still powerful enough, database user.

For our database work, we'll be using the **phpMyAdmin** tool. phpMyAdmin is part of the XAMPP installation (detailed in Appendix A), or can be downloaded from `www.phpmyadmin.net`, if you don't have it. phpMyAdmin provides a powerful web interface for working with your MySQL databases. If you're familiar with phpMyAdmin, or prefer to use the command line for working with MySQL, this section won't present any problems.

First of all, open your browser and navigate to `http://localhost/phpmyadmin/`, or whatever the location of your phpMyAdmin installation is.

We will need to create a username for our MySQL user to access the `mambo` database. Let's call our user `mamboer` and go with the password `mambopassword`. However, in order to add an extra level of security we will introduce some digits and some other slight twists into our password in order to strengthen it, and so use the word `mamb071Passv0rd` as our database-user password.

To create the database user, click the **SQL** tab in phpMyAdmin, and enter the following into the **Run SQL query/queries on database** textbox:

```
GRANT ALL PRIVILEGES ON mambo.* TO mamboer@localhost
        IDENTIFIED BY 'mamb071Passv0rd'
        WITH GRANT OPTION
```

Your screen should look like this:

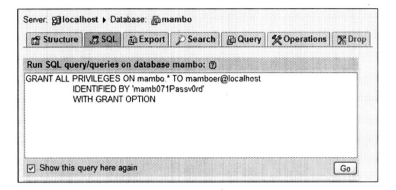

Click the **Go** button, and the database user will be created:

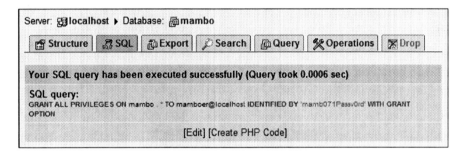

Switching to the New Database User

Now that the user is created, we'll make a quick modification to the Mambo configuration to use this MySQL user account.

Enter the URL http://localhost/mambo/administrator into your browser, and you'll be taken to the **login** page for the administrator area:

Here you need to enter the account details of the Super Administrator account that you created during the last step of the web installer. Enter the **username (admin)** and **password** (you did make a note if it didn't you!) and click the **Login** button.

You will find yourself in the Administrator area, also known as the back end of the site. From here you control your site. We'll talk more about this in the coming chapters. For now, select the **Global Configuration** option from the **Site** menu at the top of the page:

Click on the **Database** tab, and enter the details of the MySQL database user we just created in phpMyAdmin:

Click the **Save** button, and the configuration settings will be updated.

Now click the **Logout** link in the top right-hand side of the page, and you will be returned to the front end of the site.

We are ready to get started!

Still Having Problems?

If Mambo is still not working, and you have foll⟨
there is something wrong elsewhere, and it is lik⟨
scouring the forums at http://forum.mamboser⟨
many questions (and solutions) on installation (b⟨
servers) from users attempting to get their site ru⟨

okanagancomment.
ca

meladmin
miocene#223

LOG IN NAME
mel wilde
miocene #22

Summary

In this chapter, we have walked through the typical steps to install Mambo on a local machine running an AMP environment.

We looked at where you get Mambo from, and also considered the two flavors of Mambo that you can get: Complete and Lite. Lite is a cut-down version of Complete, but contains the main functionalities required to get a Mambo site up and running. We chose to install the Complete version, but if you went for the Lite version, then you can simply install all the missing features as you go. We will see how to do that as we progress.

Installing Mambo was straightforward; we extracted the downloaded files, and then copied them into a folder in the root of our web server. Browsing to that folder in our web browser brought up the installation wizard, which stepped us through the installation process.

We had to provide the details of our database server so that Mambo could connect to it and create the required database tables. We also had to provide the password for the Super Administrator account. As we will see, this account can be used to do anything on our Mambo site, so choosing a strong password, and keeping that password safe is very important.

The final step to installation is to remove a folder called `installation` from inside the folder containing the Mambo code. Once this folder has been removed, Mambo is ready for action.

We made one last change to the standard installation in this chapter; we created a new database user with access only to the Mambo database, and then re-configured to connect to the database using this account. This is a first step towards increasing the security of our Mambo site.

3
Your Frontpage

Mambo is set up and you're ready to get started. Before you can dive in, we need to .... actually, let's dive in. I like to follow Captain Kirk's approach, "fools rush in where angels fear to tread..." I'm not suggesting you're a fool, dear reader, the fact you are reading this book shows you to be a person of impeccable taste. However, diving in to make our first modifications to the site will give us a great chance to get introduced to many of the main concepts of Mambo, which you will explore in greater detail in the coming chapters.

In this chapter you'll familiarize yourself with a visitor's eye-view of the Mambo world, and then peer into the secret realm of the administration area. The Administration area is the "base of operations" for managing and controlling our Mambo site. Along the way, we'll make our first changes to the site, and edit the content displayed on the frontpage of the site, and also change the way the frontpage display is configured.

Your Mambo Site

Navigate to the frontpage of your site in your browser. For our newly installed Mambo site, this will be `http://localhost/mambo/`. You should be presented with the following screen, which we saw at the end of the last chapter:

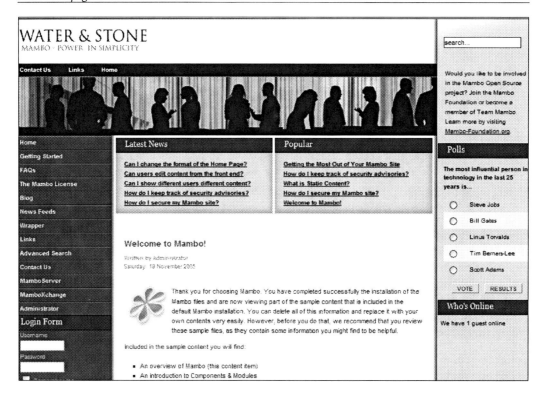

Considering that we've not really done anything, this is impressive. I'm sure you won't be able to resist clicking on some of these links and seeing what Mambo has in store for us. Of course, this isn't our site; everything that you see on the page comes from the Mambo example database, and I doubt that you plan to create a site that has the same content as this. For now, it gives us something to see and interact with to get a better feeling of how Mambo works.

Rest assured that over the next few chapters things will really start to heat up as we begin the creation of our new site.

Let's first talk about what we can see on the frontpage.

At the top, there is a site logo, a horizontal navigation menu, and a site banner image, often referred to as the masthead:

The page body begins underneath this header. You can see that the layout of the body essentially consists of three columns with a big chunk of information in the middle column. The page layout of a Mambo site need not always look this; the arrangement of the elements, the choice of color, text styles, and images is controlled by the template. A different template can be selected for the site, and immediately, the look and feel of your site is changed.

Menus

The horizontal navigation menu at the top of the page is an example of a Mambo menu:

As you would expect, a menu in Mambo is there to provide navigation for the visitor. On our frontpage there are three menus displayed:

- Top menu
- Main menu
- Other menu

The Top menu is the horizontal navigation menu we have just seen. It provides the visitor with quick access to what are considered the most important parts of the site.

The Main menu (located in the left-hand column) is the key navigation element of a Mambo site:

You will be familiar with this type of menu from almost every website that you have visited. This menu shows the main destinations within the site. The **Home** link is always found on a Mambo main menu, and returns you to the frontpage of the site, or the "homepage", however you want to call it.

Sometimes, when you visit certain pages (the **FAQs** page for example), the menu entry for that page will expand to show a list of further pages within that part of the site:

The **Other menu** (that is what it is called in Mambo; it's not just that I couldn't think of a name for it) contains other links. Currently, it is found under the Main Menu, and here it contains links to the main Mambo sites, and also a link to the Administrator area of our site.

 One thing to note with Mambo is that the Main Menu, your primary navigation object, does not automatically fill up with links to different pages on your site. After creating a page or piece of content on your site you will need to add a link to one of these menus for the visitor to find it.

However, it would be absurd if every page on your website had to appear in one of these menus. If you had a large site, your menus would become massive and also cease to be useful to the visitor. As we will see, Mambo can automatically display lists of pages that come under the current page that you are viewing.

 There is a fourth menu, the User Menu, but you can't see it on your page at the moment. It is only displayed once a visitor has logged into their user account. We'll see more of this menu in Chapter 7.

Modules

The menus that we have just seen are actually examples of a Mambo **module**. Modules in Mambo are little nuggets of information, which are scattered across the page, at the sides or above the main part of the content. They are similar to the sidebar blocks of information in a newspaper, providing weather information, brief headlines, and other snippets of information related to the main stories in the newspaper.

The menu modules for example provide navigation, linking to other parts of the site, while other modules provide a report or summary of the content that is available either on your site or, possibly, on another site. Typically, many modules are displayed on a single page.

On the frontpage, in addition to the menu modules, we can see the **Latest News** and **Popular** modules:

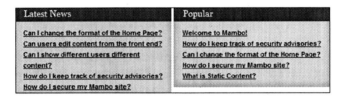

These two modules appear in the middle of the page, above the main page content. The **Latest News** module displays the titles of the most recently posted articles, and the **Popular** module displays the titles of the most viewed articles.

On the left-hand side of the page, under the **Main Menu** and the **Other Menu**, is the **Login Form** module:

This module presents a form for visitors to enter their login details, and then click the **LOGIN** button. If they don't have an account on the site, there is a **Create one** link to create an account. You will notice the **Password Reminder** link, with which (forgetful) users can be sent an email reminding them of their password. This is more evidence of how Mambo will take care of the tedious little details that are part and parcel of managing a sophisticated website.

If this module were to be removed from your pages, it would of course make it more difficult (but not impossible) for visitors to log in. If you click some of the links in the Main menu, then you will notice that the **Login Form** module does not show on all pages; in fact, it is only shown on the frontpage.

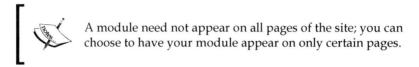

A module need not appear on all pages of the site; you can choose to have your module appear on only certain pages.

You will notice a commonality to the module display; there is a title bar, followed by the body of the module. However, not all modules need to look like this. The **Search** module (by default at the top of the right-hand column of the page) has no title bar:

Each module is configurable from the administration area as we'll see in the coming chapters. One thing that can be configured is whether or not to display the title of the module. The ability to configure each individual module like this means that there can be some variety on your page.

Components

See the bit right in the middle of the frontpage? That's the output of the current component.

Mambo is a component-based system. Each component is like a mini website in itself, performing different tasks and working with different types of content. The Mambo 'core' provides a central mechanism for handling these components, so that they work together sharing data and user information, and ensuring a consistent look and operation throughout your site. In short, the components define the functionality of your site.

The good thing with Mambo is that you can add and remove components to your heart's desire, selecting the best range of features to suit your site and its visitors. We will discuss the standard Mambo components over the next few chapters, but they are only the tip of the Mambo iceberg. There are numerous third-party components that can be downloaded and installed, covering a massive range of activities. The choice of available components is something that makes Mambo such an appealing system.

When viewing a page on a Mambo site, the component currently in play can be determined by looking at the URL of that page. For example, click on the **Getting Started** link, and the page will have a URL like this:

```
http://localhost/mambo/index.php?option=com_content&task=
category&sectionid=4&id=16&Itemid=27
```

The part of the URL after the ? character is the query string. The query string contains variables that are separated by the & character. In the above URL, the query string variable option has the value com_content. Mambo switches between components according to the value specified in the option query string variable.

Within a single component there are typically a number of different activities to be done, and the other query string variables indicate to the system which of these activities the visitor wants to perform. They also identify which item of data should be displayed. For example, on the **Getting Started** page, the URL is:

```
http://localhost/mambo46b1/index.php?option=com_
content&task=category
&sectionid=4&id=16&Itemid=27
```

Here, the task variable (which has the value category) is indicating that a list of the items in a "category" should be displayed, with the other variables specifying more information about which "category" is chosen.

The output of the component being currently viewed is displayed in the middle of the web page, and is generally the central focus of a page on a Mambo website.

The visitor isn't particularly aware of which component is being presented to them; as the visitor clicks links on the various menus and travels to different pages, Mambo will select the required component and display it to them.

Templates

The way the page has been laid out is not fixed in Mambo. The look of the page, the organization of where the modules sit, the colors, spacing, background images used, and so on, are all controlled by the **template**. Mambo allows you to select a new template, and immediately, the look of your site will be transformed.

In Mambo, there is no reason why the same template has to apply to all pages; you can assign a different template to certain pages on your site.

The default template, **Water and Stone**, looks OK (though a bit too much gray I'm sure you will agree), but there are countless other templates that you can find on the Internet, both free and commercial. You can download and install these, and give your site a completely new look. There are also a number of variations on the **Water and Stone** template that ship with Mambo itself.

Of course, there is no reason why you can't create your own template, or if you feel less bold, make some customizations to an existing template. We'll talk more about this in Chapter 11.

Viewing Site Content

Your site isn't just there to display little modules around the sides of the pages. It exists to display content to visitors, so, let's have a look at some content in Mambo. Click the **FAQs** link, and you'll see this in the middle of the page:

Although there is information here, what you are seeing isn't actually a piece of content, it's the details of a section. Mambo uses sections to organize your content into more manageable groups, and the text you can see displayed under the **Frequently Asked Questions (FAQs)** title is the section description.

Underneath the section description is a list of categories within the **FAQs** section. Categories are a further refinement of your content into groups within the sections. We'll talk more about this hierarchy of content when we come to study it in more detail in Chapter 8.

We'll click on one of the categories to see what items are held under there. Click the **Mambo and Security** link and you'll see this when the page reloads:

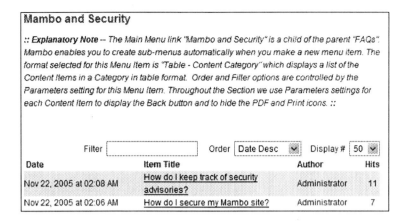

The main text we see here is the category description, the **Mambo and Security** category in this case. Underneath the description is a list of content items within this category. You can see the date the content item was created, its title, its author, and the number of times the content has been read.

Above the list of content items is a toolbar for filtering or sorting the list. If you select a new way to order the list from the **Order** drop-down box, the page will be reloaded with the new ordering of the list. The **Display #** drop-down box allows you to control the number of items displayed in the list. If there are more items than you want displayed, the items will be grouped into pages, and links will appear to take you to particular pages to see the items there.

Click the **How do I keep track of security advisories** link and we will finally see a piece of content!

That's actually a rather disappointing story, I have to confess.

In this short tour, we have seen that Mambo content is organized first into sections, which in turn contain categories. The actual pieces of content, the content items, belong to the categories. Content items do not belong to sections directly.

The good news is that we have traversed the content hierarchy to arrive at this item. There is no reason that you need to have your content "nested" like this on your site, Mambo's flexibility is too great to restrict you like that.

Looking at the content itself, you can see the title of the item in the large font (**How do I keep track of security advisories?**), followed by the text of the item (**Visit the Forums regularly and subscribe to the Mambo Security Announcements mailing list**).

Clicking the envelope graphic to the right of the content title pops-up a little window that allows you to enter details of someone you'd like to email the story to. It is possible to configure different elements to appear here; for example, there can be icons for creating a PDF copy of an article, or a printer-friendly version of it.

Note that the **Back** link at the bottom of the item has exactly the same effect as clicking the **Back** button on your browser; it takes you back to the last page you were looking at in the browser. It does not necessarily move up in the content hierarchy. This is similar to the experience when using Windows Explorer to view files on your hard drive; you can click the **Back** button to return to the folder just viewed, or you can click the **up one** button to take you to the folder containing the folder you are currently viewing.

Throughout all of this activity, if you were keeping an eye on the URLs of the pages you were looking at, you must have noticed that all of them have the value of **com_content** for the option query string variable, indicating that all of this is being done through the Content component. The Content component is the main content management engine of Mambo.

Pieces of content entered into the Content component have a fixed format. They have a title, some introductory text and then some main text. (The content item that we just saw in fact has only the introductory text and no main text!) With this format, a piece of content can be thought of as an article or story. We will often use the term article when talking about an item from the Content component. As you can see, we would otherwise end up using the word content too many times in our sentences!

This introduction to content in Mambo has also given us an idea of the administration tasks that lie ahead. We'll have to organize our content into sections and categories, manage these, and then get down to actually putting some content into the system.

Becoming the Administrator

You've had a quick play with the front end of the site, the part of the site that a standard visitor will get to see. Now it is time to enter an area that only a privileged few will be able to enter, the administration area. The administration area is your operational head quarters for actually controlling your Mambo site.

To start the journey, click the **Administrator** link in the **Other Menu**:

You will be taken to the administration login panel:

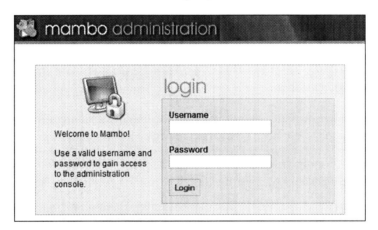

You will need to enter the administrator username and password that you created in the previous chapter, and then click the **Login** button to pass over to the other side: the administration area of your site.

Provided your credentials match and your identity is confirmed, you will get your first taste of the administration area:

Take a good look at the administration area; it will become like a second home to you as you manage a Mambo website. You are now the Administrator of your Mambo website, in fact, the SuperUser.

Like the front end of your site, the administration page has some notable elements. The first of these (under the administration banner) is the menu bar.

This menu bar contains a drop-down menu with links to the various administrative functions:

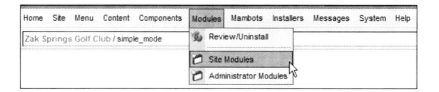

Mambo has many administrative functions, and organizing them into a familiar drop-down menu like this makes everything more manageable. One useful link is the **Home** menu entry on the administrator drop-down menu bar. That returns you to the page you are viewing at the moment, the "homepage" of the administration area.

On the right of the menu bar you can see the number of private messages waiting for you, the number of online users, and also a link to log out of the administration area.

Underneath the menu bar is a box for information rather like the navigation box in your browser. Here you will see a "path" to your current administration function.

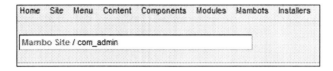

To the right of this information box is the toolbar. Currently there is only one item on that toolbar, an icon for help. When we start doing things, more icons will appear on that toolbar.

Below that, is the main part of the page, the control panel.

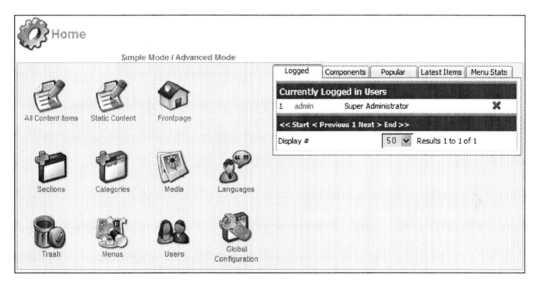

The control panel has two modes, **simple** and **advanced**. The default mode is advanced, and shows a healthy number of icons in the panel. Clicking the **Simple Mode** link restricts the number of icons in the panel. With the advanced mode and its larger range of icons in the panel, you get access to a broader range of administrative actions.

Note that each icon in the control panel is a clickable link. An advantage of the control panel over the administration menu is that you can right-click on the icons in the control panel, and open the link in a new tab or window (depending on what your browser allows). This means that you can be working on different parts of the administration area in different tabs or windows, and perform different tasks without having to go back through the menu structure to get there.

On the right of the control panel is a tabbed element with some quick links.

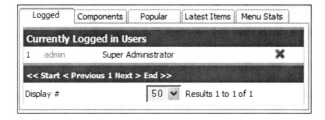

The first tab shows the list of users currently logged onto the site (and paginated so that you don't have a massive list if your site is busy), and other tabs show links to the most popular or recent articles, and links to further administrative actions. This provides yet another way to get at different parts of your site quickly.

Previewing your Site

The first function of the administrator menu bar we'll look at is site preview, from **Site | Preview | In New Window**.

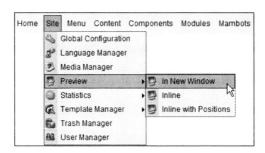

Of the three options, the first one, **In New Window,** displays the front end of your site in a new browser window. You will find yourself using this feature often to check your site as you make changes to it from the administration area.

The other two preview options, **Inline** and **Inline with Positions**, display the front of your site as a frame within your current browser window. With these options, as soon as you click on another function in the administration area, this will replace your preview of the site in your browser.

Managing the Frontpage

For the articles displayed on the frontpage of the site, their order and arrangement is controlled from the **Frontpage Manager**. This is accessed from the **Content | Frontpage Manager** option of the administrator menu bar. Selecting this option brings you to the **Frontpage Manager**:

First of all, you will notice that more icons have appeared at the right-hand end of the toolbar. You can use these icons to perform operations on a group of items listed in the **Frontpage Manager** control panel. Each item has a checkbox, where you check the items you want to act on, and then click on the icon in the toolbar to perform the action on this set of checked items. To act on all the items in one go, you can check the box in the title bar of the table to select all the items shown in the table.

The **Frontpage Manager** page shows the list of articles that will be displayed on the frontpage of the site. For each of these articles, the title and some other properties are listed. What the **Section** and **Category** properties represent should be familiar from our earlier discussion of sections and categories. There is also a column that shows the name of the **Author** of the article.

There are also drop-down boxes to filter the list of articles by section, category, or author. Also, you can enter some text into the **Filter** text box to show only articles that match the text you typed.

The remaining properties (**Published**, **Reorder**, **Order**, and **Access**) give us a good opportunity to introduce some very important concepts of a Mambo site: publication, ordering, and access restrictions.

Publishing Content

If everything that was entered into Mambo was always displayed on the site, this could lead to problems. Perhaps you have written an article to announce the imminent release of your new, top-secret, world-beating product, but it's not quite ready yet, and you don't know the exact date when it will be ready. Obviously, you don't want this displayed on your site celebrating the release of something that isn't actually available yet.

Displaying an article on the site is known as "**publishing**" the article. You can choose to enter the details of an article and not publish it, schedule it to be published at a later date, or unpublish an article, removing it from the site, but not deleting it.

The publication state of an article on the frontpage can be seen by the graphic in the **Published** column.

Published	✓
Unpublished	✗

If you hover the mouse cursor over the graphic in the **Published** column, more information about the article's publication state is displayed:

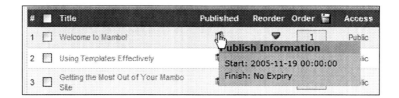

Publishing is not a concept restricted to articles in Mambo. Being published should actually be interpreted as "available on the site"; so with that in mind, it makes sense that things like modules can be published or unpublished, effectively activating or deactivating them on the site. The published property is one that you will see a lot in Mambo, across a whole range of elements, not just articles.

We can click the graphic in the **Published** column to toggle the publication state of an item. For example, unpublish the second article, then preview your site in a new window (from **Site | Preview | In New Window** on the administrator menu bar) and you will see that the **Using Templates Effectively** article can no longer be found on the frontpage, and the other articles have "moved up" to take its place. (That's an unusual task—being asked to look for something isn't there!)

You can publish single items by clicking the graphic as we did above, or you can publish or unpublish a group of items by checking their boxes in the control panel, and clicking the **Publish** or **Unpublish** icon in the toolbar:

Ordering Lists

Whenever you have a list of content items, you will probably want them displayed in a particular order. Possibly some are more important than others and you'd like these at the top of the list to catch the eye of your visitors.

Ordering also applies to things like menu entries; you don't really want the **Home** link on your main navigational menu to appear in the middle of the other links as this would rather frustrate your visitors, so being able to control the order in which things are displayed to the visitor on a page is useful. Of course, you might want to offer the visitor the option to reorder the display for their own taste, but you do want to make sure that your lists are ordered to your satisfaction.

There is a **Order** column in the table in the **Frontpage Manager** control panel. The number in this column determines the rank of that item, with the lowest ranking item displayed first in a list, and then the next highest rank and so on. It is easy to reorder items. To move an item up, simply click the up arrow in the **Reorder** column and the item will swap positions with the one above it in the list. Clicking the down arrow will swap the item's position with the one below it in the list.

In this way, you can move items up and down your frontpage.

Note that although there are supposed to be six articles displayed on the fisrt page of the frontpage (according to the table in the Frontpage Manager control panel), you didn't see all of them on the frontpage. The first article, **Welcome to Mambo!**, was displayed prominently, with the next two articles, **Using Templates Effectively** and **Getting the Most out of Your Mambo Site** displayed underneath. Only the titles of the three remaining stories could be seen, underneath these first stories.

Restricting User Access

Security in your Mambo site controls who can do what in a particular place. There are two fundamental problems of security here:

- **Authentication**: Deciding if the user is who they claim to be
- **Authorization**: What that user is able to do when browsing the website

Mambo solves the authentication problem with user accounts. It authenticates users (when necessary) by asking for a username and password combination.

Mambo solves the authorization problem by classifying the status of the visitor to your site into one of the following:

- Public: Any visitor to the site. Until a visitor registers and logs in, he or she has no identity and is simply a member of the public.
- Registered: Visitors with a user account who have logged in with a valid username and password.
- Special: This is a Registered User who belongs to a group that has certain front-end "modification" permissions. Members of these groups are able to add content, edit content, or even publish content directly to the site. We'll talk more about these groups in Chapter 7.

Anybody browsing the site falls into one of these categories, and there are many opportunities within Mambo to restrict access to content to one of these "levels". These restrictions, or 'permissions' if you like, rather than being assigned on an individual user basis are assigned to one of the above categories of users. In this way, access to parts of your site can be restricted and these restrictions can be easily managed.

Restricting access, so that only visitors from a particular group can view certain content, is commonplace in Mambo.

The current access level of a particular article can be seen in the **Access** column of that article. You can click the column to toggle between the three values we mentioned above.

For example, it is easy to make a content item accessible only to registered users of the site. To make **Need Help with Mambo?** accessible only to registered users, simply click its **Access** column until it says **Registered**. After that, preview the site in a new browser window, and you will see that that article is no longer seen on the frontpage, well, not by you anyway!

With a click (well, a couple of clicks!) of your mouse, you have already designated an item of content as being viewable only to people who actually have an account on your site. On the downside, since we don't have any user accounts set up you can't actually see it yet!

Editing an Article

Now we'll take our first steps towards editing content in Mambo. We'll change the text in the **Welcome to Mambo!** article; you can rewrite it completely if you feel inclined. To do this, from the **Frontpage Manager**, click on the title of the **Welcome to Mambo!** article, and you will be taken to the **Content Item: Edit** screen:

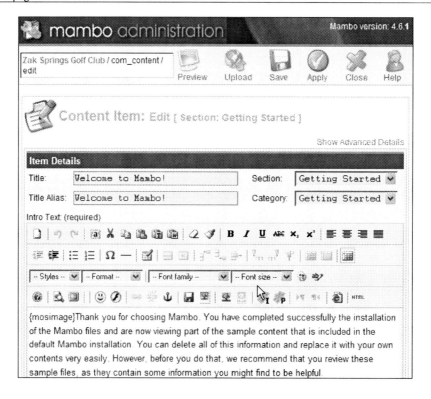

Here you can see the details that make up the content item: its **Title**, **Title Alias**, and the **Intro Text**. Scroll down your screen a bit further and you will see the **Main Text** field.

You can also see the section and category that this article belongs to in the **Section** and **Category** drop-down boxes.

You will also notice that a number of new icons have appeared in the toolbar: **Preview**, **Upload**, **Save**, **Apply**, and **Close**.

- The **Preview** icon displays the article in a pop-up window similar to how it would appear on the site. Note that the preview actually displays the current version of the article you are working on, including the changes you have made since you started editing and have not yet saved.

- The **Upload** icon allows you to add a file to the Mambo file storage. We'll skip past that for now, and think about the **Save**, **Apply**, and **Close** icons.

- The **Save** icon stores your edits in Mambo, updating the article. After it has finished saving, you are returned to the previous menu (the **Frontpage Manager** in this case).

- The **Apply** icon also saves your changes, but keeps you in the Edit screen. This can be useful if you are making a lot of changes, and want to save as you go.
- The **Close** icon cancels all your edits and returns you to the **Frontpage Manager**.

To see the importance of these icons, click the **Back** button in your browser to see the **Frontpage Manager** again. This time, you will notice a padlock icon next to the **Welcome to Mambo!** article.

This padlock icon indicates that this article has been "checked out".

You can Check Out Any Time, But You can Never Leave

When you begin to edit an item, it gets checked out. When an item is checked out, it can't be worked on by another administrator or "editor", and also, certain operations cannot be performed on the item by you until you have checked it back in.

Since the padlock icon sits on top of the checkbox to select the item for moving, copying, or deleting, these cannot be done until you have checked the item back in, and the padlock vanishes.

We've seen that leaving an item in the middle of editing leaves it checked out. To check the item back in, you will need to either use the **Save** or **Close** icons on the **Content Item: Edit** screen to terminate your editing session. Clicking the **Apply** icon will save your changes but will keep the item checked out to you.

 Another restriction on a checked-out item is that it cannot be published while it is checked out.

You can imagine that this could lead to lots of items being checked out all over your site when you have started work on them, but then decided to do something else without first using **Save** or **Close**. To take care of this, there is a feature to check in any item on the site that is currently checked out. This is done with the **System | Global Checkin** option on the administrator menu bar. The **Global Checkin** feature trawls the database looking for anything marked as checked out, and proceeds to check it in.

In the same way that the concept of "publication" applies to parts of Mambo beyond articles, so the "check out" concept also applies beyond simply editing articles. Many Mambo components use checking out to protect the "thing" you are working on. When you begin editing something from one of these components in the administrator interface, that element is marked as checked out in the Mambo database, and the same restrictions apply as when editing articles. Also, these elements will be checked in by the **Global Checkin** feature above.

Now that we've encountered checking in and out, click the title of the **Welcome to Mambo!** article again and let's get back to editing it.

Editing with the HTML Editor

Under the article details is the HTML editor for working with the article content:

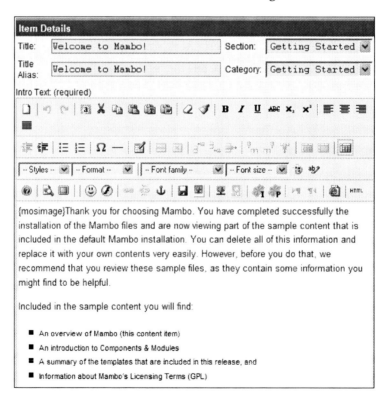

The HTML editor makes adding your article text easier, providing an interface similar to that of Microsoft Word, Wordpad, and so on.

For example, you can format your text in bold or italics, add an underline, or select a style from the **Styles** drop-down box. You can also add bullets, numbered lists, and other visual styles.

If you like, you can edit the HTML source by clicking the **HTML** button, and click the **Update** button when you're finished to return to the HTML editor.

 Note that the HTML editor is not part of the Mambo Lite package.

Adding Images

There are two ways in which you can make use of images in your content. The first allows you to add an image when you know its URL, and we'll look at that here.

The second way allows you to upload an image to the server directly, and put that into your content using the `mosimage` mambot. We'll see more of that in the coming chapters.

If you know the URL of the image you want to add, you can add it by clicking the **Insert/edit image** button:

A dialog pops up, which allows you to enter the URL where the image can be found, and also specify things like the image border and its size, among others. After you enter the URL into the **Image URL** field, click in one of the other fields, and the image will be displayed in the **Preview** pane:

Clicking the **Insert** button adds the image into your content:

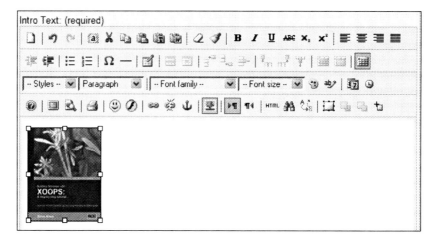

Click the image to select it, then click the **Insert/edit image** button again, and you can edit the properties of the image, such as setting a border, or setting the style from the **Appearance** tab. Here we set the **Style** of the image to give it a dashed border. The information we use here is the CSS (Cascading Stylesheet) syntax for setting a border:

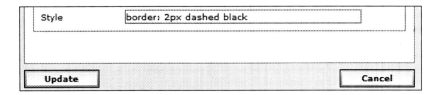

Click **Update**, and our image is modified:

Cascading Stylesheets allow you to format your HTML in different ways. You can find more examples of CSS at `http://www.w3schools.com/css/css_examples.asp`.

Adding Links

Adding a link to your content is straightforward. Simply select the text for the link:

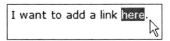

Then the link icons will become active in the editor:

Click the left-hand of the above icons, the **Insert/edit link** button, and a dialog will pop up into which you can enter the URL for the link:

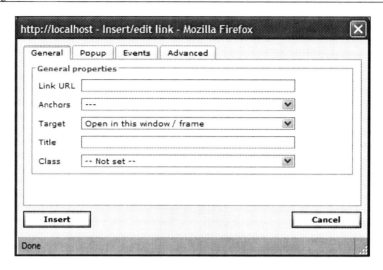

You enter the URL into the **Link URL** field and click **Insert**, and the text you selected will be made into a link:

If you want to edit the link, click on it, then click the **Insert/edit link** button again. From the **Insert/edit link** dialog, you can modify other properties of the link, such as the window in which the link will open from the **Target** option.

Note that if your URL does not begin with **http://**, then by default, the editor will convert the URL into an absolute URL with **http://<server>** added to the front. This means if you were trying to link to a page on your site, it will have the current server hardcoded into the link. If you were working locally before deploying to a remote server, you would find that your links still point to the local machine! You can turn off this feature from the configuration of the HTML editor, which you find under **Components | MOStlyCE Admin**. There are a number of configuration settings that can be made here, including turning off this feature to **Convert Absolute URLs**:

The **Insert/edit link** dialog allows you to specify a huge number of options for your link if desired, including a popup to display when the link is clicked.

Email Addresses, Spam, and Mambots

Instead of entering a URL into the **Link URL** field of the **Insert/edit link** dialog, you can use **mailto:** followed by an email address to produce a link that will open the user's email client when clicked, ready to send a mail to that specified email address. Including email addresses like this in page output is a notorious source for "spam harvesters", who collect such email addresses and add them to mailing lists for rather undesirable mails.

However, Mambo comes to your rescue here. If you create a **mailto:** link in this way, say for the email address doug@packtpub.com, Mambo will include something like this in the HTML of the page, which is almost impossible for a spam harvester to decipher:

```
<script language='JavaScript' type='text/javascript'>
<!--
var prefix = '&#109;a' + 'i&#108;' + '&#116;o';
var path = 'hr' + 'ef' + '=';
var addy78528 = 'd&#111;&#117;g' + '&#64;' + 'p&#97;cktp&#117;b' +
'&#46;' + 'c&#111;m';
var addy_text78528 = 'd&#111;&#117;g';
document.write( '<a ' + path + '\'' + prefix + ':' + addy78528 + '\'>'
);
document.write( addy_text78528 );
document.write( '<\/a>' );
//-->
</script>
```

Mambo keeps you safe like this through the **Email Cloaking** mambot. Mambots appear every so often in Mambo; they are hooked into various parts of the system and perform a single task, in this case formatting some output. When Mambo wants to display some content, it sees what "content" mambots are plugged in, and passes them the content for some processing. The Email Cloaking mambot for example looks for any HTML of the form `<a href=mailto:` (which would be an email link), and processes that into something like the form above.

You have already seen some other mambots in action. This **Write Comment** link is produced by a mambot, and can be seen under some of the content items:

Write Comment (0 comments)

Last Updated (Nov 23, 2006 at 08:49 PM)

Read more...

Controlling Article Display on the Frontpage

Remember we said you can control how many articles are displayed on the frontpage? Well, let's see you try to find the function to change that in Mambo. It's not done from the **Frontpage Manager**; that only manages the articles on the page, not their layout. Have a look round the administration area and see if you can find something that looks like it could solve our problem. You probably won't find what you're looking for.

Let's think about this another way. How do I get to the frontpage? Well, one way is to click the **Home** link in the main menu. Thinking about it further, it makes sense that the "menu item" could, in some way, have some influence over the way things are displayed on the page it is pointing to. That's exactly right!

Select **Menu | mainmenu** from the administration drop-down menu. You'll see the **Menu Manager** for the **mainmenu**:

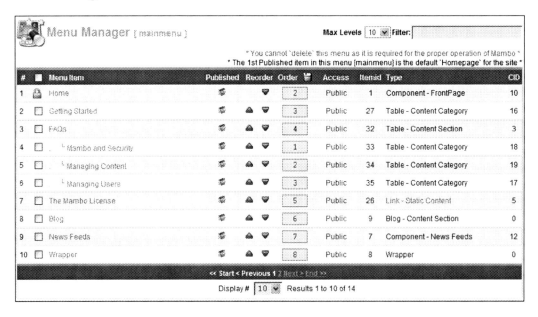

This shows all the items on this menu, and information about them. Again we see things like the publication state of the menu item, its order, who can access it, and so on. The **Home** menu item is the one that takes our fancy here. Click on the **Home** menu item, and you'll be taken to the Edit **Menu Item** page (like the **Content Item: Edit** page we saw for the frontpage content item earlier):

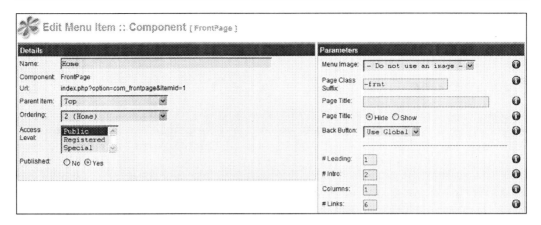

The **Details** of the menu item are on the left-hand side of this form, and the **Parameters** table on the right is what we're after. In general, each menu item has two bits of information.

- Details of the menu item itself: its **Name**, URL (where it points), **Parent Item** (where it sits in the menu hierarchy), **Access** (who can see it), and whether it's published or not.

- Data that controls how the target page of the menu item should be displayed. This is what the **Parameters** table takes care of.

There are many, many options in the **Parameters** table so we won't look at all of them here; we'll focus instead on the **# Leading, # Intro, Columns**, and **# Links** fields. In general, there will be different options in the **Parameters** table depending on what the menu item is pointing to. For example, if the menu item isn't pointing to the frontpage of the site, it wouldn't really make sense for you to be able to control the number of items on the frontpage from the parameters of that item. And in Mambo, if it doesn't make sense, that's not how it works!

We'll see more about menu items and the **Parameters** table in later chapters when we create new menu items.

The **# Leading** field determines how many stories are displayed at the top of the page. These stories are displayed underneath each other. After that, the number of stories defined by the **# Intro** field are displayed. These can be put into columns, the number of columns controlled by the value in the **Columns** field. Finally, the **# Links** field controls the number of article titles that will be displayed underneath this.

We're going to keep **# Leading** at **1**, so there is one story displayed prominently, but then we're going to have four articles displayed under that, across two columns, so we set **# Intro** to **4**, and **Columns** to **2**. We'll leave **# Links** as it is for now.

Make these changes, click the **Save** button, and then preview your site in a new window. Now you will see the change in frontpage configuration.

Summary

OK, we dived in. We had a look round the example Mambo site, and got ourselves acquainted with menus, modules, components, and templates. We saw how content appears on the site, and how you navigate around content structures to find articles.

That was a rather passive activity. Next we actually did some things. We logged into the administration area, and had a look around. We met the concepts of publishing, ordering, access restrictions, and checking in (and out!).

Finally, we started editing one of the articles that appears on the homepage. This was done from the **Frontpage Manager.** We saw the HTML editor that makes it easy to enter formatted text into Mambo, and finally, modified the way articles are displayed on the frontpage of the site, introducing us to Mambo menu entries.

4
Configuring the Site

In this chapter, and over the next few chapters, we will begin to acquaint ourselves with Mambo's administration area, which allows you to manage your site from the comfort of your web browser. We'll look first at the site configuration settings. These options control many global properties of the site, such as the name of the site, mail server setup, and some default options for displaying content, among others. We conclude the chapter with a quick look at the Private Messages functionality that is used to send notifications to back-end users in many parts of Mambo.

We will also create a new installation of Mambo without the sample data. This new installation will be our Zak Springs site that we will gradually add to as we progress through the chapters.

After we've mastered site configuration in this chapter, we'll move on to look at module and component administration, followed by menus and templates in the coming chapters.

Your Site, Your Database

The database that we created when we installed Mambo in Chapter 2 is Mambo's storage repository.

That may sound like a rather trivial remark; we know Mambo is a database-driven web content management system. However, it is worth understanding the nature of what Mambo stores. It stores not only information about registered users of the site, and things like your content items, features about you, your company, or your club, your photos and other images, but also stores information about the layout of your site, which features are enabled, how they are configured, and so on.

There are many more things Mambo squirrels away into its database, but the point in general is that your site is determined by the contents of its database.

This may sound rather overwhelming, particularly if you are new to databases — but this is precisely where the real power of Mambo lies. You don't have to be a MySQL master or know anything about the finer points of database theory; in fact, you generally won't be touching the database yourself. Mambo's powerful and easy-to-use web-based administration tool lets you control and maintain your site through the comfort of your web browser. Through it you are effectively managing the database; but this happens behind the scenes and it is not something that you need to overly concern yourself with.

This also suggests that maintaining your database is very important; if the database is, in some sense, your site, then you need to make sure that you make backups of the database regularly, ready to restore if some problem presents itself. Lose your database, and you have lost your site!

Starting Afresh

We've installed Mambo once, and used the sample data to guide our first steps. However, from now on, we're going to work with a clean installation; with virtually nothing in the database to start with. We will be adding everything ourselves. This will give you a good feel for the process that takes you from "zero to site".

Install Mambo again; this time, copy the files to a folder called `zaksprings` in the root of your web server. You can start the web installer from:

    http://localhost/zaksprings/

As you step through the web installer, this time call the database `zaksprings`, and uncheck the **Install Sample Data** checkbox on the Database Configuration step:

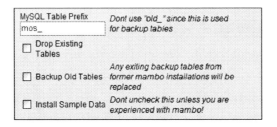

Yes, you are experienced with Mambo, so go ahead and uncheck it! If you do not think you are experienced with Mambo, you will be — you will be.

Also during installation, set the name of the site to be **Zak Springs Golf Club**.

Once the installation is complete, you will find that there is very little in this new site, and only two entries on the menu. Never mind, we'll soon have things livened up.

Visiting the Administration Area

With Mambo's administration features, you manage your site through your browser, controlling every aspect of its behavior, as well as adding and maintaining the content that is displayed. This doesn't mean that anyone can mess with your site; access to the administration area is restricted. You, the Super Administrator, as head of administrators, have supreme power and can even appoint other people to act as administrators, with specific abilities to manage certain parts of the back end of the site.

Mambo's administration area is sensibly organized, especially considering the range of activities that can be done from there. The actions you perform, the icons, menus, and the way that you interact with the system when doing these things is pretty consistent. Over the next few chapters we will get to grips with the administration area, since in your role as a Mambo website administrator, it is where you will spend most of your time (the administration area, not these chapters!).

The first thing to do is to log in to the administrator area. Enter the following URL into your browser:

```
http://localhost/zaksprings/administrator/
```

If you are not already logged in, you will be prompted for the administrator username and password created earlier. Enter these values and click the **Login** button to proceed.

You will be brought to the home page of the administration interface:

This is the central hub of the administration interface. The icons in the control panel in the centre of the screen, and the menu entries from the drop-down menu that link to specific parts of the administration area, are responsible for the control and management of particular features.

Note that if you do not have JavaScript enabled in your browser, then you will find that most of the administration area does not work. For example, the main administrator menu will not display, let alone present the drop-down options, and the toolbar buttons will not do anything. Make sure that JavaScript is enabled in your browser to use the administration interface.

Global Configuration of your Site

Our first task is to make some global settings. Many of these are to do with the underlying platform on which Mambo is running (web and database server, and mail server setup, among others), some specify system-wide defaults.

These settings are the first step in getting the site to work the way you want it to.

The **Site | Global Configuration** menu option allows you to make these configuration changes that will apply "globally" to your site.

The configuration options are carefully organized into tabs based on the task or service to which they relate. You click on one of the tabs to bring up the options for that task:

Above the tabs you can see the standard toolbar buttons for saving your configuration changes (**Save**), applying your changes (**Apply** for "*save* and *continue*"), canceling your changes (**Cancel**), and getting more help (**Help**).

Although you can see lot of tabs, the Global Configuration manager is a single page. When you click one of the tabs to view its options, the new tab is selected by some JavaScript code in the page. This means that if your browser has JavaScript turned off, you simply won't be able to access any of the tabs other than the **Site** tab. Should you be experiencing this, then you can turn JavaScript back on in your browser to get things going.

Another consequence of all the tabs being on the same page is that you can modify some options on one tab, then you can then click on another tab to modify an option there without having to save your changes first. As long as you remember to save all your changes once you're done, all the changes you make will be persisted.

How the Options are Stored

After you save changes in the Global Configuration manager, Mambo actually creates a new version of the `configuration.php` file in the root of your Mambo installation. This file contains all the configuration options in a form that can easily be used by the system without having to go and retrieve these settings from something like the database. This does mean that your `configuration.php` file has to be writable by PHP in order to save any new configuration settings.

If the file isn't writeable, you will see this message at the top of the Global Configuration manager:

Global Configuration **configuration.php is** : Unwriteable ☐ Override write protection while saving

In this case, you will need to check the **Override write protection while saving** checkbox before you save your changes. Provided that PHP is able to change the permissions of the file, this will allow the changes to be written to the `configuration.php` file, and will then set the file back to read-only once it is finished. On a remote server, PHP may not be able to change the permissions of files on the server. We talk more about this in Chapter 12.

These are the tabs in the Site Configuration manager:

- Site
- Locale
- Content
- Database
- Server
- Metadata
- Mail
- Cache
- Statistics
- SEO

We aren't going to cover all the possible configuration options. There are simply too many of them, and for most of them, their relevance to you at this point will be unclear.

As we move through the chapters, we will meet a number of the global configuration options as and when we need. Then, we will discuss them in more detail.

Note that if you hover your mouse cursor over the **i** icon at the end of each option, a message describing the option will be displayed to you. The image at the top of the next page shows the message describing the **Show UnAuthorized Links** option on the **Site** tab:

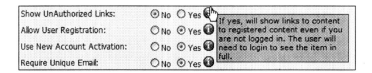

The Site Tab

The configuration settings on the **Site** tab are the most general ones. This tab allows you to turn your site on or off (the front end that is; turn off the back end and you're in trouble!), as well as the message to display when the site is offline.

The **Site Name** is also here; this goes into the page title in the browser, and is included in emails sent out by the system.

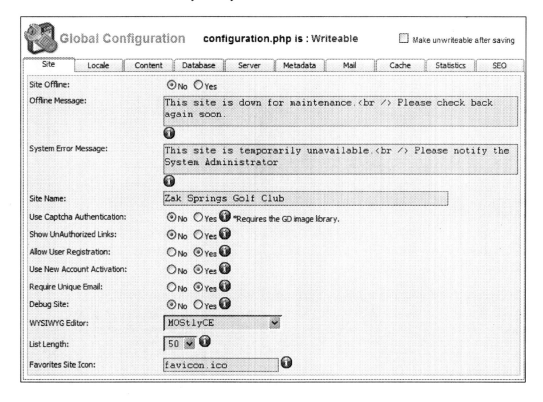

We'll meet many of the other options later in the book.

Locale

The **Locale** tab controls the default language setting for your site, and the time offset. The main use for the time offset value is when your server and your main audience are in different time zones. For example, if you are running a site for a UK audience with a server based in the US, the time on the web server would be different from the time of the site's usual visitors, and you would use the **Time Offset** property to ensure that these match up. If the server is in a time zone 6 hours behind the UK time say, then you would want to select **6** from the **Time Offset** field. If somebody was on the site at 12 pm UK time, this would be recorded as 6 am in the server time zone, so 6 would need to be added to that value to make it the actual time.

The default language is **en**, which is English. The available languages are shown in the drop-down box. Selecting a new language will change the "interface" language.

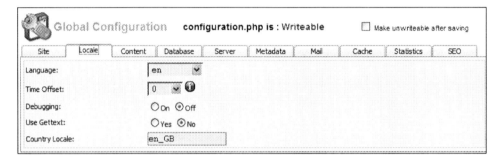

Content

The **Content** tab contains a number of options that will be applied to the display of individual content items. As we'll see later, there is an opportunity to override these global options in specific cases.

The options on the **Content** tab control things like showing the email, PDF, or printer-friendly icons for the content items, as well as things like showing the number of times a content item has been read, when the item was created, and so on.

Database

The database tab contains the settings for connecting to the system database. If you change the **MySQL Database** option, make sure it points to another Mambo database, or you will break your site! If you want to change this setting, you will have to go into `configuration.php` file, and change the `$mosConfig_db` variable to the name of your working Mambo database.

```
<?php
$mosConfig_offline = '0';
$mosConfig_host = 'localhost';
$mosConfig_user = 'mamboer';
$mosConfig_password = 'password';
$mosConfig_db = 'mambo';
$mosConfig_dbprefix = 'mos_';
```

Changing the **MySQL Database** option is useful when you want to choose a new MySQL user to access the database, or move your site information and contents (or data) to a new database, without modifying the existing one.

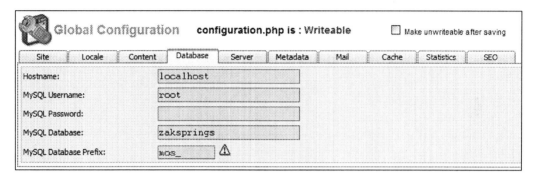

Mambo accesses your database server through the root database user, which has complete control over the entire database server. You may want to use a different database user, which has power only over the Mambo database. You can specify this user here.

The database user needs to be root at installation since it creates a database, and then creates and fills lots of tables. This is more power than you would normally want from a database connection from your live website, so you can move to another MySQL user here.

Configuring the Web Server

The **Server** tab displays options related to PHP settings on the web server.

The **Login Session Lifetime** option determines the length of time that a session can remain inactive before it is removed from the server. The default value is 15 minutes (**900 seconds**). Each time a user logs into your site, a session is created on the web server. The **Login Session Lifetime** option value means that if a logged-in user does nothing on the site for 15 minutes, the next time they attempt to do something they will find that their session has expired, and they will have to log in again.

The **Register Globals Emulation** option (set to **On** by default) controls whether global PHP variables should be defined from incoming request parameters (such as variables in the query string, or fields contained in a submitted form). This process, whereby variables are created without the intervention of the programmer, is generally discouraged in PHP applications. Typical security advice for PHP applications is to turn off this activity (see `http://uk2.php.net/register_globals` for example). Since many servers will have this activity turned off by default, a number of PHP applications actually simulate the activity, by explicitly creating global variables from request variables. This may seem an odd thing to do, but it is mostly due to the age of the application and a desire to keep parts of it working that might have relied on these global variables. In Mambo, setting **Register Globals Emulation** to **Off** is a security-conscious choice, but problems have been reported with some third-party components. So you will have to monitor its consequences carefully.

Error Reporting is set to **System Default**, which means the standard server options for PHP error reporting are used. When executing scripts, PHP can generate errors that do not force it to stop executing, such as notices or warnings about undefined variables. In Mambo, the display of these errors is controlled by the **Error Reporting** option here. If you find that you see messages like **Notice:** appearing on your pages, then you may want to set **Error Reporting** to **None**. The errors reported by PHP are different from any problems Mambo might encounter when running, and Mambo has its own methods for catching problems with its operation, which are not affected by this setting.

Sending Mail

This tab controls the options for sending mail from your site. Mail is sent to users when they register for an account, and also for administration notification purposes.

For mail to be sent properly (or indeed at all!), you need to have your mail server settings correctly configured on this tab. The mail server can be configured to use either the **PHP mail function**, a **Sendmail**, or an **SMTP Server**.

The choice of mail server setting will depend on the set up of your web server. To use the **Sendmail** option the web server will need access to a working installation of **Sendmail**, and for the **PHP mail function** to operate properly it has to be properly configured on the web server. For your live site, you will have to check with the system administrator of the server to see if these options are viable for you. One option that will likely always be available to you is the **SMTP Server** option.

Your ISP will probably have provided you with access to an SMTP server that you can use to send outgoing mail. Check with your ISP if you don't know the details. Once you know the details, enter them into the **SMTP** fields on this tab to get your site's outgoing mail up and running. You will need a username and password for the SMTP account, and once you've got these, enter them into **SMTP User** and **SMTP Pass** fields, and select **Yes** from the **SMTP Auth** option. You only need to enter values into the **SMTP** fields if you are using the **SMTP Server** mailer option.

You also specify the email address that the mails will be sent from, and the name (name displayed in the recipient's email client) of that account.

Enter the details of your SMTP server here, and for our Zak Springs site, we'll enter **Zak Springs Golf Club** into the **From Name**.

Cache

Whenever a page is requested from your Mambo site, the system does a lot of work, retrieving things from the database, getting and displaying content items, and then preparing the page for viewing. To decrease the load on the database, and improve the response time of your site, Mambo can cache (save) the HTML output of some items to the disk. These items can then be retrieved immediately rather than having to get raw data from the database and then build some new HTML output.

Another reason for using caching is that the content items on your site will likely not be changing that often. If you only update the site every few days, why would you need the system to go to the database, grab a content item, and format it every time the item is requested, when it hasn't changed the way it looks in a while? This is a good situation for caching.

You turn on the cache by setting **Caching** to **Yes**. The cache needs a folder on the server that can be written to. The default folder is the `cache` folder in your Mambo installation. You can set this location from the **Cache Folder** option. If you put your cache elsewhere, ensure that the directory is writeable by PHP.

The **Cache Time** is the number of seconds that something will be stored in the cache before it is freshly generated. The default value is **900 seconds**.

Module output is cached, and caching is used by some components like the Content component, to cache content items. Items that depend on the current user will not be cached, as this could mean that someone other than the current user could see them. Nothing related to the administration area is cached.

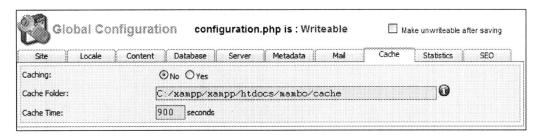

If you hover your mouse cursor over the **i** icon at the end of the **Cache Folder** option, instead of seeing a message about what the **Cache Folder** is, you will see the current status of that folder's writeability. This happens for a number of options in the **Global Configuration**; the text isn't necessarily a help message, it's a status message.

Visitor Statistics

By default, Mambo keeps basic records of who visits your site, what browser they're using, and so on. (This is enabled with the **Yes** value of the **Statistics** option.) The other options enable different kinds of records to be kept, such as when a particular content item was viewed, or what terms were entered into your site search facility. This will allow you to build up a richer picture of what is happening on your site.

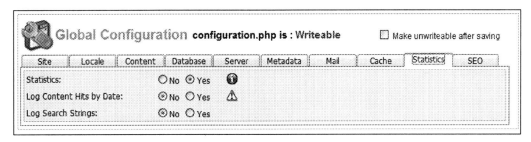

The statistics themselves can be viewed from the **Site | Statistics** option of the administration drop-down menu.

Making Mambo-Search Engine Friendly

Your site isn't really of much use unless people actually visit it. One way for people to find your site is through web search engines. However, getting the pages on your site near the top of the returned results for particular searches is not a random matter or luck. It is the end of an activity called Search Engine Optimization (**SEO**). This discipline involves a number of alterations to your site, including the way it presents content, in order to get high ranking results on search terms.

Two things Mambo can help you with are creating search-engine friendly URLs, and page titles that are related to the content of the page.

Search engines supposedly have difficulty with page URLs that contain lots of query string variables (the form of the URL suggests that the content has been created dynamically, and so the page may change again soon). For example, the URLs on a typical Mambo site look something like:

```
http://sitename.com/mambo/index.php?option=com_content&task=view&id=13&Itemid=27
```

which contains several query string URLs. Setting **Search Engine Friendly URLs** to **Yes** means that links like the one above would now be in a form like this:

```
http://sitename.com/mambo/content/view/13/27/
```

Basically, the query string variables have now become part of the "path" to the page, and Mambo is able to work out which variable is which based on its order in this "path".

If you select **Yes** for **Search Engine Friendly URLs**, then you will prompted when you save your settings to rename the `.htaccess.txt` file in the root of your Mambo installation to `.htaccess`. This file is used by the Apache web server to "prepare" the search engine friendly URLs into a form that can be processed by Mambo. If you are running on Windows, you might find it unusually difficult to rename the `.htaccess.txt` file to `.htaccess`. You may find it easiest to open the file in a text editor, and then save it with the new name of `.htaccess` (note the dot in front of `htaccess` here!).

The **Dynamic Page Titles** option is best left to **Yes** since this means that Mambo should put the title of the current content item into the page title bar in your browser. This page title will also be in a search engine listing when the page is found by the engine in response to some search term.

Away from the **SEO** tab, Mambo can also help with further aspects of search engine optimization.

Metadata

The **Metadata** tab allows you to create `meta` description and keyword tags that appear in the `<head>` of the HTML page output. These tags are used (to a certain extent) by Internet search engines.

```
<head>
<title>Zak Springs Golf Club</title>
<meta name="description"
      content="Mambo - the dynamic portal engine and content
management system" />
<meta name="keywords" content="mambo, Mambo" />
```

For example, the text in the `description` tag will be displayed by certain search engines when a result is returned from your site. The `keywords` tag is where you would list keywords or keyword phrases that relate specifically to the content on the page. However, it is generally held that search engines are not too fussed about this tag anymore; but there's no harm in putting keywords in anyway! Do not overdo the keywords, since many search engines simply view this as keyword "spam", and will not look kindly upon on your page.

You fill up the `meta` tags in your page by using the values from the fields in the **Metadata** tab:

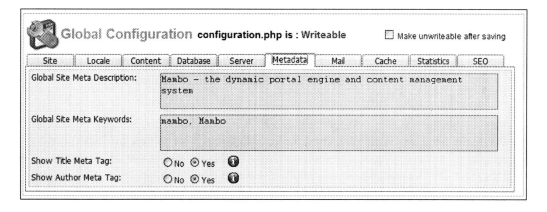

These values are "global", in the sense that they apply to your whole site, so the keywords and description here should reflect your site as a whole, and not individual pages. Keywords and a description can be added for individual content items as we'll see later.

Private Messages

The Private Messages feature of the Mambo back end allows you to send messages to other back end users. Each back-end user is provided with an "inbox" where they can see and reply to private messages that have been sent to them.

Private messages are also used by Mambo to notify various back-end users when content items have been submitted to the site.

The configuration for private messaging is done from the **Messages | Configuration** administrator menu option. There are two options; one is to send an email notification when a private message arrives (the default is to send), and the other locks your inbox (the default is **Yes**):

 The **Lock Inbox** setting really should say "Receive Messages". If you set **Lock Inbox** to **No**, then you will find that you cannot receive Private Messages! To make sure you can receive Private Messages, you must set **Lock Inbox** to **Yes**.

For this exercise, make sure **Mail me on new Message** is set to **Yes**, and then click the **Save** icon in the toolbar to save the settings. Until you save the configuration settings, they are not actually stored in the database. The settings you see when you first go to the page are just default settings, and not your current values. Once you save the settings and they are stored in the database, they will function properly. If you do not save any changes to the configuration, you will receive private messages, but you will not be notified by email when they arrive.

Now we're configured, let's send a message. Select **Messages | Inbox** from the administrator drop-down menu, and you'll see your Private Messages Inbox. It's not much to look at right now, you don't have any messages! Click the **New** button in the toolbar, and we'll proceed to send ourselves a message.

Select your username from the **To** drop-down box, and enter a **Subject**, and some text in the **Message** field. After this, click the **Send** button in the toolbar, and your message is sent to yourself. You will see the received message in your Private Messages Inbox, from where you can delete it, read it and then delete, or reply to it.

Also, if you open up your mail client and check your mail, you should find a message from your site with the subject **A new private message has arrived**. Intriguingly, the body of the mail is also **A new private message has arrived**. If you don't receive this mail, then check your mail server setup from the **Mail** tab of the **Global Configuration**, and then send yourself another private message.

Summary

This has been a short chapter, since we've only been concerned with one activity, exploring the basic configuration options of a Mambo site.

We started the chapter by creating a fresh Mambo installation, called `zaksprings`. This installation will be added to as we go through the chapters, building up our **Zak Springs** website.

We looked at the global configuration options from the **Site | Global Configuration** administration menu option. These options are presented in a tabbed format, and require JavaScript to be working in your browser to function properly. Once you make changes to the configuration options, the `configuration.php` file in the root of your Mambo installation is updated, which means that PHP must be able to write to this file. Failure to write to the file will display warnings.

The global configuration options control a number of properties of the site, such as the name of the site, how the mail server is set up, how long items should be stored in the cache, and what form the URLs of pages should be.

We concluded the chapter with a look at the Private Messages functionality. This is used not only by back-end users to send messages to other back-end users, it is also used by Mambo to send system notifications to various administrators, so it's important to have this set up and ready to go. Our look at the Private Messages feature was also used as a quick test to see if our mail server configuration was correct.

5
Managing Media, Modules, and Components

In this chapter, we'll look at module and component administration. With Mambo, you can configure the modules as a whole; their position on the page, who can see them, and so on. Also, the modules themselves are configurable, which allows you to control whether the title of the module is displayed on the page, and also make some settings specific to that module.

After that, we'll see an overview of component management, although management of individual components is a topic that will occupy much of the rest of the book. We'll have a look at the Universal Installer, which allows you to install any type of Mambo add-on with ease.

Before we move on to module and component management, we'll start with a quick look at the Media Manager. This allows you to add files directly to the server, for use in your content items.

Managing Media

The Media Manager allows you to upload resources (images, PDF, and Office documents) that can be used (linked to) in your content. To help with organizing these resources, the Media Manager allows you to create directories on the server. The Media Manager allows you to upload images in either GIF, PNG, JPEG, or Windows BMP format, PDF documents, Flash movies (SWF format), and Microsoft Office documents (Word documents (.doc), Excel spreadsheets (.xls), and PowerPoint presentations (.ppt)). The type of the file is determined from its extension.

Note that you cannot use the Media Manager to upload plain text files to the server.

The Media Manager can be accessed from **Site | Media Manager**.

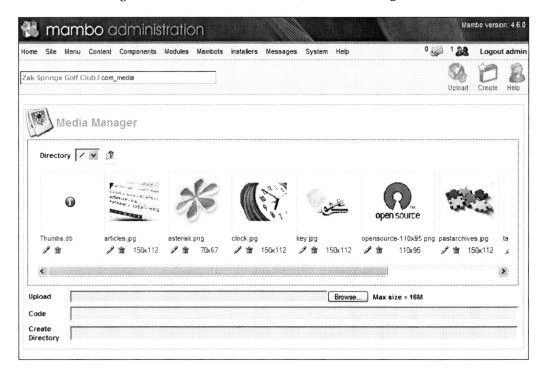

Here you can see a gallery of the images and other resources currently stored in this "root" folder. You can upload a new media resource to the folder by clicking the **Browse** button, selecting the file you want to upload, and then clicking the **Upload** button to send the file to the server.

You can create a new directory on the server by entering its name into the **Create Directory** field and then clicking **Create** in the toolbar.

The "root" directory for this store of media resources is the `stories` folder within the `images` folder of your Mambo installation. This means that any directory you create in the Media Manager will become subdirectory of the `images\stories` folder. Note also that you cannot upload any resources using the **Media Manager** to any folder above `images\stories`. You can change to a new directory in the Media Manager structure by selecting it from the **Directory** drop-down box.

Note that creating a new directory inside your "root" directory requires Mambo to have full write access to the `images\stories` folder. We talk more about setting up these permissions in Chapter 12. On your local testing machine, you should not encounter problems with permissions on this folder.

If you click on the image of the resource in the **Media Manager**, the HTML to add a link to this resource will appear in the **Code** field. (Clicking on the *pencil* icon of the resource will also make this HTML appear.)

Clicking the *trash* icon under the resource thumbnail allows you to delete that resource from the server. You will be prompted to confirm your decision before the file is deleted. The file will be removed from the server if you choose to go ahead with this action. Since you can only operate on files or folders within the images\stories folder in your Mambo installation, you can't delete any important Mambo files with this feature!

Before going any further in the chapter, we'll try out the Media Manager by uploading an image to the server. You can find the Zak Springs logo image (zaksprings_logo.png) in this chapter of the code download, so get it ready.

Select the Media Manager from **Site | Media Manager**. Click the **Browse** button, and then navigate to the Zak Springs logo graphic (I told you to have it ready), and select it. After that, click the **Upload** button in the toolbar, and your image will be uploaded to the server, and displayed with the other images:

Managing Modules

Modules are a key part of the layout and operation of a typical Mambo website. You can customize the individual properties of a module, and also choose where and how the module is displayed on the page.

Installed Modules

Module management begins from the **Modules** section of the administration menu:

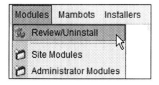

The **Review/Uninstall** menu option displays the list of modules that are currently installed on your system:

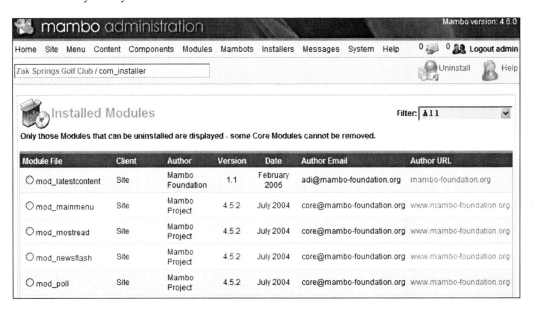

This list provides some basic information about the installed modules, and allows you to uninstall a module by selecting the radio button the left of the module file name, and then clicking the **Uninstall** icon in the toolbar. Be careful; this will physically remove the module files from the `module` folder. In other words, it will remove the module from the server. A module actually has a pair of files that go in the `modules` folder. One of these files is a PHP code file, the other is a configuration file. The filename corresponding to a particular module is shown in the **Module File** column.

There are two types of module, **Site** and **Admin**. **Site** modules are for the front end (the publicly visible portion) of your site, and **Admin** modules are only used on the back end of the site. You can use the **Filter** drop-down box if you only want to view one of these types of module.

Note that this list of modules is only a list of the physical module files stored on the server; it's not the actual list of modules displayed on your site. There isn't much you can do with this list other than delete files from the server. To really do things with modules, we need to move to the Module Manager.

Managing Site Modules

Select the **Modules | Site Modules** menu option to visit the **Module Manager**, and begin the administration of the front-end modules of your site.

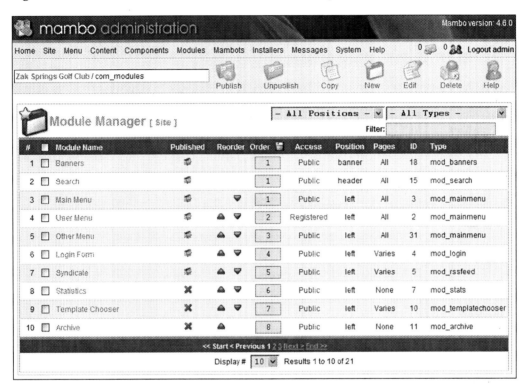

Now this really is a list of the modules on your site. Each of these is an "instance" of a module that we saw in the **Installed Modules** list. Instance here means an individual "object" based on the "parent" code. Once the instance has been created, it can be given its own configuration, and you can have several module instances of the same "parent" code on your site. You can see the "parent" code that the module is an instance of from its **Type** column. The value in this column indicates the code file that is the module's "parent".

You should be familiar with many of the columns in the table from the last chapter. We saw the **Published, Reorder, Order,** and **Access** columns in the **Frontpage Manager,** and discussed what those concepts meant in relation to content items there. We also mentioned that these concepts applied generally throughout Mambo, and here we're seeing proof of that already. Modules can be activated (published), reordered, or restricted to certain groups of users by editing values in these columns.

Exactly what "reordering" means in this module context, we'll be exploring in a minute.

The **Position** and **Pages** columns suggest that there are two dimensions to the location of a module:

- Where on those pages is it displayed?
- Which page(s) is it displayed on?

The **Pages** column may not look quite so helpful, as it seems to have only the values of **All**, **None**, or **Varies**. That suggests that a module can appear on all pages, no pages, or some pages, which is probably what you would have guessed anyway! We'll have to look more closely at the individual module to find out what **Varies** means exactly. It doesn't really mean **Varies**, it actually means "Some". It doesn't mean the module appears on one page on Tuesday, and another page on Wednesday!

The **Position** column specifies one of the "module positions" for the module to be displayed in. These are various places on the page (their exact location is specified in the template) where sets of modules can be displayed. Select the **Site | Preview | Inline with Positions** menu option to see the placement of module positions:

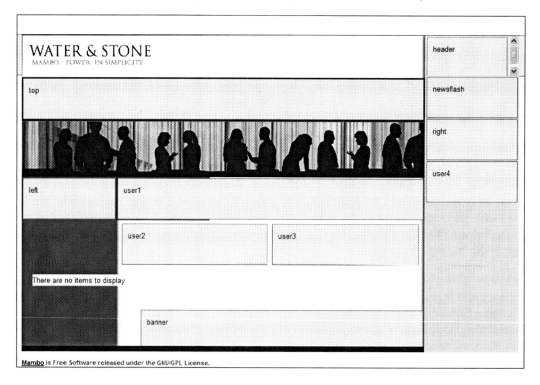

We haven't added the boxes onto this image ourselves (except to emphasize their outline), in fact Mambo has actually drawn these for you. Each of these boxes is a **module position**, and the name of the position is shown in the box.

If you click the **Back** button in your browser to return to the **Module Manager** page (or refer to the earlier screenshot), you will be able to build a mental picture of the page from looking at the value of the module in the **Position** column, and checking where that position is on the **Preview | Inline with Positions** map. For example, the Main menu and User menu have the position of **left**, so these will be displayed in the left-hand column of the page.

The **Position** of the module goes with the **Order** of the module. The order of the module actually means "order within that position". Reordering a module means moving it up or down within the set of other modules that are displayed in the same position as that module. The module with the lowest order value (**1**) will be displayed first in that position, the one with the next highest order is shown next, and so on. Note that a checked-out module can't be reordered directly, although you can move it by moving the module above or below it.

You can use the drop-down box with **All Positions** in it to view only the modules that are in a particular position.

From our experience with the **Frontpage Manager** in the previous chapter, we know that we can click in the **Published** column of a module to publish or unpublish it. An unpublished module is never seen on the public side of your site. You can also check the boxes next to the module titles, and click the **Publish** or **Unpublish** toolbar icons to affect several modules in one go.

Clicking on the arrows in the **Reorder** column moves a module one position up or down, and clicking in the **Access** column toggles the user access restrictions for that module.

One thing that may initially disorientate you is, when there is more than one page of modules, and you make some changes to a module on a page after the first one. For example, say you deactivate (unpublish) a module. After you click to deactivate the module, you will find yourself back on the first page of the list, and the module you were just looking at is nowhere to be seen on the current page. You will have to click the paging links to get back to the page that had your module.

The paging links are displayed under the list of modules (and generally in Mambo you will find paging links at the bottom of a list in the administration area). The current page is highlighted (in the image below we are on the second page, so **2** is highlighted), and there are links to each of the available pages, and also to the next or previous page:

The number of elements to display on one of the pages is controlled from the **Display #** drop-down box.

Editing Module Properties

You can edit the properties of a particular module by clicking on its name. This brings you to the **Site Module: Edit** page. Let's click on the **Login Form** module for now, and see what comes up:

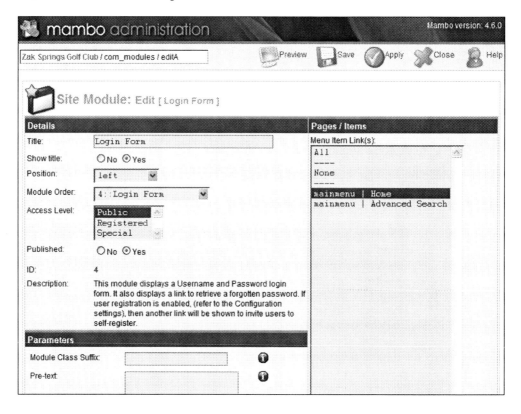

There are three panels on this page, **Details**, **Pages/Items**, and **Parameters**.

Module Details

The **Details** panel holds the module properties that we saw displayed in the **Module Manager** table: the **Title**, the **Position**, the **Module Order**, the **Access Level**, and the **Published State** of the module.

Something that you can't get from the table in the **Module Manager** is the **Show Title** field. Remember we saw the **Search** module in the previous chapter, and mentioned that it seemed to have no title—no banner saying **Search**. Remember I also said you could control that? Well, you do that with the **Show Title** field. Setting it to **No** will mean the module is displayed without its title, as the **Search** module was.

The Access Level field allows you to show the module to anyone (**Public**), logged-in users (**Registered**), or one of the other front-end user groups we will meet in Chapter 7 (**Special**):

Pages/Items

The **Pages/Items** panel explains the **All**, **None**, **Varies** values for the **Pages** column in the **Module Manager**. From this panel, you set the pages on which the module will appear. Select the **All** entry, and the module will appear on every page; select **None** and it will not appear on any page on your site.

If you want the module to appear on only some pages, then you simply need to select those pages. You select multiple pages in the way you usually select multiple items on your computer (on Windows for example, hold down the *Ctrl* key as you click on each page you want).

Actually, you don't see all the pages on the site in the **Pages/Items** panel; you only see the menu entries. We'll talk more about menu entries in the next chapter, but for now, we'll just say that menu entries point to pages. However, there will be more pages on your site than have menu entries, and as we'll see, certain pages will "inherit" settings from their parent page, which will have a menu entry.

Currently, since our database is pretty empty, there are only two menu entries, **mainmenu | Home** and **mainmenu | Advanced Search**. If you have a look at your previous installation, with the sample data, you will see that there are more menu entries, and more pages to add the module to.

The image here shows the **Pages/Items** panel from our previous, sample data installation. We've selected the **Mambo and Security** menu entry.

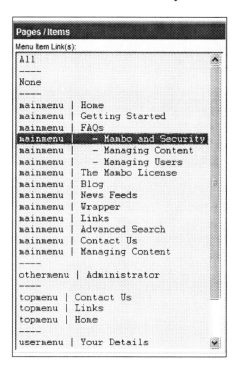

If you do the same, click **Save**, preview the site, and browse to the **FAQs | Mambo and Security** menu entry, you will see that **Login Form** is indeed displayed on the page. Now click on one of the item titles displayed on that page, and you will see that the **Login Form** is still displayed on this new page. This is because this page inherits the **Login Form** module from its "parent". In this way, modules can be added to pages that are not directly linked to from the menus.

Module Parameters

The panels we've just seen are the same for every module. What you see in the **Parameters** panel depends on the module you are working with. This panel handles the configuration specific to that type of module. Here we see the **Parameters** for the **Login Form** module:

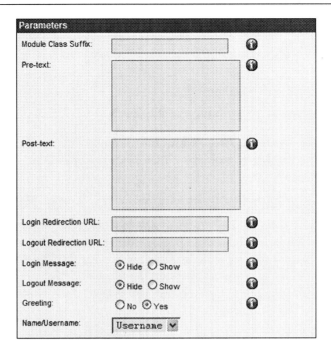

Most of these fields are specific to the **Login Form** module. They allow you to do things like choose the text that is displayed before the **Username** box to customize the **Login Form** module. Again, there are little **i** icons for you to hover the cursor over to get field-specific help information. If you make changes to these fields, you will need to click **Save** or **Apply** in the toolbar to persist your changes.

The **Module Class Suffix** generally appears in most module **Parameters**. This allows you to specify a string that will be placed on the end of all the CSS class names in the output of the module. With this suffix, the classnames used in the module output can be unique, which means that you can define CSS styles specifically for this module, which can give your module an extra level of visual customization.

Note that if you click the **Back** button while editing module details, or leave the page by some other means, that module will be checked out, and the familiar padlock icon will appear next to the module in the **Module Name** table.

When a module is checked out, you can't publish, and you can't re-order it, although if you move the module above it down (or the one below up), then the module will move by itself!

All of this means that there are three aspects to module management:

- General module details: its name, where it's displayed on the page, who can see it
- Which pages it is displayed on
- Configuration specific to that type of module

All of this can be done from the **Site Module**: **Edit** page. This "general" and "specific" control over a module makes Mambo modules extremely flexible.

Adding a New Module Instance to your Site

You can add a new module instance to your site in of one two ways: you can either use an existing module as a "template", or you can create a more basic module. The first way involves "copying" a module, the second is simpler. The words "template" and "copying" here could give the impression that this is a rather involved process, but it isn't. It simply involves a couple of clicks in the **Module Manager** and you're away.

Creating a basic module offers limited functionality for the module. It can do these things:

- Display RSS feeds from other sites
- Display custom HTML stored in the database

We'll create two new modules. The first will display a news feed of golf headlines from the BBC Sport website, and the other will display the Zak Springs logo using simply HTML.

Adding an RSS Feed Module

From the **Module Manager**, click the **New** button in the toolbar. This brings up the **New** module page. We'll begin by entering the title of the module, **BBC Golf News**, but we'll also set it to not display this title:

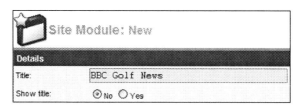

We will leave the other fields in the **Details** panel as they are.

Click the **Apply** button in the toolbar to save our changes before we move on. You will see this text displayed below the toolbar once the page reloads:

Successfully Saved changes to Module: BBC Golf News

Now scroll down the screen to the **Parameters** panel. We enter the URL of the RSS news feed, `http://news.bbc.co.uk/rss/sportonline_world_edition/golf/rss.xml` into the **RSS URL** field, and we set the other options as follows:

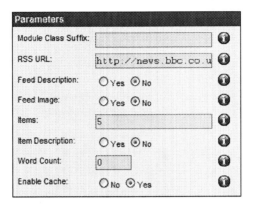

We don't want to show the feed description, as this is quite a long piece of text, which will make the module take up a lot of space, and we won't show the feed image either for the same reasons. We also set the **Item Description** to **No** so as only to show the headline of the story. The **Item Description** will again be a chunk of text that bloats the size of our module.

Finally, we set **Enable Cache** to **Yes**. This means that the output of the module will be cached. By doing this, our site will not have to make a request to the target website to grab the RSS feed every time the module is displayed. (We don't really need to make a fresh request all the time, as we don't require the information to be completely up to the minute). Removing this overhead will make our page display faster, and reduce the overall load on our system.

Note that the caching of the RSS feed will still work even if the global site caching is not enabled. The data from the RSS feed is cached using a different caching "engine", and the cache will remain fresh for an hour. There isn't any way to change this value directly from the administration area of Mambo.

Click **Apply** in the toolbar to save the changes and continue working. There is one more thing to do.

The final activity is to set which pages this module will be displayed on. This is done from the **Pages/Items** panel (above and to the right of the **Parameters** panel). We will set the module to display only on the homepage. We do this by selecting the **mainmenu | Home** option:

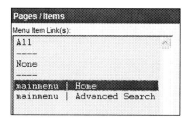

That's it. Click the **Save** button in the toolbar, and you will return to the **Module Manager**. Your first module is now displayed in the list of site modules:

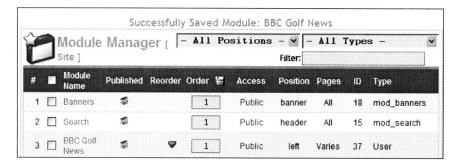

You will note from the **Type** column that this module is of type **User**. This is because it isn't based on any of the installed custom modules.

Now if you preview your site, you will see your module at the top of the left-hand column:

This was of course the news from that feed at the time of writing; you will very likely see something different, unless the world of golf has drawn to a complete standstill since this moment. Click on any of these links and you will be taken to the relevant story on the BBC News website, with the story opening in a new browser window.

Adding a Custom HTML Module

This time we'll enter some HTML that will be used directly for the module output. This will be stored in Mambo's database, and retrieved and displayed when the module is output on the page. Such an HTML module cannot take advantage of any "server-side" PHP processing, so the output is always fixed. The module output will always look the same, whenever you look at it, whoever you are.

To get started, you click the **New** button in the toolbar of the **Module Manager** (again!). We'll start with the module details, we'll give it a title of **Zak Springs Logo**, and again set the title to not be visible as we did above.

This time, scroll down past the **Parameters** panel to find the **Custom Output** panel:

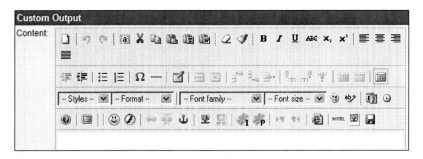

This panel contains a single HTML editor, for a field called **Content**. This is where we enter the HTML for our module. We aren't even going to type in any text; we're just going to insert an image. We're going to add the Zak Springs logo that we uploaded to the server earlier in the chapter with the **Media Manager**. If you didn't do it then, now is a good time to go back and do that!

Prior to version 4.6 of Mambo, there was a feature that allowed you to browse through your media in the **HTML** editor, and select the image to insert. From 4.6 onwards, this feature has been relegated to a plug-in rather than a standard feature, and currently it has not been completed. This is a shame, since it means that you have to know the URL of the image you want to insert before you start attempting to add it.

For our logo image, its path on the server will be `images\stories\zaksprings_logo.png`, so we'll just have to remember that.

Click the **Insert/edit image** icon in the HTML editor:

A dialog pops up, where you have to enter the URL of our image (`images/stories/zaksprings_long.png`) into the **Image URL** field (note the `/` character in the path for the URL instead of the `\` character for the file path), and add a title and description as below:

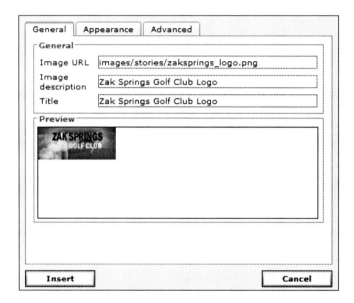

After that, click the **Insert** button; the dialog will close, and the image will be added to the **Content** field. Click on the newly inserted image, then click the centering icon in the text editor to centre the image:

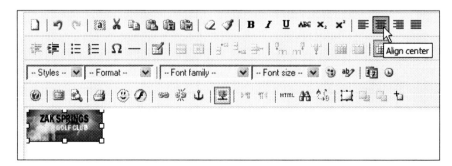

Click the **Save** icon in the toolbar, and you'll return to the **Module Manager**. Our new logo module is now shown in the list of modules:

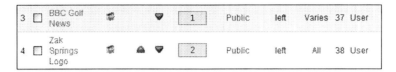

You will notice that the module has been placed below the **BBC Golf News** module we created previously (we can move it up if we like with the reordering arrows) and that it is also of type **User**. We left the logo module to be displayed on **All** pages; that is the default value in the **Pages/Item** panel.

Preview the site, and the logo can be seen in all its glory:

That's all there is to creating a module to show a piece of custom HTML. The HTML we used was very simple, only consisting of a single image reference, but of course it can be more complex (and useful!) than this.

 Note you can combine an RSS feed module and a custom HTML module. Enter the details for the RSS feed into the **Parameters** panel, and enter some text into the **Content** field of the **Custom Output** panel, and both will be displayed. The HTML from the **Custom Output** panel will always be displayed before the start of the RSS news feed.

Creating a Module Copy

The other way to add a new module instance is to base your module on an existing one. This is done by "copying" one of the current site modules. "Copy" actually means "create a blank copy"; all the *values* of the fields of your new module are reset to their default state, and your module copy will have the same fields as the source module.

We'll create a copy of the **Random Image** module. This module shows an image at random from a folder of your choosing. We'll use this module to show thumbnails of some of the holes at Zak Springs.

First of all, grab the thumbnails of the holes at Zak Springs from this chapter in the code download, create a folder called `holes` in the `images` folder of your Mambo installation, and copy all the images into there. (Alternatively, you can upload the thumbnails with the **Media Manager**; create a folder called `holes` with the **Media Manager**, and then upload the images.)

Creating a module copy begins by selecting your source module. If you can't find the type of module you're after, you can use the drop-down box with **All Types** in it to filter for a particular type of module. The **Random Image** module is of type **mod_random_image**, so select that from the drop-down box and the module you're after will be shown:

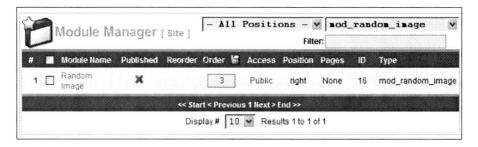

Check the box next to the name of the module, and click the **Copy** button from the toolbar.

After you click **Copy**, you might be surprised to not be confronted with a **Site Module: Edit** page. Instead, you're still in the **Module Manager**, and you will see this text below the toolbar:

Module Copied [Copy of Random Image]

Filter again by **mod_random_image** and you will discover your newly copied module:

Note that our copy is unpublished. Regardless of whether the module we copied is published or not, our copy will always be unpublished by default. We will have to set it to **Published** once we are finished with it.

Now you can click on the **Copy of Random Image** module name and actually start editing your module:

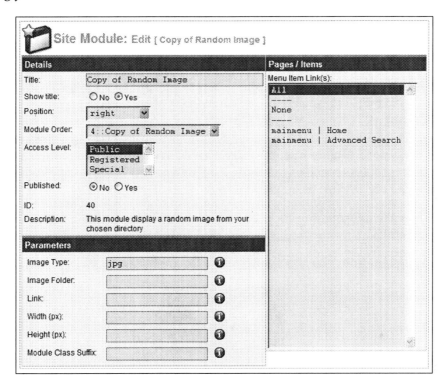

The title has already been conveniently created for you (very cleverly the words **Copy of** were added to the front of the title of the module you copied).

We'll change the **Title** to **Holes at Zak Springs**, and also set the **Position** to **left**. You will note that as soon as you change the position, the **Module Order** dropdown will change, to display only the modules that are in the left position. We will also change the position, so that this module is displayed after the **Zak Springs Logo**. We'll set the dropdown to **2**.

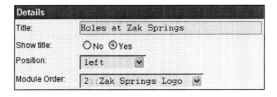

Set the **Published** field to **Yes**, so that the module will be displayed as soon as we finish entering our details.

Scroll down the screen to the **Parameters** panel. The only thing we need to specify is the **Image Folder**; this needs to point to the folder containing the images from which the random selection will be made. We use a relative URL for this, rather than the full `http://localhost/` form of the URL, since Mambo will add the path to our live site onto the front of the URL anyway. Enter `images/holes/` into this field. (If you followed the alternative suggestion above and uploaded the images using the **Media Manager**, the path you need to enter will be `images/stories/holes/`.)

We could specify a **Width** for the images to be resized to when displayed, and if no width is specified, the width will be set to 100 pixels. Note that no thumbnail of this size is generated; the images in the folder you have specified will be displayed to the visitor, and simply resized in the browser. If you have large images, even though the visitor sees them at a smaller size, the large images have already been downloaded for the visitor, so this can make your page load slower. The images supplied in the code download are already thumbnail-sized.

After entering the information, click the **Save** icon in the toolbar, and our module copy is fully done.

When you preview your site now, you will see the random image:

If the image is not displayed, edit the module details and check the **Image Folder** field.

If you click **Refresh**, a new image will be displayed (probably... it is random!).

This **Random Image** module is very rudimentary—we had to add our own specially prepared thumbnails to the image, and then there isn't really much for the user to do other than look at the image. It would be good if they could click the image to see a full-size version of it. This will all be made much easier when we use the specially created module for the zOOm Gallery in Chapter 10.

That just about wraps up our discussion of adding new modules to the site; now we can move on to deleting module instances.

Deleting Module Instances

To create a copy of a module, there needs to be an instance of that module already defined on the site (it need not be published of course). That does mean that if you delete the last remaining instance of a particular module, you won't be able to create a new one.

This does seem to be the case. In fact, worse than that, delete the last remaining instance of a module from the site and the module itself will be uninstalled.

So watch out! Unless you have a good reason to delete a module, it is best to leave a module unpublished and simply ignore it. You never know when you may want to use it again!

Administrator Modules

So far we've looked at the **Site Modules** option of the **Modules** menu, which controls the modules that appear on the front end of your site.

As you would expect, the **Administrator Modules** option allows you to control the modules that appear in the administration area.

The Administrator Modules are different from the site modules in terms of the type of functionality they offer, and where they are stored in the Mambo file structure. Moreover, very few administrator modules offer their configuration parameters. Also, there is no option to display the modules on certain pages; administrator modules are displayed on all pages of the administration area.

However, the templates that control the administration area do not usually make use of such a wide range of module positions as the site modules.

The Administrator Module management page, obtained by selecting the **Modules | Administration Modules** option on the administration menu, works in an identical fashion to the Site Module management page, and you can bring the skills that you learned from our exploration of that page to bear on the Administration Module management page.

One difference is that if you want to create a new administrator module, there is no option for an **RSS feed** module; you can either create a module consisting purely of HTML, or else copy an existing administrator module to create a new instance. You cannot copy a site module to create a new instance of an administrator module, and there is probably little reason you would want to. Site Modules are designed for the front end of the site, for visitors, and Administrator Modules are designed for the back end of the site, for administrators.

The main module positions for administrator modules are:

- **cpanel**: the tabbed element in the Control Panel on the administrator home-page. Selecting a module with this position will add a new tab to that element on the administrator homepage. A module in this position is only shown on the administrator homepage.

- **top**: where the administration menu is displayed. A module in this position will be shown on "most of" the pages of the administration area.

- **header**: to the right side of the top position, where the number of online users is displayed.

Component Management

Components are the main units of our site's functionality, but there isn't really much to do for their general management. Unlike modules, which have properties like position, pages, and so on to set, components can either be installed or uninstalled from the **Components | Review/Uninstall** menu option, and that's about all you do with components in general:

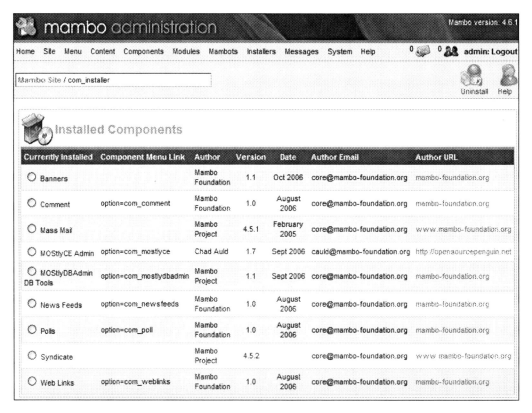

Management and configuration of the components themselves is done from the **Components** menu. Each component that has any kind of configuration will provide a menu entry on this menu, and you use that to set up that component in the way you want. This is specific to each different component, and we will talk about configuring individual components when we look at the functionality of that component in the coming chapters.

Installing Mambo Add-ons with the Universal Installer

In Mambo 4.6 onwards, there is a new "universal" installer that allows you to install a component, a module, a template, a mambot, or other feature of Mambo easily from a single place.

Mambo add-ons are packaged up into a single ZIP file, and this is done by the person or individual who produced the add-on; this isn't something you have to do.

This ZIP archive contains all the files required for that add-on, and unlike many other systems where installing add-ons requires you to copy lots of different files into different places on your server, installing a Mambo add-on with the Universal Installer simply requires you to upload this single ZIP file onto the server running your Mambo site. Mambo will automatically put the required files into the right place, and advise of any errors.

You upload the file from the **Installers | Universal** page. Whatever type of add-on you want to install, Mambo will work it out once you upload the file.

The easiest way to install an add-on is with the **Upload Package File** panel on the **Installers | Universal** page:

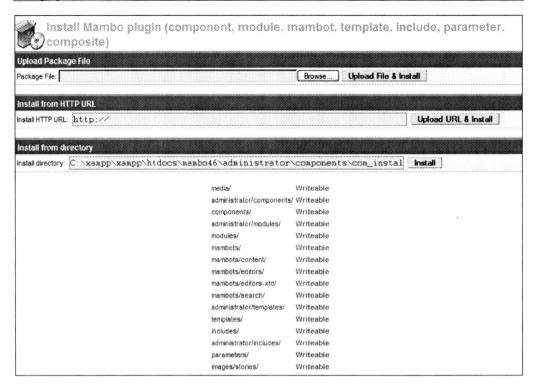

You click the **Browse** button and navigate (on your local machine) to the ZIP file containing the add-on you want to install, click the **Upload File & Install** button, and the file will be uploaded to the server. Mambo will extract the contents of the ZIP file, work out what type of add-on you've uploaded, and begin the process of copying the files to the correct place on the server. If the file you upload isn't a Mambo add-on you will be advised of this and nothing will be copied into your Mambo installation.

For this to work, it does mean that Mambo will need to be able to write to the folder into which the add-on is being placed. You can see the write status of all the Mambo folders on the **Installer | Universal** page. While attempting to install any add-on, if the installation process cannot write to any folder it needs to, an error message will be displayed, and the installation will not succeed.

Installing Directly from a URL

In fact, you don't even have to get the ZIP file yourself and upload it to the server. If you know the URL from where an add-on can be downloaded, you can simply point Mambo towards that URL, and it will download the ZIP file itself, extract, and distribute the files accordingly. It couldn't be easier!

This does mean that you have to know what you're downloading. You could be downloading absolutely anything to your server. For example, you could be downloading a component that seems to work fine, but it could have replaced the login component with something that sends passwords off to some evil location on the Internet (I hope I haven't given anyone an idea there...).

While such things might seem far fetched, if you are not downloading from somewhere that you completely trust, it may be wise to download the ZIP file manually and check it out yourself, and it's worth doing this for any add-on that you install using the ordinary method we just described as well. The same risks apply; the difference between the URL method and the previous method is that with the URL method you have no opportunity to look at what you're installing before its get installed.

Having mentioned all that doom and gloom, one thing that installing from URL is great for is downloading Mambo add-ons from the MamboXchange website, especially the add-ons for Mambo Lite.

Installing the ExtCal Event Component

The **ExtCal** event component adds a calendar to the front end of your site, to which users and administrators can add events. At Zak Springs, this component will be used to provide a calendar of up-coming club events, such as tournaments. We'll talk more about using the calendar in a later chapter, but for now, let's get it installed!

The ExtCal Event component can be downloaded from:

```
http://mamboxchange.com/projects/extcalendar/
```

If you enter this URL into your browser, you will be taken to this component's page on the MamboXchange website, where you will see some links to download it:

Latest File Releases

Package	Version	Date	Notes / Monitor	Download
ExtCalendar Component	ExtCalendar Component v0.9.1	May 27, 2005	📑 - ✉	Download
ExtCalendar MiniCal Module	ExtCal MiniCalendar Module v0.8.2	May 27, 2005	📑 - ✉	Download
ExtCal Latest Events Module	ExtCal Latest Events Module v0.7.2	May 27, 2005	📑 - ✉	Download
ExtCal ScreenShots	Various ExtCal Screenshots	May 27, 2005	📑 - ✉	Download
	[View All Project Files]			

The component also comes with some supporting modules; we'll install one of them in a moment. Click the **Download** link for the **ExtCalendar Component** and you will see the released files for this package. The most recent stable version is highlighted:

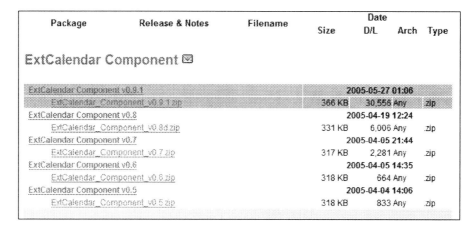

Click the link for **ExtCalendar_Component_v0.9.1.zip** and the file will begin downloading to your hard drive.

Once the file has finished downloading, return to your Mambo administration area, and select **Installers | Universal** from the administration menu:

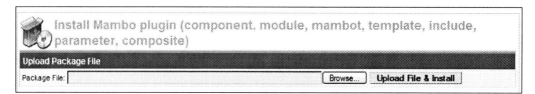

Click the **Browse** button next to the **Package File** field, and navigate to the ZIP file you just downloaded, select it, and then click **Upload File & Install**.

When the page reloads, you will see a long message about the installed component, which begins like this:

Scroll down the screen, and you will see the successful upload information:

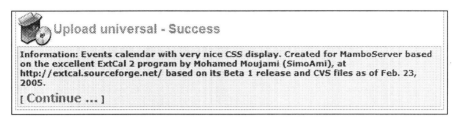

If something has gone wrong with the installation, you will be advised of that here. Any problem with the installation will be reported.

Click the **Continue** link to return to your component administration. You will now be able to see that the **ExtCal** component has been added to the **Components** administration drop-down menu:

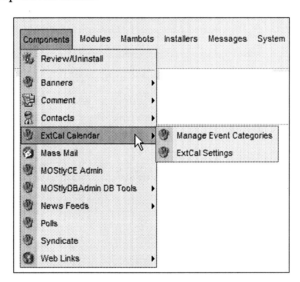

Installing an ExtCal Module from a URL

Now we've got the **ExtCal** component, let's download the **Latest Events Module** to go with it. This time, we'll install the component directly from its location on the MamboXchange website.

If you return to the homepage of the ExtCal add-on at the MamboXchange website, and this time click the **Download** link for the **ExtCal Latest Events Module**, you'll see the list of files for the module:

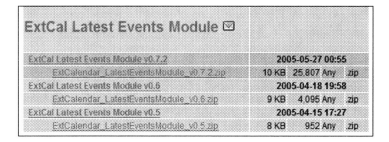

Rather than clicking the **ExtCalendar_LatestEventsModule_v0.7.2.zip** link to download the ZIP file, we'll need the full URL of the link. This can be obtained directly from your browser:

- In Firefox, right-click the link and select **Copy Link Location** from the pop-up menu. This will copy the full URL of the link to your clipboard.

- In Internet Explorer, you can right-click on the link and select **Copy Shortcut**, and the full URL of the link will be copied to your clipboard.

- In the Opera browser, you can do the same by right-clicking the link and selecting **Copy link address**.

In other browsers, you can get the URL of a link in a similar way. Once you've got a copy of the full URL of the link, return to the Universal Installer page, and then paste the link into the **Install HTTP URL** field:

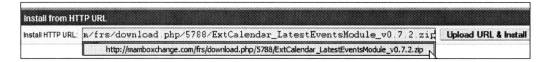

Once you've done this, click the **Upload URL & Install** button. When the page reloads, you'll see the upload success message:

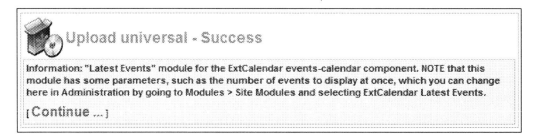

Click the **Continue** link. If you return to the **Module Manager** page (**Modules | Site Modules**), you can see the newly installed module in your list of modules:

Both ways of installing these add-ons were pretty straightforward. Installing from the URL required us to grab the URL of the ZIP file we wanted, which we could do straight from our browser.

The installer has made a rather tedious process very simple. Installing a Mambo add-on would otherwise require copying files to a range of different places in the Mambo installation, adding some new tables to the database, and then updating some existing tables. It's much easier to just put in the URL of the package you want to download and click a button!

Interlude: Web Links

The Web Links component provides a repository for links (unsurprisingly) organized into categories. For each link, you provide a URL, the target for the link, a name for the link, and a description of the link.

For the Zak Springs site we will use the Web Links component to create a simple directory of local hotels and other leisure partners. The link will point to the website of the relevant business to enable visitors to the course to book accommodation.

For now, we'll create one category, called Hotels within 10 Kilometres, and add a single link to that category for the Hotel De Fear.

Creating Web Link Categories

To create a **Web Link** category, select **Components | Web Link | Web Link categories**, and then click the **New** button in the toolbar.

Now enter **Hotels within 10 Kilometres** into the **Category Title** and **Category Name** fields. Leave the other options as they are. Scroll down and enter **Quality hotels within 10 kilometres of Zak Springs Golf Club** into the **Description** field:

After entering these details, click the **Save** button in the toolbar.

Your first category can now be seen:

Creating Web Links

Now we can create a link to go in this category.

Select **Components | Web Links | Web Link Items** from the administrator menu, and click the **New** button in the toolbar.

Enter **Hotel De Fear** into the **Name** category, select the category we just created from the **Category** drop-down box, and enter **www.hoteldefear.com** into the URL field. In the **Description** field, enter something like:

4 star accommodation in picturesque hamlet of Draxville

167 Darkness Boulevard

Draxville

Leave the other options as they are, and click the **Save** button in the toolbar. Your newly created **Web Link** can be seen:

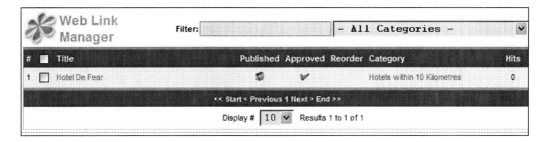

That'll do for now. That's given us a quick experience of managing other components. Since **Web Links** comes with Mambo you would expect it to behave in a very similar way to Mambo in general, and it does. The process we've just gone through to enter data is one that we will be doing over and over again in our Mambo lives.

Summary

In this chapter we looked at managing media, modules, and components.

Mambo has a **Media Manager** that allows you to upload directly to the server without the need for a separate FTP client. We used the **Media Manager** to upload the logo for Zak Springs golf club.

Next we looked at module management. Modules are generally PHP files that go in the `modules` folder of your Mambo installation, and the actual modules on the site are "instances" of these bits of codes.

We saw three aspects to module management:

- General module details: its name, where it's displayed on the page, who can see it
- Which pages it is displayed on
- Configuration specific to that type of module

We also created a couple of new module instances. We created an RSS feed module to grab some golf headlines, a custom HTML module to display the Zak Springs logo, and then created a copy of the **Random Images** module to display some holes from the Zak Springs golf course.

We looked at component management next. In general, there isn't much to general component management, and the management of individual components is really the key to managing your Mambo site, and we'll spend time on that over the remaining chapters. We concluded the chapter with a quick look at the Web Links component, to add details of hotels near to the Zak Springs course.

We also looked at Mambo's powerful Universal Installer. This allows you to install any kind of Mambo add-on from a single page, and provides a range of different ways of installing the add-on. We looked at the basic way, whereby you select the package containing the add-on (a ZIP file), and it is uploaded to the server, and Mambo takes care of the rest. We also saw how to install an add-on directly from a remote URL. This is certainly a feature for the future for Mambo, since it does open up the possibility of remote updating of add-ons on your site, to keep them up to date in the same way that your virus checker keeps itself up to date. Mambo isn't there yet, but there is a definite possibility for that in the future.

6
Managing Menus and Templates

In this chapter, we will look at managing menus and templates. Menus contain links to pages on your site, but more than that, these links also control the way the page will be displayed. Mastering Mambo's menu management is a must to making your site useful for visitors. We'll also have a look at the proposed menu structure for Zak Springs.

Templates control the look and layout of your site pages. Later in this chapter we'll have a quick look at how to select different templates, and assign them to different pages on the site.

Menus

Without menus, visitors will have a very difficult time finding anything on your site.

You can see all the menus currently set up on your site from the **Menu | Menu Manager** option of the administrator menu:

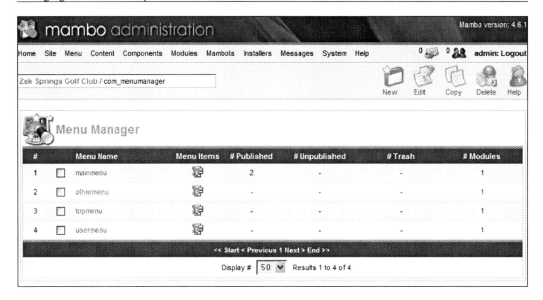

From here you can rename the menus by clicking on their titles (or checking in the box next to the title and clicking the **Edit** icon), delete menus, or create a copy of an existing menu.

If you click the graphic in the **Menu Items** column, you can begin editing the individual menu items of a particular menu.

Alternatively, you can get to the menu items of a particular menu directly by selecting its name from the **Menu** administrator drop-down menu.

We'll start with the **mainmenu**.

Menu Items

A menu is made up of menu items. Menu items point to pages on your site. However, they don't just point to a page, they define how the target page should be displayed. This control over the display is determined by the type of the menu item.

Creating a menu item involves two stages.

1. Choosing the type of the menu item
2. Providing a name for the menu item, and then some configuration specific to the type of menu item

After these two stages are complete you are ready to save your menu item.

 Be careful! After you have chosen your menu type, done the second step, and then saved your menu item, you cannot change the menu type, unless you delete it and start all over again.

The **Menu Manager** for the **mainmenu** currently looks like this:

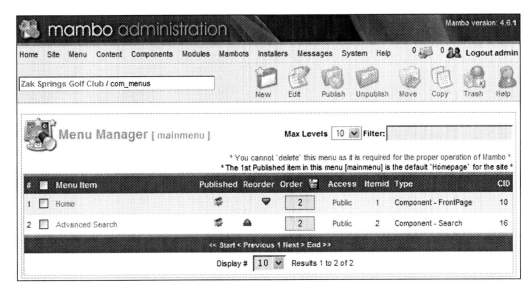

It's a familiar looking table. You can see the publication state of the menu item, its order on the menu, who can access the menu item, and also its **Type**.

You can configure individual menu items to be visible to the **Public, Registered** users, or **Special** users.

 Who can access the menu as a whole can't be found in any of these menu management screens. Since a menu is actually a module, access to the whole menu is determined by the properties of the corresponding module.

The modules for the standard menus have names like Main menu (**mainmenu**), Other menu (**othermenu**) and so on.

Let's get straight into creating a new menu item. We'll create a menu item to point to our Web Links.

Click the **New** button in the toolbar to move to the **New Menu Item** page to choose your menu type:

Menu Item Types

The **New Menu Item** page has four panels that group the menu types:

- Content
- Components
- Links
- Miscellaneous

Within these panels, there are a number of different menu entry types:

- **Link**
- **Component**
- **Blog**
- **Table**
- **Wrapper**
- **Separator/Placeholder**

As we look at the panels, we'll get an idea of what these menu types mean, and follow that with an illustration of the difference between the menu types.

Content Menu Type

Menu items created from the types found in the **Content** panel are for displaying content items. The Content panel contains menu entries of type **Blog, Link,** and **Table**. Content is obviously very important to your site; so that explains why it has its own panel! We'll talk about this type of menu items in more detail in Chapter 8, when we really get to grips with content management in Mambo.

Components Menu Type

The choices in the **Components** panel create menu items that allow you to jump straight into some part of a component.

- The **Component** option creates a menu entry that takes the user of the site to the main page of a particular component.
- The **Link** options create menu entries that take users to a single published item in the component (**Contact Item** and **Newsfeed** are there by default).
- The **Table** options create menu entries that take users to some "list" in a component (**Contact, News Feed,** and **Weblinks** are there by default).

Links Menu Type

The choices in the **Links** panel create menu items of type **Link**. These take you straight to a published item in a component. There is also a **Link – Url** option that allows you to explicitly specify a target URL. This can be used to link to places external to your site.

From reading the above paragraph, you would think that the description of the **Links** panel is almost identical to the **Link** options in the **Components** panel, and you might wonder what the difference is. Essentially, the **Links** panel is a collection of all the possible **Link** options, hence you are basically seeing repeated options in the **Links** panel.

If you were to create a **Link – Contact Item** menu entry from the **Links** panel, and a **Link – Contact Item** menu entry from the **Components** panel, and start digging around the Mambo database, you would find that there seems to be no difference between the way the two are stored, and also that there is no way the system could distinguish whether the menu entry came from the **Links** panel or the **Components** panel.

The important thing to bear in mind is that the **Links** panel is more or less a "recap" of the **Link** options available in the other panels.

Another thing to bear in mind is that a **Link** menu entry points to a published item in a component, and that likely only that item will be displayed on the page. The menu types in the **Components** panel (such as **Table**) offer wider views from components, such as lists.

Miscellaneous Menu Type

The first of the two menu types here, **Separator / Placeholder,** allows you to add a separator to your menu, to break the menu items up. The second type, **Wrapper,** will create an **IFRAME,** which can hold a complete page from another website. This is one way that you can "wrap" output of another application or even another website to make it look as if it is integrated into your site.

Adding a New Menu Entry

We're going to choose **Table – Web Link Category** from the **Components** panel. Either click that link, or select the radio button next to it and click the **Next** button in the toolbar.

If you have made some mistake, you can click the **Back** button in the toolbar and change your menu type. If you carry on and click the **Save** button to save your changes, there is no going back!

Add Menu Item Page

The **Add Menu Item** is the second step of the menu item creation process. Here is the page for the **Table – Web Link Category.**

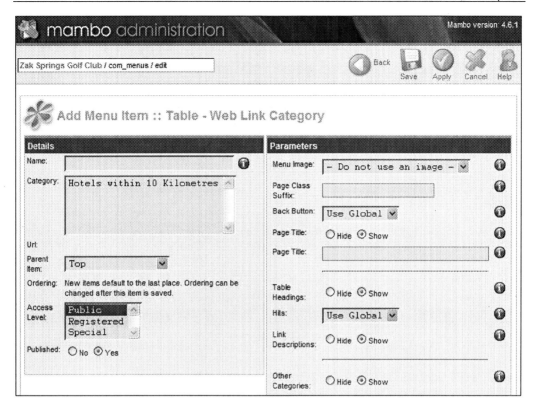

You can see the **Details** panel, which holds the information about the menu item, and the **Parameters** panel, which holds information specific to the menu type we chose. The **Parameters** panel we see here allows us to show the link descriptions for example. We will leave these as they are for now.

A menu item always needs a name, so let's enter **Accommodation** into the **Name** field. We need to select the category from the **Category** box, so click on our solitary category and it will become highlighted.

The **Parent Item** allows you to define a hierarchy in your menu. The default is **Top**, which means the menu item is at the top level of the menu. You can nest a menu item by selecting another menu item to be the parent from the **Parent Item** dropdown.

You can determine who can access this menu entry from the **Access Level** list, by selecting one of the user groups. If a visitor does not belong to the required group, then, by default, they will not even see the menu entry. This behavior is controlled by the **Show UnAuthorized Links** option on the **Site** tab of the **Global Configuration** (by default this set to **No**). Should a visitor find their way to a page corresponding to a menu entry that they cannot access, they will see a message of the form: **You are not authorized to view this resource.**

Let's leave everything else as it is, and click the **Save** button. Our first new menu entry is created:

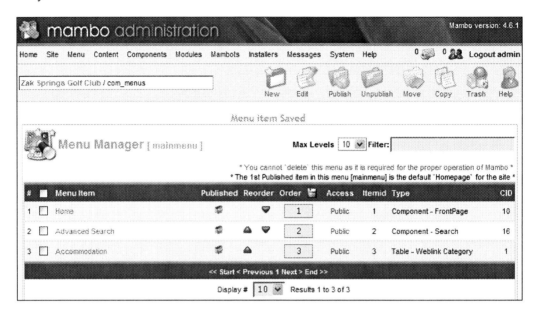

Now if your preview your site, you will see your new menu item:

Click the **Accommodation** link, and the list of Web Links (namely the hotels within 10 kilometres) is displayed:

News Feeds Component, Link, Category

Now that we've had an overview of the menu entry types, and seen how to create a menu entry, we'll now have a look at an example of the different types of menu items that can be created for the **Newsfeeds** component. In the **Components** panel, there are a couple of options for menu entries linking to parts of the **Newsfeeds** component. These options produce different looking pages, and also, different information is required to set up the menu item. Not only that, we will see different **Parameters** panels for the different types of menu items, presenting options relevant to that menu item type.

Note that this example actually works with the sample data site, and does not contribute anything to the Zak Springs site.

The **Newsfeeds** component organizes a list of sites into categories, and when a site is selected, the news feed from that site is grabbed and displayed on your site.

In the Components panel, there are two types of menu items for a News Feed:

- **Link - Newsfeed**
- **Table - News Feed Category**

There is also a third type that we can use, **Component**. As we mentioned earlier, this displays the homepage of a component. When you create a menu item of type **Component**, you obviously have to specify the component:

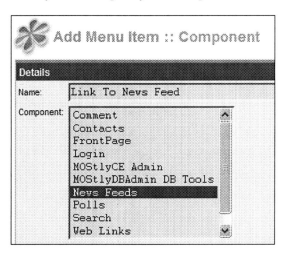

Once you supply the details for the menu item (you must always supply a **Name**), the page on the front end of your site will look something like this:

This just shows a list of the available News feed categories. It makes sense that if we created a menu item of type **Table - News Feed Category**, it would display a list of sites in a category.

When you create a menu item of type **Table - News Feed Category** you are prompted to select the category from the available list:

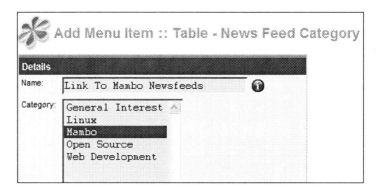

Once you select a category, and provide the rest of the details for the menu item, the page on the front end of your site will look something like this:

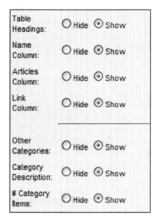

This page shows a list of sites within the category (along with the list of other categories underneath).

If you were to edit this menu item, you would see that it's **Parameters** reflect its table layout:

Here you can see options to control the way the list of sites in the category is displayed. By contrast, the **Component** menu item previously has no options like this in its **Parameters** panel.

We should be able to predict what will happen with a link of type **Link - Newsfeed**. The page will display the news feed from a single site, and we will be asked to select that site from the list when the menu item is created. That's exactly what happens when you create a menu item of type **Link – Newsfeed**:

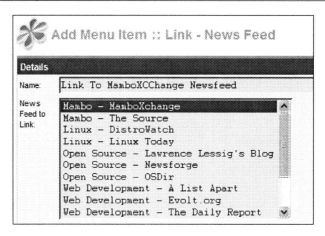

After you've selected your site, and filled in the rest of the details for the menu item, the page on the front end of the site will look something like this (we selected **Mambo – MamboXchange**):

Exactly as we predicted! Also, the **Parameters** panel for this menu item is relevant to showing the news feed of a single item:

Here we see options for displaying the description of the News Feed and so on. These can be used to change the look of the page.

On the sample data site, there is a **Newsfeed** link, of type **Component**. It displays a list of the categories; you click them to see the list of sites in the category, and you click one of the sites to see its News feed. This is an example of how there can be pages on your site that do not have menu items pointing to them, and yet they are still accessible. There is only one menu item pointing to the **Newsfeed** component on that site, and yet it is possible to see any of the news feeds by following links in the component.

Planning the Zak Springs Menu Structure

We've leapt ahead and added a menu item for the Zak Springs site without too much discussion of the menu structure we'd like to end up with, so we'd better catch up!

We'd like to have three menus, a top (horizontal) menu, a main navigation menu, and a menu at the bottom of the page.

From our requirements in Chapter 1, we'll make a quick list of the kind of menu items we'd like our menus to have. However, this is just a rough sketch at this point, since we don't yet have a clear view on how we'll create the pages for most of the menu items. Also, since Mambo doesn't allow you to edit the type of a menu item after you've created it, we can't even rush off and create the menu structure and then add the types of content later. For now, we will have to content ourselves with this plan.

Top Menu: This menu will provide quick links to the main parts of the site:

```
Home    News    Courses    Pro-Shop    Members
```

Main Menu: This is our main navigational element. The indented elements below would be nested menu items:

```
Home

News
    Course Information
    Membership
    Tournaments

About Zak Springs
    History
    Location
```

```
Golf Club Staff
    President
    Administrative Staff
    Golf Staff
    Hospitality Staff

The Courses
    Rates
    Scorecards
    Gallery

Professional's Shop
    Meet the Team
    Equipment
    Lessons

Membership
    Membership Rates
    Membership Terms and Conditions
    Apply for Membership

Events and Tournaments

Blogs
    President
    Professional

The Facilities
    Bar and Catering
    Weddings

Accommodation

Contact Us
```

Bottom Menu : The bottom menu will be another horizontal menu.

```
Home        Contact Us    Membership    Accomodation
```

We'll create the Bottom Menu now. The other menus we will create as we go, in later chapters.

Creating the Bottom Menu

From **Menu | Menu Manager**, click the **New** button to create a new menu. We'll give this menu the Name **bottommenu**, and the module corresponding to this menu will be called **Bottom Menu**:

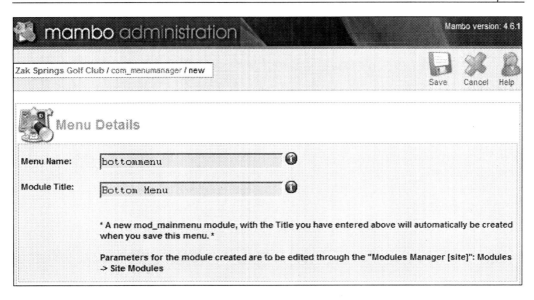

Click the **Save** button and our menu is created:

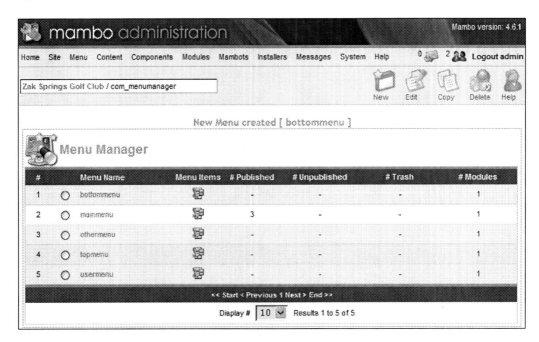

To get on with adding the menu items to this menu, click the graphic in the **Menu Items** column of the **bottommenu** row:

Now click the **New** button in the toolbar, and we can add our first menu item, **Home**, which will point to the homepage of the site. This menu item will be of type **Component**, because it will point to the homepage of a component — the **FrontPage** component.

Check the **Component** radio button, and click the **Next** button in the toolbar:

Enter **Home** into the **Name** field and select the **FrontPage** component from the **Component** list. Everything else can be left as it is if for now.

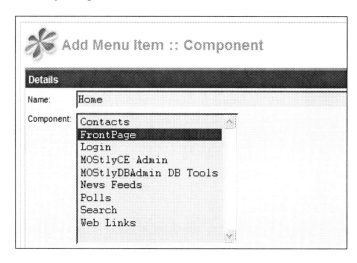

Click the **Save** button in the toolbar, and our bottom menu is underway:

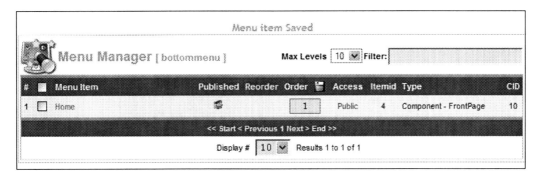

There isn't much else to add to this menu at the moment, other than the **Accommodation** link, pointing to the Web Links component as earlier, so add that, and let's move on to see how to display the menu on the page.

Assigning the Menu to a Module Position

The display of a menu is determined by the module that corresponds to it. Right now, the module corresponding to our **bottommenu** menu has not been published, so we can't see it anyway. If you go to **Modules | Site Modules**, you will also see that its default position is **left**, which is not where we want the menu displayed. We want the module displayed somewhere near the bottom of the page, ideally in the middle.

Click the **Bottom Menu** link, and we can see about a better position for this module. If you have a look on the **Position** drop-down list, there is a position called **footer** that sounds pretty hopeful:

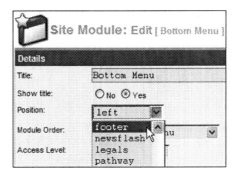

Select **footer** from the **Position** dropdown, select **Yes** for the **Published** option. We want this to be a horizontal menu, so let's scroll down the screen, and select **Horizontal** from the **Menu Style**:

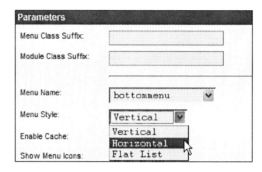

Click the **Save** button in the toolbar.

As we created this menu, there were two things to notice:

- The menu is just a holder of menu items, links to "pages".
- How the menu is displayed is controlled by the corresponding module.

Thus if you find yourself puzzling over why a menu looks the way it does, then you need to look into the module corresponding to the menu rather than the menu itself.

Returning to our bottom menu, if you preview your site, you won't see your menu. The problem is that the current template does not support the **footer** position.

If you use **Site | Preview | Inline with Positions** to see the modules positions supported by the current template, you don't see footer! This is rather unfortunate at the moment, but not a big problem, and we'll overcome it in Chapter 11, and reveal our Bottom Menu in all its glory.

If you are desperate to see your new menu, you could change its position to **banner**, which is where advertising banners are displayed (it's at the foot of the page in the default themes).

The Wrong Homepage?

If you have a look at your new **bottommenu**, and click the **Home** link in it, you may notice something odd. It looks like the front page of the site, but you won't see the **Login Form** module; but it should be there. Why is not there? It's because the Login Form module is displayed on the **mainmenu | Home** page, and this is different from the **bottommenu | Home** page. To have the **Login Form** module displayed on your **bottommenu | Home** page, you will need to set this from the **Pages / Items** panel of the **Login Form** module:

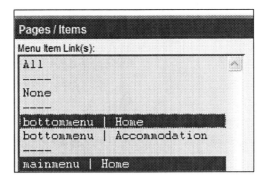

This might seem like a slightly confusing aspect of Mambo; you have created menu links that should point to the same page, but the pages aren't the same! However, it does make sense; the page is "defined" by the menu item, and two menu items would define two different pages. It might just happen that at some point, you want those pages to be the same, so this means that you have to modify one of the menu items to make it the "same" as the other menu item, so the pages the menu items point to will actually be the "same".

Managing Templates

Templates control your site's look and feel. We'll take a brief look at the overall management of templates, before we have a deeper look at them in Chapter 11.

There are two types of templates: templates for the site (front end), and administrator templates, for the backend. We'll look at site templates here.

Template management begins from **Site | Template Manager | Site Templates** from the administrator drop-down menu. The currently installed templates are listed:

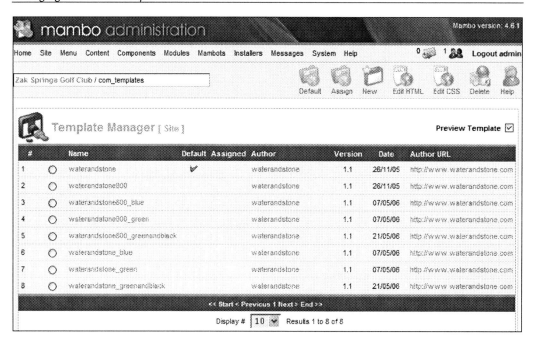

The name of the template is shown in the **Name** column, and hovering your mouse cursor over one of the entries in that column brings up a preview of how the template looks:

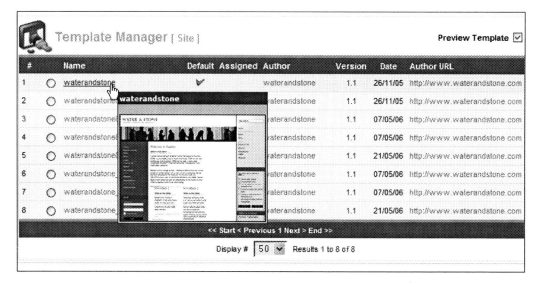

The default template for the site is marked in the **Default** column. All of the templates installed by default are variations on the "**Water and Stone**" template, with different colors, or optimized for different screen sizes. To select a new template for your site, simply check the radio button next to the template name, and click **Default** in the toolbar, and your entire site will be transformed.

Installing a new template is done through the Universal Installer that we covered in the previous chapter when looking at installing Mambo add-ons.

Assigning Templates to Pages

Setting a template as the default means every page on the site will use this template. However, you can specify a different template to be displayed on a particular page, so that your site can have different templates on different parts of the site, so not every page need look the same.

You assign a template to a particular page by checking the radio button next to the template name, and then clicking **Assign** in the toolbar. A list of the pages on the site, or more accurately, a list of menu items, is displayed.

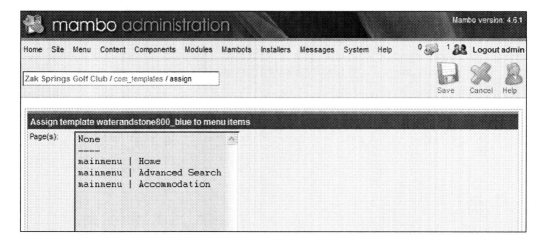

To assign a template to a particular page (or a set of pages), simply select the pages you want in the **Page(s)** box, and click the **Save** button. On the face of it, this looks like it only allows you to assign templates to a small number of pages, namely the ones that correspond to menu items. However, when we look at managing content in Mambo, we'll see that it is more flexible.

Summary

In this chapter, we looked at managing menus and templates. Without menus, visitors will have a very difficult time finding anything on your site. A menu is made up of menu items. Menu items point to pages on your site. However, they don't just point to a page, they define how the target page should be displayed. This control over the display is determined by the **type** of the menu item.

We saw the two stages of creating a menu item:

1. Choosing the type of the menu item
2. Providing a name for the menu item, and then some configuration specific to the type of menu item

We saw how the type of menu item affects not only the way the page is displayed, but also the options that are available to control that display.

We also saw the difference between pages and menu items. You might think you have two menu items pointing to the same page, but in fact the pages are slightly different. The page is "defined" by the menu item, and two menu items would define two different pages, so you may need to adjust one of the menu items to make it like the other page.

We finished the chapter with a look at template management. We saw how to select different templates, and assign templates to different pages on the site.

7
Managing Users

Mambo enables visitors to your site to create and maintain their own user account, and maintain their personal details. Those annoying little tasks like managing lost passwords are also taken care of for you by Mambo.

User accounts can be created in two ways:

- By the user registering on your site
- By the Super Administrator (that's you)

The first method involves a confirmation email sent to the user's email account. This email contains a link for them to click and confirm their registration to activate their account (although this feature can be turned off).

In this chapter, we will walk through the creation of new users, both by registering as a new user from the standard visitor interface on the site and by the Super Administrator.

We will also look at the features for managing users from the back end of the site, and look at the different types of back-end user that can be created, and what power they have.

We conclude the chapter by exploring the users and roles we will need to set up for the Zak Springs site.

User Groups

Not all users of a Mambo site are equal; different users can have different "permissions". Some can just read the text on the web pages, click links, and generally just "see" things and interact in a limited way. Some users are able to "do" things, and actually able to change things.

Rather than managing these permissions at the level of individual users, Mambo has **groups** of users, and certain permissions are assigned to these groups. When a user is a member of a group, they get the permissions of that group.

Groups in Mambo are divided in two types, front-end groups and back-end groups, and this determines where they can do their stuff.

- The front-end groups are **Registered, Author, Editor**, and **Publisher**. The **Registered** user is a standard site user, with a username and password. There isn't much else they can do, other than enjoy reading the content of the site. The **Author, Editor**, and **Publisher** groups deal with the submission of content through the front end of the site. We'll talk more about these in the next few chapters when we start managing content.

- The back-end groups are **Manager, Administrator**, and **Super Administrator**. We'll meet these later in this chapter.

The Special Ones

We have seen in the last few chapters that for published items on our site, we can restrict access to one of three sets of users: **Public, Registered**, and **Special**. We explained who users in the **Public** and **Registered** set were, but we were not so forthcoming about this **Special** set. This consists of users who are an **Author, Editor**, or **Publisher**.

Ingredients of a User

Every user, front end or back end, requires a certain amount of information to uniquely identify them in Mambo. There are three things required of every user in Mambo:

- **A username**: This identifies who the user is, and is their online identity in Mambo.

- **A password**: This is required to verify that the user is who they claim to be.

- **A valid email address**: A confirmation email is sent to this address.

Once the user account is created for a user, the user is of course able to modify their details.

Registering as a User

The first thing we'll do is to create a user account by registering on the front end of the site as a normal visitor would. We'll call the user account `testuser`.

Before doing this, make sure you have configured your mail setup properly from the **Mail** tab of the **Global Configuration** settings. You will need this because a confirmation email will be sent to the email address you specify for the user. The confirmation email sent by Mambo is a key part of the registration process, and includes a special link for the visitor to click to activate their account. If you can't get your mail setup working, you can follow the text and screenshots for now. Configuring mail from a desktop, test environment is not always so easy. Don't worry though, when your site is live on a web-hosting account, you will undoubtedly be able to access a mail server.

1. First of all, make sure you are on the site's homepage, so that you can see the Login module. Click the **Create one** link after the **No account yet?** text at the foot of the Login module. If for some reason, you can't see the Login module (you should be able to!), then you can use the direct URL of the registration page:

   ```
   http://localhost/zaksprings/index.php?option=com_registration&t
   ask=register
   ```

   This brings you to the **Registration** page:

2. Enter the **Name** as **Test User**, and **testuser** for the **Username**.
3. Enter your own email address into the **E-mail** field.
4. For convenience, we are going to use **testuser** for the password as well as the username. If you can think of a better password at this point, enter it instead. Enter the password again into the **Verify password** field.

> The password needs to be more than 6 letters, and should contain only alphanumeric characters and no spaces. If your password does not conform, a dialog box will pop up advising you of this, and you will not be able to submit your details until you have chosen a suitable password.

5. Check the box next to **Yes, I Accept** to accept the **Disclaimer and Privacy Policy**. If you don't check the box to accept these terms, you will not be able to register.

6. Click the **Send Registration** button. You will see a screen asking you to confirm your details. You can click the **CORRECT YOUR DATA** button to go back and change the details, or click **CONFIRM REGISTRATION** to move on:

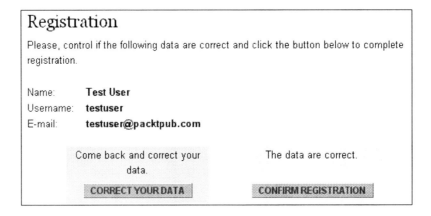

7. Once you click **CONFIRM REGISTRATION**, you will see a message like this:

Registration Complete

Your account has been created and an activation link has been sent to the e-mail address you entered.

Note that you must activate the account by clicking on the activation link before you can login.

8. Open up your email client, and log in to check your mail. You should find a mail with the subject **New User Account Activation** waiting for you. It will be from the email address you specified in the **Administrator Email** field in the **Site Configuration Menu**. The body of that email will look something like this:

Hello Test User,

Thank you for registering at Test Site. Your account has been created but, as a precaution, it must be activated by you before you can use it.

To activate the account click on the following link or copy and paste it in your browser:

http://localhost/zaksprings/index.php?option=com_registration& task=activate&activation=b157f6e453fba6cbe91ae337ace64d57

After activation you may login to http://localhost/mambo46 using the following username and password:

Username – testuser

Password – testuser

9. Click the link in the email, or copy the link and paste it into your browser, and you will be taken to the activation page on your Mambo site where you will see a message of the form:

   Activation Complete!

   Your account has been activated successfully. You can now login using the username and password you chose during registration.

10. You are now ready to start using the username and password to log in. Note that you will have to return to the front page of your site to use the login module to log into the site.

That's all there is to creating a new user account. You will have done it hundreds of times on different sites across the Internet, and Mambo's user registration is no different.

Note that only one occurrence of a particular username is allowed; the system will check the uniqueness of the username before creating the account.

Also, the **Disclaimer and Privacy Policy** is currently "hard-coded" into the page output; at present, it is not configurable. If you're interested, the text to modify to add your own disclaimer can be found in the file `registration.html.php` in the folder `components\com_registration`, on line 139:

```
<?php echo T_('put your disclaimer here..'); ?>
```

In the mail sent to the visitor, you will notice that the link to activate the account contains the URL of your Mambo site:

```
http://localhost/zaksprings/index.php?option=com_registration&
task=activate&activation=b157f6e453fba6cbe91ae337ace64d57
```

Note that the URL of the site is taken straight from your Mambo setup, so the activation link is certain to point to the right site!

The **activation** part of the URL is what identifies the unregistered visitor to the system. When the visitor registers their details, Mambo stores them in the database along with the **activation** value. When the visitor visits the above link, Mambo will check the value of **activation** against the values stored in the database, and if it finds a match, that user account will be activated.

This is the last time a user will be able to see the password they entered. Mambo sends the password now, before it is stored in the database. The password itself isn't stored in the database, but a one-way encoded form is. This means that the original password cannot be retrieved. Except possibly by some super-sophisticated hacker like you see in movies, or some secret government agency, also like the kind you see in movies.

Should a user forget their password, a new one can be sent to them. They can click the **Password Reminder** link on the **Login Form** module (or enter the URL `http://localhost/zaksprings/index.php?option=com_registration&task=lostPassword` on your site), and then enter their **username** and **E-mail address** to receive a mail with a new, automatically-generated password. The visitor can now log in with this password, and change it to whatever they like (hopefully something they won't forget this time).

Note that unlike some other systems, the activation link does not expire.

Front-End User Goodies

Now that you have created (and activated!) a front-end account on your site, you could log in to see what goodies await you. If you return to the front page of your site, enter the **Username** and **Password** into the **Login Form** module, and click **LOGIN,** you should be logged in.

If you can't see the Login module, enter this URL instead:

```
http://localhost/zaksprings/index.php?option=com_login
```

This will take you to page with a form for entering your **Username** and **Password** details, and a **LOGIN** button to log in. The **Login Form** module bypasses this page, and goes straight to the authentication of your account details.

To be honest, there isn't much to see on the blank site!

Go ahead and create the **testuser** account on our previous sample data installation. After you're done there, and you log in, the User module is much more appealing:

Your name is now displayed in the Login Form module, and the User Menu module has appeared, including some links to your details, and to submit some pieces of content (a FAQ or a WebLink). You are able to edit all your details from the **Your Details** link (which takes you to the page index.php?option=com_ user&task=UserDetails), including changing your username.

User Management

Let's move on to user management at the back end of the site. User management starts by selecting the **Site | User Manager** option on the Administrator menu bar, or clicking the **Users** icon in the Control Panel:

This brings up the **User Manager**. The list of currently registered users is displayed.

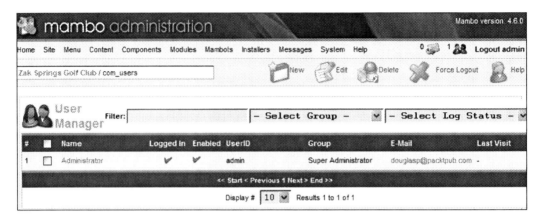

There is a text box to enter some text to **Filter** the usernames by — this allows you to search for users whose name matches your text.

The two drop-down boxes allow you to select users who are in a particular group, or show the users that are currently logged in, or not logged in.

For each user, the **Logged In** column is ticked if the user is currently logged in. The **Enabled** column indicates if the user account is activated. The **UserID** column shows their username, and their **Group**, **E-mail** address, and the time of their **Last Visit** is also shown.

Right now, we have only two users. One is your Administrator account, the other is the **testuser** account we just created. Since you activated the **testuser** account, there is a tick in its **Enabled** column.

While a user is in the limbo between registration and activation, their status would look like this in the **User Manager**:

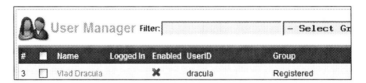

The red **X** in the **Enabled** column indicates that this user account isn't activated. By clicking this icon, you can activate an account, or deactivate an account that is currently operational. Deactivating an account will allow the user to continue to operate on the site, but once they are logged out, they will not be able to log back in again. Activating an account before a user activates it themselves will not cause problems for the user.

You can log out a particular user by checking the box next to their name, and clicking the **Force Logout** icon in the toolbar. The user will then find they are logged out (as soon as they attempt to access another page on the server).

If you have taken a sudden dislike to a particular user, check the box next to their entry in the **User Manager** and click the **Delete** icon on the toolbar, and they are gone forever (the user account, not the person).

 You can't delete a Super Administrator account. This not only applies to your Super Administrator account, but any other Super Administrator account.

User Details

Clicking on a user's name in the **User Manager** brings up their details:

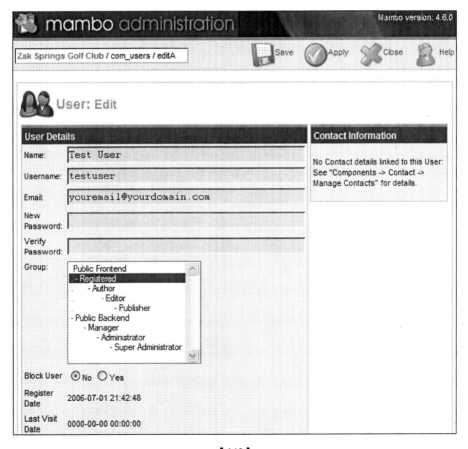

The user's **Name** and **Username**, **Email** address, and **Group** can be clearly seen, along with some information about when they registered on the site, and the date of their last visit.

The group to which this user belongs is shown highlighted in the **Group** text box. To select a group, simply click on the desired one and it will be highlighted. Note that **Public Frontend** and **Public Backend** are not actually groups you can select; they are simply bits of text to identify what the groups beneath them apply to.

You can't see their password (since Mambo doesn't store the actual password in the database; it stores a one-way encoded version of the password), but that doesn't matter; if you want to change the password, simply enter the new password into **New Password** and **Verify Password** text boxes.

If you want to make changes to these details, you will either need to enter the same text into the two password fields or leave both blank. If there is text in either of the password text boxes, the text will need to match or else you will not be able to submit your changes. If you find text has been entered into the text boxes (this may be done automatically by your browser), then you can simply delete that text from the box and save your changes. The password will not be changed.

If you want to make changes to a user's details, you do so in the usual way by clicking either the **Save** or **Apply** button in the toolbar, or **Cancel** if you want to abandon the edits and return to the User Manager.

Login Module Configuration

When a user logs in, their username is displayed in the **Login Form** module. This feature can be changed from the **Parameters** for the **Login Form** module. From **Modules | Site Modules**, select the **Login Form** module, and scroll down to see its **Parameters**. Here, we are changing the message to display the user's **Name**, rather than their **Username**.

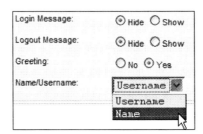

Adding a Logout Link

Once you a user has registered on your site and logged in, the User Menu will be displayed to them (it's for Registered Users). However, by default, there is nothing in that menu. A Logout link would be helpful, since there is no other obvious way for the user to log out (unless that is your plan: to trap users logged in forever!).

We'll add a **Logout** link to the User Menu now.

From **Menu | usermenu**, click **New** in the toolbar to create a new menu item, and click on the radio button beside **Component** from the **Components** panel:

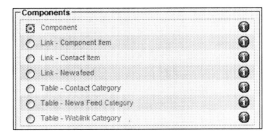

Click the **Next** button in the toolbar (or you can simply click on **Component**).

Enter **Logout** into the **Name** field, and select **Login** from the **Component** list. Set the **Level** to **Registered**:

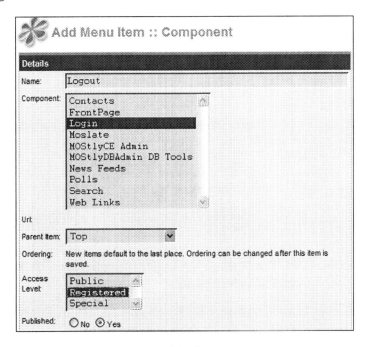

Now click the **Save** button in the toolbar. You will notice that apart from the **Name** we gave this menu item, there was nothing to suggest it actually will log the user out. The **Logout** link will not log the user out straight away; it will display a page with a button for them to click to log out. The direct URL to log out is:

```
http://localhost/zaksprings/index.php?option=logout
```

You can control some aspects of the page that displays the logout button by editing the menu item, and making use of the **Parameters** (scroll down to find them):

These options allow you to specify things like the page to redirect the user to after they have logged out (the default is the homepage of the site).

Super Administrator Details

If you look at the details of a Super Administrator account, you will see some minor differences between their details and "ordinary" users:

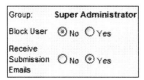

First of all, the **Group** cannot be changed. A Super Administrator cannot become anything other than a **Super Administrator**.

The next thing to note is the **Receive Submission Emails** option. When set to **Yes**, this account will receive notifications (as we'll see later, actually private messages) when certain content items are submitted to the site. We'll see this in action in the coming chapters.

Creating New Users at the Back end

The Super Administrator is able to create new users from the **User Manager** area. Click the **New** button in the toolbar to bring up the **User: Add** screen, which is almost identical to the **User: Edit** screen:

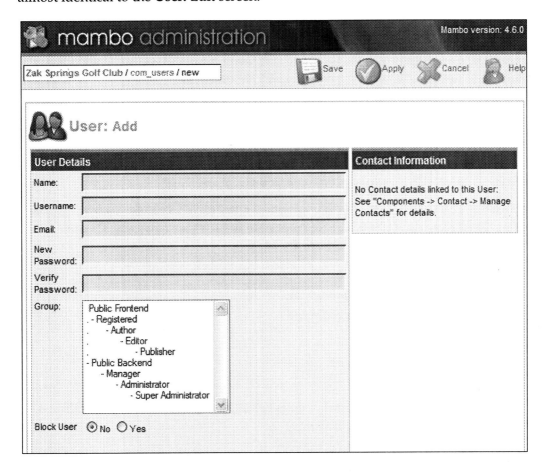

You enter the user's details here (remember the passwords need to match), select their group, and click **Save** or **Apply** to store the user.

When you create a user in this way, you (the Super Administrator) will not receive an email informing that a new user has been created (well, you did just do it yourself...). However, an email will be sent to the email address you specified for this account, informing the person that an account has been created:

> You have been added as a user to Zak Springs Golf Club by an Administrator.
>
> This email contains your username and password to log into the http://localhost/zaksprings
>
> Username - testuser
>
> Password - testuser
>
> Please do not respond to this message as it is automatically generated and is for information purposes only

Unless you specify **Yes** for the **Block User** option (its default is **No**), this user account will be enabled as soon as you click **Save** or **Apply**. Selecting **Yes** for the **Block User** option will mean the account isn't activated, but an email will be sent to the user anyway.

The Registration Process

We went through the registration process as a normal visitor, but we didn't really talk about the Super Administrator's role in this.

Whenever a user attempts to register on the site (before the account is activated), an email notification, with a title like **Account details for <Username> at <Name of your site>** is sent to the Super Administrator.

> Hello The Administrator,
>
> A new user has registered at Zak Springs.
>
> This email contains their details:
>
> Name - Test User
>
> e-mail – theiremailaddress@theirsite.com
>
> Username - testuser
>
> Please do not respond to this message as it is automatically generated and is for information purposes only

Registration Options

The administrator can control aspects of the user registration process from options on the **Site** tab of the **Global Configuration** control panel:

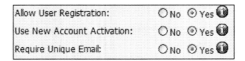

The first option, **Allow User Registration**, actually allows the above procedure to be carried out. If this option is set to **No**, then new users cannot register on the site, and only the administrator can create users. The default value is **Yes**.

The account activation stage can be bypassed by setting **Use New Account Activation** to **No**. If it is set in this way, then no email to activate the account will be sent, and the user account will be activated as soon as the details are entered. The administrator will still receive the email confirming the registration of a new user. The default value for this option is **Yes**.

By default, only one occurrence of an email address is allowed on the system; if someone uses an email address that belongs to another user account, then that address will be rejected, and the user will have to choose another address. This can be turned off by setting the **Require Unique Email** option to **No**, and future visitors will be able to register even if their email address is already in the database. The default value for this option is **Yes**.

Even an administrator is unable to assign the same email address to two different user accounts if the **Require Unique Email** address is set to **Yes**.

Managing Other Administrators

The Super Administrator account that you have been working with has complete control over the entire site. Super Administrator is actually a group, and your account is a member of that group.

As your site grows, it is possible that you may wish to get other people to help you out with some limited administration of the site, or you may even want to have different administrators for different tasks from the outset. Mambo lets you do this.

In addition to the Super Administrator group, Mambo provides two other types of groups with control over certain parts of the site back end. These are the **manager** and **administrator** groups. The manager group is concerned with content management; the administrator group is concerned with site administration.

A user in either of these groups is able to access the administration area of your site with these accounts. Obviously, no one can create an account like this for themselves; the account would have to be created by a Super Administrator, or an Administrator user.

A back-end user account is also valid on the front end of the site. Once you log in to the front end of the site with a back-end account, you will find that your front-end account has the same privileges as a **Publisher**. Exactly what a Publisher does will be seen in the next chapter.

Note that if you are logged into the front end of the site with a back-end user account, you will still have to log in from the administrator login page before you can do work on the back end.

The Administrator

Back-end users in the Administrator group have pretty comprehensive power, including administrative control over users, modules, and content among other things. However, they cannot manage the site templates, nor can they change the Global Configuration.

An administrator can create new users, and edit user details, including assigning users to different groups. An administrator cannot create a Super Administrator account, nor can they assign another user to Super Administrator status, nor can they even see the identity of the Super Administrators. In other words, they can only manage users who are "less than or equal to them".

Administrator accounts are "equal", which means you can't delete another administrator, but you can modify their details. You can change the password of another Administrator.

Users in the Administrator group have the **Receive Submission Emails** option available in their user details, so they can receive notifications about content submissions. Actually, they will receive private messages when a content item is submitted, as we'll see in the next chapter.

The Manager

Back-end users in the Manager group are able to manage content. Their administration toolbar is limited to only a couple of options, and the control panel shows only options for working with content:

A manager's attempts to access any other parts of the administration area will fail. In particular, a manager cannot administer users or modules; nor can create other front-end users.

 Users in the Manager group do not have the **Receive Submission Emails** option available in their user details.

Summary of Permissions for Back-end Groups

The table overleaf shows a quick summary of what a user in each back-end group can do:

	Manager	Administrator	Super Administrator
Content	X	X	X
Templates			X
Users		X	X
Modules		X	X
Components		X	X
Install		X	X
Receive Notifications		X	X
Edit Users		X	X
Delete Users			X

Zak Springs Users and Groups

We'll continue with the Zak Springs site, and create some users in various groups that correspond to the requirements of the site. When you create these users, you may want to add your own email address for the users, and, for convenience, before you start, you may want to set the **Require Unique Email** address option to **No** in the **Global Configuration** to allow to you to use the same email address for them all.

Here is the statement of the permissions and privileges mentioned in the original site requirements:

- "Weblog" for Club Professionals, offering equipment and game tips
- "Weblog" for Club President
- Administrative Staff to be able to publish and amend news items
- Hospitality staff to be able to publish and amend content for hospitality facilities
- Marketing Manager to be able to amend any content on the site
- Nominated member of Administrative Staff to have full control over site
- Ability to amend these permissions in future
- Club President to have full control over site

From this, it looks like we'd want to set up a Super Administrator account for the Club President (well, he is paying our bill...), and also a Super Administrator or Administrator account for one of the members of the Administrative Staff, Edgar Hooch.

From the looks of it, the Administrative Staff would probably want to be set up with a Publisher account on the front end.

The Marketing Manager only needs to amend, so Editor seems like a good choice for him. However, it may be best to give this user a Manager account, to manage content on the back end. This would put him in total control of the site's content.

However, further discussion reveals that the Marketing Manager should check all the content before it goes onto the site. This would certainly mean the Marketing Manager would need a Manager back-end account.

We'll create these accounts:

Name	User name	Group
Otto Simplex	osimplex	Super Administrator
Edgar Hooch	edgarh	Administrator
Brad Visionary	bradv	Manager
Marie Flame	marief	Frontend – Editor
Audrey Pores	audreyp	Frontend – Author
Neil Vortex	neilv	Frontend – Publisher

There are more accounts to create, but these will do for now. You may prefer, for the sake of your convenience, to give these accounts more memorable names, such as **admini** for the administrator, **manager** for the Manager, **editor** for the Front-end Editor, **author**, **publisher** and so on.

Set up these accounts, and your list of users should look as follows:

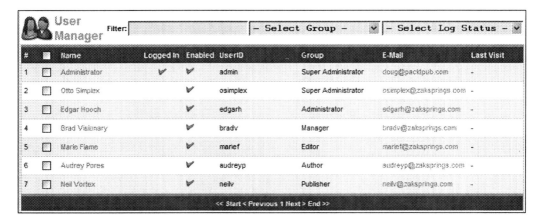

We'll also set the Administrator account (Edgar Hooch) to receive Submission Emails.

Summary

In this chapter we have seen how users are able to register themselves on your site, and how you as the Super Administrator manage them from the back end of the site.

We walked through creating a new user account on the site, and saw the mail received by new users with their account details, and also the other administrator mails that are triggered when new users register themselves on the site.

We also saw how to create a back-end user, a user in the Administrator or Manager group. Each of these groups has limitations on the back-end tasks that they can do; an **Administrator** "manages" the site, a **Manager** "manages" content.

We also looked briefly at the so-called **Special** front-end users, users in one of the **Author**, **Editor**, or **Publisher** groups. We'll see more of these as we move into content management in the coming chapters.

Finally, we ended the chapter by creating a number of user accounts for key personnel on the Zak Springs site.

8
Managing Content

So far our site is pretty empty. The middle bit of our homepage still seems pretty empty. It feels like there is something missing. That's right, the content.

Mambo does not summon content from the darkest regions of the universe to appear on your site by magic (I'm sorry to disappoint you there). In this chapter, we will begin the journey of managing content with Mambo, or, in other words, getting stuff up on the site.

Here we're going to look at the fundamental type of Mambo content, the content item. Content items are the most versatile type of Mambo's content, and have probably the richest set of features of all its available content types. In fact, there are so many features and options that it can make you dizzy. That is what this chapter is for. No — not making you dizzy, but helping you avoid the dizziness by guiding you through all the features of Mambo content management.

In this chapter, we will look at the back-end details of content item management. We will cover:

- Organizing content items into sections and categories
- Managing sections and categories
- Adding, deleting, and archiving content
- Adding content items to menus
- Adding images to content with the mosimage mambot
- Different views of content

In the following chapter, we will look at content item management from the front end of the site.

Organizing Content

Mambo has two schemes for entering content in the Content component: **organized content** and **static content**. Static content is content that is "not organized"; that doesn't necessarily means it's disorganized. It simply means that the content items in this scheme are not intended to fit into any particular organization of hierarchy; they are a kind of floating content if you like. This kind of content would be used for one-off pieces of content that don't particularly relate to or fit with anything else on the site directly.

We'll actually spend most of our time talking about "organized content", since this is the way that you will mostly be storing your content in Mambo.

Before you start entering content, you need some form of organization for it. Mambo organizes content into sections and categories, following this hierarchy:

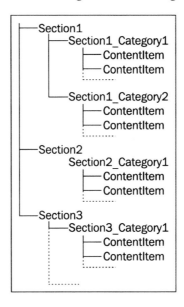

This diagram shows that sections contain categories, and categories contain the content items. Sections do not contain content items directly.

What is also implied from this diagram is that a content item can belong to at most one category, and a category belongs to at most one section. Categories cannot contain other categories.

A way of thinking about sections and categories that you will often see is that sections are like the drawers in a filing cabinet, categories are the folders within those drawers, and the content items are the documents within the folders.

Why Organize Content?

Organizing content makes it easier for the visitor to find something; if they were looking for an article about Tyrannosaurus Rex, and they saw you had a collection of articles about dinosaurs, they would probably expect to find the article in that collection.

Organizing content also makes it easier to decide where content should go, and it also has benefits in terms of how you manage the display of the content, and help the visitor navigate through the structure.

For example, you can display a list of all the content items in a category, which will be automatically updated as soon as you change the details of a content item, delete it, unpublish it, and so on. Similarly, lists of all the categories within a particular section are also generated by Mambo, so that you can very easily create a navigational structure for your content.

You can create a menu entry that will display a list of all the categories in a particular section. The exact display of this list can be controlled from the administration area of course. When a user clicks on one of the categories, all the content items in that category will be displayed; again, the display of this list can be controlled from the administration area. In this way, you will have created a navigational structure for everything in a particular section simply by adding a single menu entry. That's it; and when you update your content items, your lists get updated automatically. We'll see more about this later in the chapter.

Planning the Zak Springs Content Structure

While this all seems straightforward, it is not entirely clear how this organization will relate to the kind of content you plan to add to your site. So let's see how we would organize the planned content for Zak Springs into sections and categories.

Let's review the requirements from Chapter 1 that look as if they might relate to content items:

- Categorized news publishing; course news, membership information, competition results
- Weblog for Club Professionals, offering equipment and game tips
- Weblog for Club President
- Content for hospitality facilities
- Information about the club and its history

The first requirement suggests that we would want a News section, with categories like Course Information, Membership, and Tournaments.

The Club President's Weblog is a collection of articles written by the club president, he wants to write about his vision for the future of the club, the course and so on. It sounds like we'd want a section devoted to the president, say From the President.

The Club Professional will also need a Weblog, so we can have a From the Professional section. That section would have categories like Equipment, Game Tips, Special Offers (advising of the latest offers available in his shop).

A Hospitality or Facilities section seems to fit the bill as well. This would contain categories like Restaurant, Bar, Weddings, among others.

Finally, the "Information about the club and its history" requirement is quite interesting. This suggests a section like About Zak Springs, but since content items can't belong to sections directly, we would need some categories there. We could have a category called History, and a category called General Information.

However, these categories for About Zak Springs seem like adding an unnecessary number of categories—the only reason we want to add them is because the system forces to add them because we can't attach content items directly to sections. Also, the club's history does not change that much from week to week, even with the Club President's highly revisionist view of his own achievements and importance to the club, so the benefits of the automatic list of content items wouldn't really be felt here. All of this suggests that the standard section-category model of content organization isn't really what we want here. We will look into using the other way of managing content, static content, for this.

In this chapter we will create a number of these sections and categories as we go, and also add a couple of content items to the categories to get the site warmed up.

Creating Sections

The first step on the road to creating content is to create your sections. Section management can be started from one of two places:

- Clicking the **Sections** icon in the control panel of the administration homepage:

- Selecting the **Content | Section Manager** menu option of the administrator menu

Both of these will bring you to the **Section Manager** page.

Since we currently have no sections, there isn't much to see on this page, so let's get cracking with creating a new section.

Click the **New** icon in the toolbar on the **Section Manager** page.

All a section needs is a **Title** and a **Section Name**. The Title of the section is how the section will be displayed on the front end of the site. The **Section Name** is how the section will be identified in the back end of the site.

Go ahead and create the sections for the Zak Spring site. After entering the title and section name, click the **Save** icon in the toolbar, and then click the **New** icon from the **Section Manager** toolbar to create the next section.

Zak Springs Sections

For the Zak Springs site, we will add these sections. We will give each section the same title and section name:

- **Club News**
- **From the President**

The **From The President** section is for the president's blog.

Section Manager Page

Now that we have some sections, the **Section Manager** screen looks a bit more interesting:

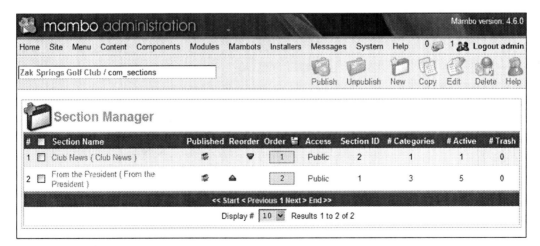

This kind of table is probably becoming very familiar to you now. We see the **Section Name** (the title of the section is in brackets), whether the section is published, its order, who can access it; and also:

- # **Categories**: the number of categories contained within that section

- # **Active**: the total number of content items which are not "trashed" in the categories within that section

- # **Trash**: the number of things "trashed" from that section

I've used the word "things" to describe what the **Trash** column represents. Things actually means categories here. When we delete a category in a section, it doesn't actually get deleted straight away, but instead goes into the trash (like the **Recycle Bin** on your computer), from where it can get removed from the system entirely. The number of categories sitting in the trash that belong to that section is shown in the **Trash** column.

You can publish, unpublish, and edit the details of sections in the usual way from the **Section Manager**. We'll return to other operations with sections later in the chapter.

Creating Categories

Now that we have some sections, we can add some categories, and assign these to some of our sections.

General category management can be started from one of two places:

- By clicking the **Categories** link in the control panel of the administration home page:

- From the **Content | Category Manager** menu option of the administrator menu

There is a third way to manage categories, and this takes you straight to the categories within a particular section. When you select the **Content | Content By Section** menu option of the administrator menu, each section is listed as a menu option. Each of these sections in turn expands to provide a link to the all the content items under that section, as well as a link to **Add/Edit** the categories in that section:

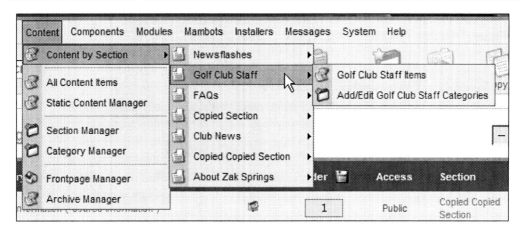

All of these options bring you to the **Category Manager**. Choosing the category from the **Content | Content By Section** menu option will show only the categories within your chosen section.

Initially, the **Category Manager** display is empty, so let's press straight on with creating categories.

Before we get into the mechanics of creating a category, it's worth bearing this fact in mind. Remember we said that categories are assigned to exactly one section? You would be correct in thinking that you assign the section at the time you create the category. What may be more surprising is this:

Once a category is created and assigned to a section, that assignment cannot be changed. The only way to reassign a category to a new section is to move the category, which we'll cover later in the chapter.

To begin creating a category, click the **New** icon in the toolbar of the **Category Manager**, and you will find yourself at the **Category:New** page.

The **Category Details** panel is similar to the **Section Details** panel we saw earlier. An important field is the **Section** field. You select the section you want to assign this category to from the list of sections in the drop-down box. If you discover that the section you want hasn't been created yet, it will be easiest to cancel creating your category, and instead create the section first and then return to creating the category.

You must specify a section; if you do not, you will be not be able to create the category.

If you chose to do your category management through the **Content | Content By Section** administrator menu option, the section will already be chosen for you.

Zak Springs Categories

For the Zak Springs site, we will add these categories, and assign them to the following sections:

- Membership (Membership), assigned to Club News
- Tournaments (Tournaments) , assigned to Club News
- Course Information (Course Information), assigned to Club News
- The Future (The Future), assigned to From the President
- The Course (The Course), assigned to From the President
- Fun and Trivia (Fun and Trivia), assigned to From the President

Category Manager Page

Now that we have some categories, the **Category Manager** page is a bit more lively:

Once again, it's a familiar table. You can see if a category has been published, its order, which group of users can view the category and also how many published content items belong to that category, and how many content items from that category are waiting in the trash.

The section to which the category belongs is also displayed. Clicking on the name of the section takes you to the **Section Edit** page, from where you can edit details of that section. Note that after finishing your edits on the section, you will find yourself in the **Section Manager** rather than the **Category Manager**.

You can use the drop-down box to restrict the categories to only those from a particular section. We'll return to the other operations you can perform with categories later in the chapter.

Entering Content

Perhaps this section should really be called "Finally we get to type stuff into the system". Now that we've done sections and categories, we're ready for what you have been waiting for—entering content into the system. Actually, typing in the content isn't the interesting bit of this section, we've already seen the basics of entering content in Chapter 3, along with a look at the HTML editor.

What is interesting here is the set of options Mambo provides for:

- Adding images to the content item
- Adding the content item to an existing menu
- Entering information about the content item to help it get indexed by search engines
- Controlling when the item is published to the site
- Controlling the elements that are displayed along with the content item

These options move Mambo beyond a simple system where you just enter some text that gets displayed on a web page, and make it an extremely flexible content management system.

Content Items Manager Page

The **Content Items Manager** page is the your place for adding or editing content items.

It can be reached by:

- Clicking the **All Content Items** icon in the control panel of the administrator home page:

- Selecting the **Content | All Content Items** menu option of the administrator menu.

- If there already is a content item in a category belonging to a particular section, there will be a content items menu entry for that section under the **Content | Content By Section** menu option of the administrator menu.

Any of these will bring you to the **Content Items Manager** page. The third option will restrict you to content items in the categories belonging to the chosen section.

Initially, the **Content Items Manager** page is empty, so we will postpone our discussion of it for a moment.

Creating a New Content Item

Creating a new content item begins with clicking the **New** icon in the toolbar of the **Content Items Manager** page.

This brings you to the **Content Item New** page:

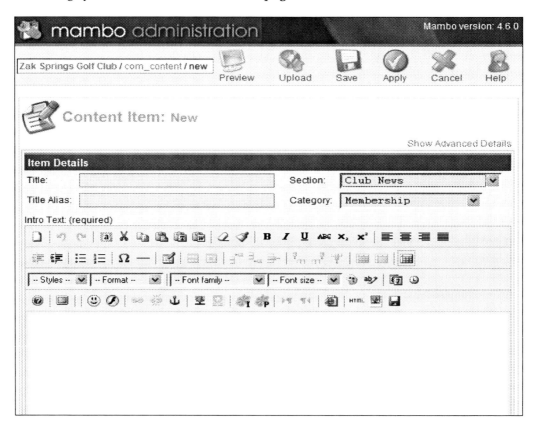

Here you can see the HTML editor for the **Intro Text** field, and some text boxes for the **Title** and **Title Alias** fields. The **Title** of the content item is, well, the title of the content item. It is used to identify the story, and also in the `<title>` element of the HTML for the page, which appears in the title bar of your browser.

The **Intro Text** is the introduction to your piece of content. Usually, this is a "teaser", encouraging the reader to read the rest of the content. The "rest of it" is contained in the **Main Text** field, which is underneath the **Intro Text** field (and not shown in the image on the previous page).

There are drop-down boxes for you to choose the **Section** and **Category** to which this content item will belong. When you select a section from the **Section** dropdown, the **Category** dropdown will update to show the categories from that section. You must select a section and a category from these boxes before the content item can be saved.

The image opposite is not exactly what you will see when you click the **New** icon on the toolbar; we have cheated a bit for the sake of making the image simpler. Instead of the **Show Advanced Details** link that you can see in the image, you will see a tabbed panel on the right-hand side of the screen, with a link above it saying **Hide Advanced Details**. That link was clicked before the screenshot was taken to avoid overcomplicating the initial discussion. We will come to these "advanced details" in a moment.

First of all let's press on with entering some content. We'll add a content item that will go into the **Course Information** category of the **Club News** section. Select these from the relevant drop-down boxes, and in the **Title** field, enter **Back Nine Closed for one week**.

In the **Intro Text** field, enter:

```
The last nine holes will be closed for one week due to an
incident involving a large fanged beast attacking golfers.
The holes will be off limits for a week, while
the Military attempt to apprehend the beast.
```

In the **Main Text** field enter:

```
All golfers are advised to return briskly from the ninth
green to the clubhouse, and certainly not to venture out
onto the back nine after dark.
```

Click the **Apply** button in the toolbar and our first content item is saved, and we can continue. We've seen the **Save**, **Apply**, and **Close** toolbar buttons a number of times over the last few chapters, so there isn't much to say about them now.

The tabbed panel on the right-hand side of the **Content Item New** page holds a number of options for the content item. You can hide this panel by clicking the **Hide Advanced Details** link, and reveal it by clicking **Show Advanced Details**. We'll cover the options available on this panel now.

Adding the Item to a Menu

The **Link to Menu** tab allows you to add your content item as a top-level menu item to one of the existing menus. You select the menu you want to add the item to from the **Select a Menu** list, enter the name of the menu item, then click the **Link to Menu** button:

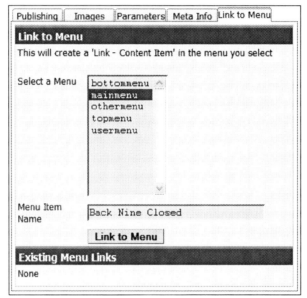

 The menu item will only be added after you click the **Link to Menu** button; saving the content item will not add the menu item unless you have done this.

Once you click the button, the list of **Existing Menu Links** is updated:

If you want to add a content item to the top level of a menu, this tab is for you. Creating the menu item at this point saves you having to go the **Menu Manager**, specify the type of the menu item, select the content item, and so on. However, you can only add a top-level menu item from this tab; you can't create a "nested" menu item directly from here. After you've created a menu item from here, you can edit it in the **Menu Manager** (as you would with any other menu item) and change its **Parent** item to nest it.

Having added the content item to the **mainmenu**, you will be able to see the content item if you preview your site now.

We'll look at more sophisticated ways of adding content items to menu items later.

Adding Images to the Item

In an earlier chapter we saw how to add an image into the text of the HTML editor using the **Insert/edit image** button of the editor. There is another way to add images into your content, and that is to use the mosimage mambot.

Before we add an image using mosimage, save the content item, and then we'll create a folder using the **Media Manager** to store the images for our news stories. Go to the **Media Manager** page (from **Site | Media Manager**), create a directory called news, and upload the backnine_beast.png file from this chapter's code download to that directory. Once you've done that, get back to the content item we were working on.

We'll add the image we just uploaded into our content item. Under the HTML editor for the **Main Text**, you can see the button for adding the mosimage mambot:

The mosimage mambot is the I button; the other button is a mambot for adding pagebreaks. Click the mosimage mambot button, and the word {mosimage} will be added to your **Main Text**.

Now we have to associate an image to go with this occurrence of the mambot. Mambots are a sort of filter, that run when Mambo wants something particular done, like displaying a piece of content or searching. The mosimage mambot works by replacing each occurrence of the string {mosimage} in a piece of content with an associated image, adding some further formatting and possibly a caption. We associate images to the mosimage occurrences using the **Images** tab of the **Advanced Details**.

The first thing to do is to select the directory containing your image (it uses the same directory structure as the Media Manager). We want the image we uploaded to the **/news/** folder, so we start by selecting this from the **Sub-folder** dropdown. Once you select the **/news/** folder, the list of files in that folder will be displayed. When you select one of the files, a preview of the image is displayed:

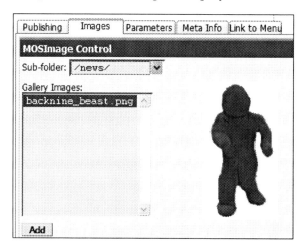

Select the image you want (in this case we have only one), and click the **Add** button. The name of the image will be added to the **Content Images** box underneath the **Add** button:

You can add several images to this box by selecting them from the list in **Gallery Images**. The order of the images in the **Content Images** list determines which mosimage they will be associated with. The first image in the list will go with your first mosimage occurrence, the next image will go the next mosimage occurrence in your text, and so on. You can reorder the images in the box with **up** and **down** buttons, or you can **remove** an image.

We're still not done yet. Make sure you select the image you want in the **Content Images** box, because there is still more to do. When you select the image, another preview of the image will appear next to the box.

Under the **Content Images** box is another set of options for controlling the formatting of the image, and an important button, **Apply**.

Edit the image selected:

Source:	backnine_beast.png
Image Align:	Right
Alt Text:	Eye Witness Account
Border:	
Caption:	A Model of an Eye Witness Acco
Caption Position:	Bottom
Caption Align:	Center
Width:	

Apply

We've set the **Image Align** to **Right**, so it will appear on the right-hand side of our content, and added a caption **A Model of an Eye Witness Account**, and some **Alt Text** for when the image isn't displayed.

Once we're happy, we need to click the **Apply** button. Until you click the **Apply** button, your image will not be associated with your mosimage mambot and your formatting options will not be preserved. Even if you save at this point, none of this information will be saved. If you have not selected the desired image in the **Content Images** box, you will be prompted to do so.

Once you've clicked **Apply**, now it's time to click the **Save** icon in the toolbar to save your content item. The next screenshot shows how our new content item looks on the site; we've added a bit more text to the content item (you can find this in the code download for this chapter):

Back Nine Closed for one week

Club News - Course Information

Written by Administrator

Aug 27, 2006 at 04:09 PM

The last nine holes will be closed for one week due to an incident involving a large fanged beast attacking golfers. The holes will be off limits for a week, while the Military attempt to apprehend the beast.
There is very little further information available about the nature of the beast. Some members have reported seeing it lumbering around, but their descriptions are rather confused, and contradict each other. One witness spoke of a huge hairy beast like a giant dog, while another described a humanoid form, but with slow, shambling movement.

All golfers are advised to return briskly from the ninth green to the clubhouse, and certainly not to venture out onto the back nine after dark.

A Model of an Eye Witness Account

Should any golfer find themselves bitten by the beast, they should report this at once to the relevant authorities immediately.

Last Updated (Aug 27, 2006 at 05:39 PM)

Back

The mosimage mambot makes adding images to your articles pretty easy. Also, when you come back to edit the content item, and you select the image in the **Content Images** box, all of the formatting and other options you set for that image will also be displayed ready for editing.

Remember that the images replace the **{mosimage}** occurrences in the order they appear in the text, not the order you added them to the text. This means that any mosimages in the **Intro Text** will have their images first. You will notice that you can use mosimage mambots in both the **Intro Text** and the **Main Text**, and yet there is only one **Content Images** box for both bits of text, so you may want to take care if you are using mosimages in both of these fields.

Keywords and Description for SEO

We encountered the `meta` tags in Chapter 4 when looking at the **Global Configuration**, and mentioned that they might be used by search engines when indexing your site's pages. You can take this one step further to help improve the indexing of the page with your content item by specifying keywords and a description that reflect the "content" of the content item. Keywords are words that you think reflect the search terms that people could use to find your content.

You add these keywords and a description in the **Meta Info** tab of the Advanced Details panel. If you can't think of any keywords, you can click the **Add Sect/Cat/ Title** button, and the section and category names, and the title of the content item will be added to the **Keywords** field. The keywords are entered as a list, with each list item separated by a comma. Thus, for our content item clicking the button gives:

```
Club News, Course Information, Back Nine Closed for one week
```

There is no need to go overboard with the number of keywords you use, and many search engines may regard an excessive number of keywords as spamming, and treat your page less favorably. Exactly what an "excessive number" means is hotly disputed, but you probably don't want to be using more than a dozen.

Publishing Information

The publication details of the content item are configured from the **Publishing** tab. These are the usual suspects, should the item be shown on the front page (default **No**), should it be published (default **Yes**), which group of users can see it (default **Public**):

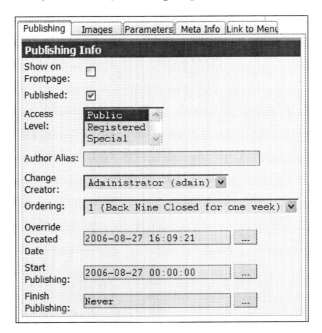

You can also change the original author of the content item, and the date it was originally created.

If you do not want the item to be available immediately, you can schedule it to be published at a particular time from the **Start Publishing** box. Click the button next to this box, and a calendar pops up, from where you select the date when you would like the content item to be published. Only the date is added by the calendar, if you want to specify a time, you need to add this after the data in the format HH:MM:SS.

To set the item to be published at a particular time, you need to set it to published first. Once you do this, and set a time for it to become available, the graphic in the item's Published column would indicate that its published, but is "pending":

If you want the content item to expire after a certain date, you can set this date in the **Finish Publishing** field. The default value is **Never**, so that an item will never expire.

Expiry will happen as soon as someone attempts to access the content item after the expiry date. The time of expiry is checked whenever a content item is accessed, and if it has passed, the item is expired and won't be displayed on the front end. Content items that have expired have this graphic in their Published column:

Controlling How the Item is Displayed

When the content item is displayed to the visitor, there are a number of other elements that can go around it. These are controlled from the **Parameters** tab, and also from the **Content** tab of the Global Configuration.

These elements can be things like:

1. An icon to email a content item to another (potential) visitor
2. An icon to display a printer-friendly version of the item
3. An icon to display a PDF version of the item
4. Who created the item, and when it was created
5. The rating of the item
6. The section name or category name
7. Details of the last update
8. A **Back** button to help the reader navigate through your content organization

Each of these can be controlled from the **Content** tab of the Global Configuration. (We won't describe which option on that tab corresponds to which item in the list above, the names of the options are a giveaway, and there is always the **Help** to help...)

The diagram on the next page shows how some of these options relate to the display of the content item:

Back Nine Closed for one week

Club News - Course Information **6**

Written by Administrator **4**
Aug 27, 2006 at 04:09 PM

The last nine holes will be closed for one week due to an incident involving a large fanged beast attacking golfers. The holes will be off limits for a week, while the Military attempt to apprehend the beast.

All golfers are advised to return briskly from the ninth green to the clubhouse, and certainly not to venture out onto the back nine after dark.

Last Updated (Aug 27, 2006 at 04:49 PM) **7**

Back 8

These options on the **Content** tab of the Global Configuration set site-wide defaults. The options on the **Parameters** tab can be used to override these defaults. Most of the options on the **Parameters** tab have values like **Use Global**, **Hide**, and **Show**. The **Use Global** value, which is the default for the options on the **Parameters** tab, means that the global defaults are used.

You can experiment with these; select different values for the options, click **Apply**, then view the page with your content item to see how the values affect the display of the content item.

Deleting Content Items

Deleting content items requires a number of steps, since Mambo uses a trash can to hold deleted items before they are completely removed from the system, in a way similar to the Recycle Bin on your desktop.

Starting from the **Content Item Manager** page, the first thing you will do is to trash the content you want rid off.

Check the boxes next to the content items you wish to delete, then click the **Trash** icon in the toolbar:

Trash

You will see a message indicating you've trashed some content; there is no opportunity for you to confirm this action:

1 Item sent to the Trash

At this point, the item has not been deleted, it has been sent to the trash. To dispatch this content item completely, we have to get our hands dirty, and delve into the trash.

The Trash Manager

The **Trash Manager** is accessed from the **Site | Trash Manager** menu option of the administrator menu:

It has two tabs, one showing the **Content Items** that have been trashed, another showing the **Menu Items**. From here, you can **Restore** an item to its original location, or **Delete** it completely from the system. You can click the checkbox in the header of the table to select all the items in the table, or check the box next to individual items to select only certain items. After you've done this, you click the **Restore** or **Delete** icons in the toolbar, depending on what the fate of these items is to be.

For either action, you will be presented with a confirmation screen. Here is the **Delete Items** screen:

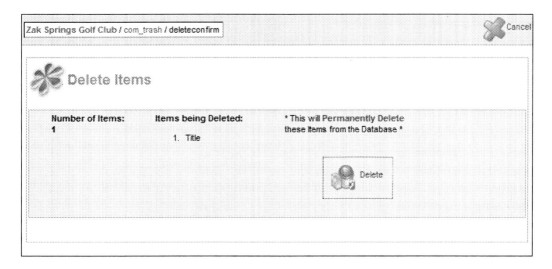

If you don't want to go through with this, click the **Cancel** button in the toolbar, or else click the **Delete** icon in the middle of the page. Clicking the **Delete** icon gives you yet another chance to be sure you know what you're doing:

Click **OK** now, and the item is finally gone.

That will remove a content item (or menu item) from the system; there is no way back for it now. You will need to do this to empty categories should you wish to delete them, as we mentioned earlier.

Archiving Content Items

If you don't want to delete old pieces of content, but want them moved off the site, you can move them to the archive. Note that moving an item to the archive does not move it to another table in the database, and does not make the size of your main content table in your database smaller. The content item doesn't really go anywhere, it just gets marked as being in the archive.

You move an item to the archive by checking the box next to its title in the **Content Manager** page, and then clicking the **Archive** button in the toolbar:

You can see the content items in the archive in the Archive Manager, accessed from the **Content | Archive Manager** administrator menu option. Alternatively, you will find that for sections where some of the items have been archived, a link to that section's archive appears in the **Content | Content By Section** menu for that section.

Content can be moved back from the archive by clicking the **Unarchive** icon in the Archive Manager. Content in the archive will still prevent the category it belongs to from being deleted.

Different Views of Content

Now that we have some bits of content, we turn our attention to the question of directing visitors towards the content.

There are essentially two ways that content can be displayed on a Mambo site, as single items or in a list. The front page of the site for example can show a list of content items. Click on one of the content items and that single content item is displayed to you.

There are essentially three views of content Mambo provides:

- Display a single item of content.
- List all the content items in a particular category (or in all the categories of a particular section).
- Display all the content items in a particular category (or in all the categories of a particular section). In other words, list them and display their introductory text.

There is a fourth view provided by Mambo, which is to list the items on the homepage.

To choose a view, you choose a different type of menu entry from the **Content** panel of the **New Menu Item** page:

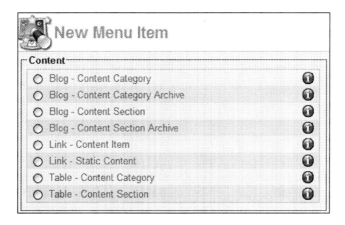

There are three types of menu entry corresponding to the three views we mentioned before:

- Link
- Table
- Blog

Single Item (Link) View

This is the standard way of linking a single item of content to a menu entry. The visitor clicks the menu entry and they see a single item of content. This is the type of menu entry that is created when you add a link from the **Link to Menu** tab of a content item's Advanced Details that we saw earlier.

Table Views

Table views list the titles of all the content items in a particular category, or in all the categories of a particular section.

Content Category View

The image overleaf shows a **Table – Content Category** view from the standard Mambo installation with the sample data:

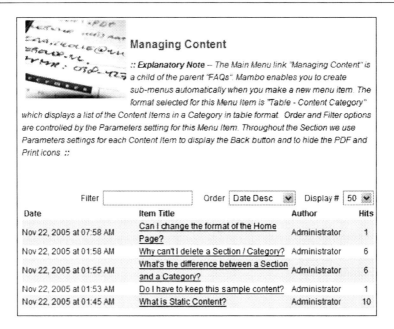

Here you can see the category description, the category image, and underneath, the list of the content items in the category.

The presence of the **Filter** box, and the **Order** and **Display #** drop-down boxes, can be configured from the menu entry.

Clicking on the title of any content item will bring up that content item. If you like, the **Table – Content Category** view defines "virtual" menu items for its "children", namely the content items in the category.

We will add a **Table – Content Category** view for the Course category of Club News.

From the **Menu | mainmenu**, click the **New** button in the toolbar, and select **Table – Content Category**:

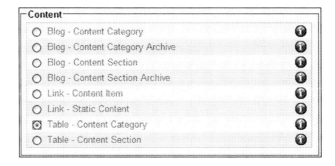

Click the **Next** button in the toolbar, enter **Course** into the **Name** field, and select the **Course Information** category from the list:

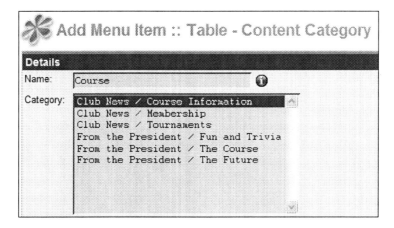

Click the **Save** button and your Content Category menu item is created.

Content Section View

Here we see a **Table – Content Section** view:

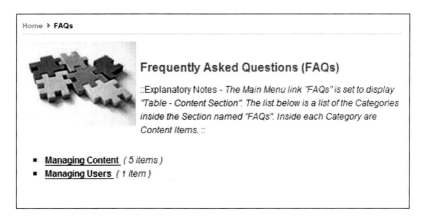

This time, as you would expect, the categories in this section are displayed, along with the section description, and its image.

Again, this display can be configured from the menu entry. One of the things that can be done is to display the description of the category in addition to its title.

Clicking on the title of the category brings up a **Table - Content Category** view of that category.

Like the **Table – Content Category** view, the **Table – Content Section** view defines some "virtual" menu entries for its children, in this case the categories in the section.

We will add a **Table - Content Section** view for the **Club News** section, and afterwards, make our Course Category View a child of that menu item to nest it.

From **Menu | mainmenu**, click the **New** button in the toolbar, and select **Table – Content Section**:

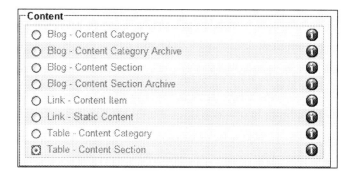

Click the **Next** button, enter **Club News** into the **Name** field, and select the **Club News** section from the list:

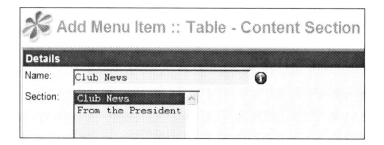

Click the **Save** button in the toolbar, and your new menu item is created:

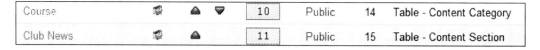

The final step is to make **Course** a child of the **Club News** menu item. Click the **Course** link in the table, and select **Club News** from the **Parent** dropdown:

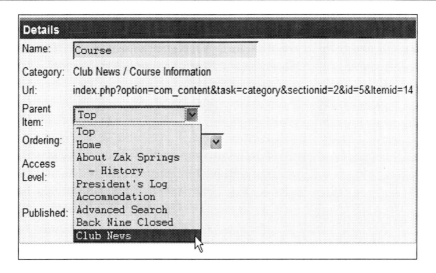

Click the **Save** button, and your menu structure is updated:

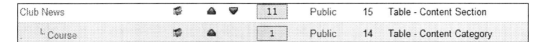

Repeat this process for the **Tournaments** and **Membership** categories; this time you can select **Club News** as the **Parent** when you create the menu items.

Assigning Templates to Table Views

Remember we mentioned in Chapter 6 that you could assign a template to a particular menu entry (which would correspond to a page)? When you assign a template to a menu entry of Table type, that template will be inherited by the "virtual" menu entries we spoke of above.

In other words, if you assign Template X to a **Table – Content Category** menu entry, then when you click the title of one of the content items to see that content item, the page template will still be Template X.

Similarly, if you assign Template X to a **Table – Content Section** menu entry, then clicking the title of one of the categories in the section would give you Template X for the list of content items in the category.

Blog Views

The Blog view presents the content items in a category or section like a weblog. This means that not only is the title of each item in a particular category or section displayed, but the introductory text is shown too.

There are three things that can be displayed in Blog format: categories, sections, or the archive.

We will add a **Blog – Content Section** menu item to display the President's blog. We created a section called **The President** for him earlier, and added his categories, **The Future, The Course, Fun and Trivia**. We still need some content items for those categories. The text for these content items can be found in this chapter's code download, so go ahead and create them.

To add the menu item, from **Menu | mainmenu**, click the **New** icon in the toolbar and select **Blog – Content Section**:

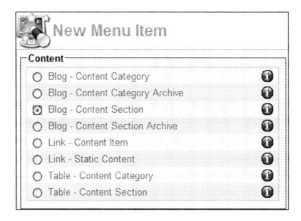

Click the **Next** button, enter **President's Log** into the **Name** field, and select **The President** from the **Section** list.

By default, the blog is displayed as two columns, but we're going to change that to a more familiar one-column layout for the items, so set **Columns** in the **Parameters** panel to **1**.

Click the **Save** button.

When you preview your site, click the **President's Log** menu entry, and provided you've added the categories and the content, you will be able to enjoy the wisdom of the Club President:

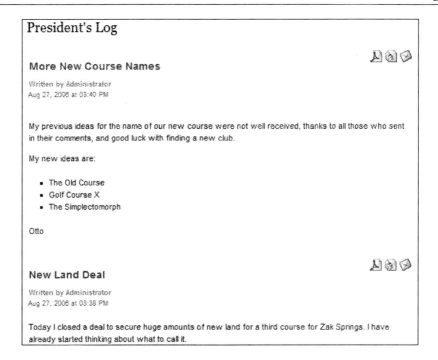

If you like, you can edit the **President's Log** menu item, and use the **Parameters** to further change the way the items are displayed.

Static Content

Static content items are created in the same way as the content items we have just been describing. Static content items do not have any section or category organization, and are typically used for "standalone" pieces of content, like an "About Us" page, or as in the case of the standard Mambo installation, **The Mambo License**. They are used for "standalone" pieces of content because there is no support for creating an automatic listing of static content items in a particular place, because of their lack of section-category structure.

Static content items are managed from the **Content | Static Content Manager** menu option of the administrator menu. This manager is very similar to the Content Manager that we have spent time looking at, so we won't spend much time talking about it in detail, we'll just see how to set up an "About Zak Springs" area.

One drawback with static content items is unless they are going to be linked to from another piece of content, they will need a menu item for the visitor to find them. This is fine if the static content item is going to be a top-level menu item (like the Mambo license) but if you intend to have static content items nested, then you will need to create a parent page for them.

We will do this to create the "About Zak Springs" part of our site, including the "History of Zak Springs" page, and the "Location of Zak Springs" page.

This is the menu structure we're after:

```
About Zak Springs
    History
    Location
```

Both History and Location will be static content items, but we will also need to create a "holding" page called **About Zak Springs**, similar to the page displayed when you view a category.

From the **Static Content Manager**, click the **New** icon in the toolbar, give our new static item a title of **About Zak Springs**, and add the text below:

> Zak Springs Golf Club is located near the Skull Mountains, and boasts two 18-hole golf courses, practice facilities, and extensive hospitality facilities.
>
> The Nemesis course is a picturesque, par 72 course of over 7000 yards. The other course is the Sinistra course. Both are in excellent condition, and present a formidable challenge for even the lowest-handicap golfer.

Click the **Link to Menu** tab of the Advanced Details, and let's add a link to the Main menu:

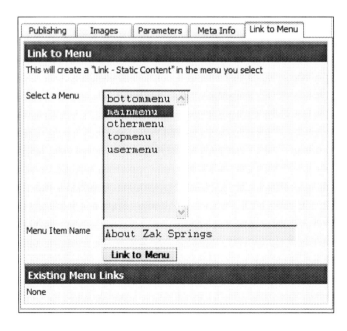

Click the **Link to Menu** button to add the link to this content item to the Main menu:

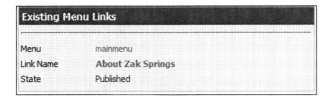

Now click the **Save** button in the toolbar.

Now we'll add the **History of Zak Springs** static content item as a child menu item of **About Zak Springs**. Click **New** in the **Static Content Manager**, and add the text for the **History of Zak Springs** item, which you'll find in this chapter of the code download. However, do not add this content item to the main menu, since you will only be able to add it to the top level of the menu. Once you've saved this static content item, select **Menu | mainmenu**, and click **New** in the toolbar to add a new menu item.

We'll add a **Link – Static Content** menu item:

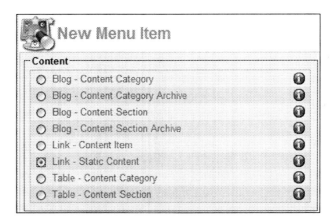

Click the **Next** button in the toolbar, and from the **Add Menu Item** page, enter the name of **History**, select the **History** static content item from the **Static Content** box, and select **About Zak Springs** from the **Parent** drop-down box:

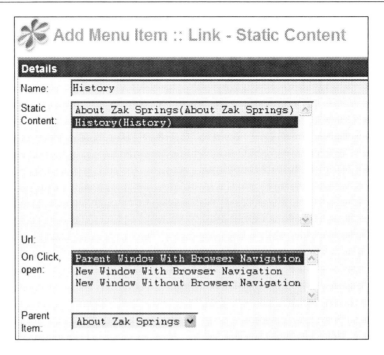

Click the **Save** icon in the toolbar, and you can see our **About Zak Springs** menu structure is underway:

Now when you preview the site, when you click **About Zak Springs**, the menu item will expand to show the **History** link. There is no link to the **History** item from the **About Zak Springs** page, apart from the menu item; there is no automatically generated list of content items like that from the content item table view. We could have used ordinary content items for this section, and got that automatic list, but we were after the nested menu structure. Even if we were using standard content items and table views, we would still have had to add the menu entries ourselves, so using static content items here has not really been too much of an inconvenience. Also, the nature of the material in the **About Zak Springs** area is that it will not change too often; we are unlikely to be adding new items here so there is no need for an automatic listing of the content.

You will find the text for the **Location** static content item in the code download, and you can add that under the **About Zak Springs** menu item to complete this part of the site.

Managing Sections

We saw earlier how to create sections. Now we return to the topic of managing categories: copying and deleting them. We saw the **Section Manager** page earlier. It displays a list of the currently defined sections, and from here you perform the section management tasks.

Copying Sections

You can copy everything in a section (its categories, and the content items in those categories) by checking the box next to the section and clicking the **Copy** icon in the toolbar.

You will then be prompted to enter the name of the target section into which these contents will be copied, and then click the **Save** icon in the toolbar. You can only copy sections to new sections, you cannot copy sections to another, existing section. If you enter the name of an existing section to copy to, this will be rejected, and you will have to enter another section name.

A section will be created with the name you specify, and will contain everything from the original section. We said that categories belong to exactly one section, and to ensure this rule is followed, you will find that copies are actually made of all the categories, and all the content items within those categories.

Deleting Sections

Sections are deleted by checking the box next to their name and clicking the **Delete** icon in the toolbar. However, a section has to be completely empty before it can be deleted. This means it can't have any categories assigned to it. If there are categories that were assigned to the section, but have been trashed, they have to be completely removed from the trash before the section can be deleted.

In other words, the **# Categories** and **# Trash** columns have to be showing **0** before you can delete a section.

Managing Categories

We saw earlier how to create categories. Now we return to the topic of managing categories: copying, moving, and deleting.

Copying Categories to Different Sections

From the **Category Manager** page, a category can be copied by checking the box next to the category you want to copy, and clicking **Copy** in the toolbar. You select the section to which you want to copy the category (the section must already exist), and a new category is created and assigned to the target section. The name of the new category is the same as the old category, with the words **Copy of** put at the start. Copies of all the content items in the category are created, and assigned to the copied category.

Moving Categories to Different Sections

We mentioned that you can't change the section a category is assigned by directly editing its details. To assign a category to a different section, you have to move it.

You can move a category by checking the box next to it in the **Category Manager**, and clicking **Move** in the toolbar.

Again, you select a target section from one of the existing sections, and the category will be reassigned to this section. There is no copy of the category created, and no copies of its content items are created.

Deleting Categories

Categories can only be deleted when they contain no content items, including content items that are in the trash. At this point in our explorations this is no problem since we've not created any content! However, the point of your site is to create some content, so generally, you will need to empty a category of content items before you attempt to delete the category.

Once a category is empty of content items, including trashed items, simply check the checkbox next to the category and click the **Delete** icon in the toolbar. The category will be deleted; there is no prompt asking you if you are sure you want to delete the category. The reason there is no prompt is that the category is completely empty; if it had content items, you already had to delete them, which involves lots of prompting as we saw. In other words, the category has no dependencies, so deleting it shouldn't cause you a problem.

Summary

In this chapter we looked at working with content items in the back end of the site. Content items are Mambo's versatile type of "content". We saw that content is organized into sections and categories, with categories sitting inside sections, and content items sitting inside categories.

We saw how to create sections and categories, and after a discussion of the section-category structure for Zak Springs, we added some of these to our Zak Springs site.

After defining our content structure, we moved on to look at creating content items. We saw the mosimage mambot that gives another way to include images in our content and also control the formatting of the displayed image. We saw the various options that are available for each content item, including the keywords and description, publishing information such as publishing on a scheduled date, and also the **Parameters** that control such things as whether icons for printer-friendly versions of the content should be displayed along with the content item.

We also looked at how you can get different views of content by specifying a different type of menu item. We saw the single item (link) view, which displays on a single piece of content on a page, the table views for showing a list of content items in a category or a list of categories in a section, and the blog views for showing a list of content items in a category along with some of their text.

There are actually two "types" of content in Mambo; organized content and static content. The first part of the chapter was devoted to organized content (with the section and category structure), and then we looked briefly at static content. Static content has no organization, and is generally intended for standalone pieces of content that do not particularly require any "hierarchy" like the section-category type of content.

Finally, we had a look at managing sections and categories: copying, moving, and deleting them.

All of this content management was done in the administration area. Mambo enables certain users to create, edit, and publish content from the front end of the site, and provides a "workflow" to ensure that only approved content is shown on the site. This is our next stop.

9
Front-End Publishing Workflow

So far, you've been writing the content yourself, as the Super Administrator of the site. In Chapter 7, we created users that were members of the front-end author, editor, and publisher groups, and we said that they will be able to add content to the site through the front end. We will look at this now.

We will first see where new content items can be added, and then look at the "workflow" involved in publishing these content items to the site. Content submitted through the front end of the site does not automatically get published; it needs to be approved by an Administrator before this happens.

Finally, we've have a look at the administration of comments.

Authoring Content

The first front-end group for working with content is the **Author** group. A user in this group once logged in can:

- Submit a new content item to the site
- Edit a content item they have previously submitted

As the name suggests, users in the **Author** group can only "author" content. This means that they can't edit any content except their own.

Log on to the front end of the site as the **Author** user we set up in Chapter 7.

The first thing you should keep a lookout for, is a link that allows you to add a new content item. However, you might not find it so easy to locate this link first of all.

Let's think about this for a moment. Suppose you were going to display a link, say **add new content here**, that when clicked will allow the author to add new content. Where would you put that link?

- If you put it on a page containing a content item, what exactly would **add new content here** mean? Content items belong to categories, they don't belong to other content items. You wouldn't expect to find your link on the page where a content item is displayed.

- Would you put it after a list of the categories in a section? If you did, then which category would the content item go into?

- If you put the link after a list of content items in a category, then **add new content here** would make sense. It would mean "add a new content item into this category". And that is exactly where you will find our mystery link.

Click on the **News | Course Information** menu link to bring up the list of items within the **Course Information** category.

Underneath the list of items in the category, you can see the **New** link:

Click this link, and you will be taken to a page with a URL of the form:

```
http://localhost/zaksprings/index.php?option=com_content&task=new&
sectionid=4&cid=1&Itemid=43
```

There are three things to note with this URL. The first is `task=new`. This indicates we want to add a new piece of content. The next things to note are the `sectionid`, which holds the ID of the section you want your content item to end up in, and `cid`, the ID of the category that the item will belong to.

On the page, you will be presented with a form similar to the **Content Item New** page in the Administrator area:

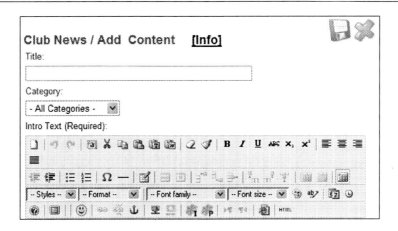

Here you see a field for entering the title of the content item and a drop-down box filled with the categories from the chosen section (the section ID was included in the URL of the page remember), from which you actually have to select the category. Although the URL contains the ID of the category you want to add your item, for some reason, this category is not selected in the drop-down box by default, and you will have to select it yourself. (This seems rather an oversight.) You can also see the familiar HTML editor for the **Intro Text**. As you would expect, you can scroll down to find the HTML editor for the **Main Text** field.

Also, there is a mini toolbar here with the **Save** and **Cancel** buttons. As you already know, you click these buttons to both save and submit your content or cancel your submission.

Scroll down the screen further and you will see something similar to the **Advanced Details** panel that we saw on the **Content Item New** page in the Administrator area:

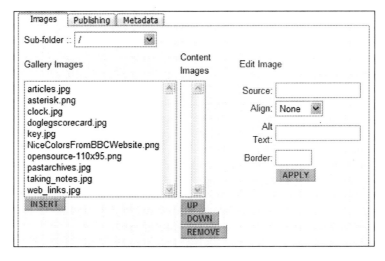

There are only three tabs here, since the author is simply entering content, not deciding where it will go or how it will be displayed. The **Images** and **Metadata** tabs are familiar, (note that in the **Content Item New** page the tab was called **Meta Info** rather than **Metadata**), and allow you to add images to the content with the {mosimage} mambot, and enter a description and keywords for the page META tags.

One thing that is noticeably absent from the **Publishing** tab is an option to publish the content item. The author cannot publish items to the site directly, and the lack of the option here reflects this.

Can't Find the Save Button?

Sometimes you might not be able to see the **Save** button anywhere on this form to enter your content. This is because of the current template, which will have a fixed width for the portion of the page in which the form is displayed. If you scroll down to the bottom of the form, you will find scrollbars for the form, and you can use these to scroll the form along to its right-hand edge. Then scroll straight back up the screen and you will see the **Save** button.

Finding Submitted Content Items

Once content has been entered through this form and saved to the system, the back-end work can begin. On the back end, either the Super Administrator or a Manager can move a submitted content item on to publication. There are a couple of ways to locate newly submitted content items:

- Navigate to the **Latest Items** tab in the control panel of the Administrator home page. Here you can click the title of the item to view its details, check or amend them, and if satisfied, set the content item to be published. This has the drawback of showing only a certain number of the most recently added content items. If you had a rush of content submitted, it is possible you might miss some of them.

- If you know who the users in the **Author** group are, you can select their names from the **All Authors** drop-down box in the **Content Items Manager** page. Then you can see all the content submitted by that author, check it, or publish it straight away.

However, how do you know when something has actually been submitted?

The Author Notification Process

When a content item is submitted by an author, a notification process begins, to advise anyone who can approve the item for publication.

It works like this:

- When the item is submitted, a private message is sent to any administrator who has the **Receive Submission Emails** option set to **Yes**. (It's only Super Administrators or Administrators, not Managers unfortunately.)
- When a private message is received (actually, when it's sent), the recipient should be notified by email if they have correctly configured **Mail me on new Message** from **Messages | Configuration**.

Thus there is no direct email notification when an item is submitted to the site. This notification process is not particularly helpful. The notification email that you have received a private message is of this form:

A new private message has arrived

The email also has this as its title. The Private Message itself looks like this:

A new content item has been submitted by [author]

titled [Again Added]

from section [FAQs]

and category [Managing Content]

None of these really say "A new content item has been submitted to the site, check it out here!", with a direct link to view the submitted item.

However, you can see the name of the user who submitted the content, so you can go to **Content Items Manager** and select their name from the **Author** drop-down box quite easily.

We played with Private Messages at the end of Chapter 4. If you sent some messages, and had a look at the email notification you received then, you would have found the text of the Private Message included in the email. This is not the case with the "front-end" notification we get after submitting a content item. That's because there are two separate Private Messages components; a front-end one and a back-end one. The Content component uses the front-end Private Messages component to send the message (and the notification), rather than the back-end component.

However, apart from the indirect notification, there is another element of frustration here:

- The Manager back-end group can manage content; the Administrator cannot.
- The Administrator back-end group can receive submission emails; the Manager group cannot.

Together, these mean that by default, Mambo content Managers cannot receive direct notification when material is submitted through the front end of the site.

Editing Content

The next front-end group for working with content is the **Editor** group. A user in this group once logged in can:

- Edit any content item on the site, provided they have access to it in the first place
- Submit a new content item to the site

Log on to the front end of the site as the **Editor** user we set up in Chapter 7.

Now, as soon as you log in, things look immediately different:

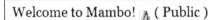

Welcome to Mambo! (Public)

Written by Administrator
Nov 19, 2005 at 07:52 AM

 Thank you for choosing Mambo. You have completed successfully the installation of the Mambo files and are now viewing part of the sample content that is included in the default Mambo installation. You can delete all of this information and replace it with your own contents very easily. However, before you do that, we recommend that you review these sample files, as they contain some information you might find to be helpful.

Included in the sample content you will find:

- An overview of Mambo (this content item)
- An introduction to Components & Modules
- A summary of the templates that are included in this release, and
- Information about Mambo's Licensing Terms (GPL)

Last Updated (Nov 22, 2005 at 07:01 AM)

Read more...

Here you can see an icon for editing the content item right next to the title of the content item.

Click this, and you'll be brought to a page where you can edit the content item:

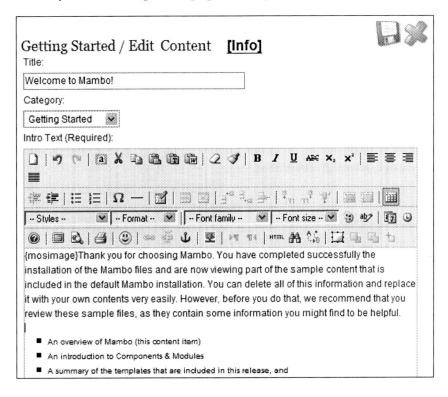

Again, the **Main Text** is underneath, along with the **Advanced Details** panel to the side.

Click the **Save** icon and the changes made to the content item are immediately reflected on the site; there is no need for approval and publishing here, since this was only editing. The content item just edited was not written by the editor; the editor is able to any edit any content item they can lay their hands on, and the handy **Edit** icon is positioned next to the item.

An editor is also able to create new content items. You will find a similar link to the one you saw for the author earlier.

Click that link to add a new content item and the editor follows the same process as the **Author** for entering a new content item. If the item is submitted, it will need approval before it can be published to the site. The editor still cannot publish new content items to the site directly.

Publishing Content

The third front-end group for working with content is the **Publisher** group. A user in this group logged in can:

- Edit any content item on the site, provided they have access to it in the first place

- Submit a new content item to the site and have it published immediately

We won't go through all the details of this; it is similar to everything we have seen above. The one difference is the **Publishing** tab of the **Advanced Details** when editing or creating a new content item:

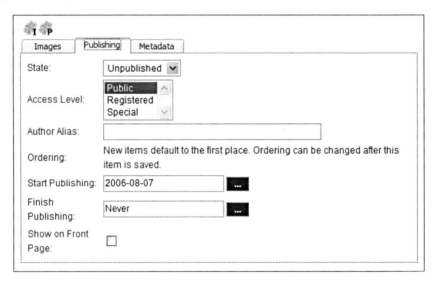

You can set this item to be published directly to the site by selecting **Published** from the **State** drop-down box. Also, you can unpublish an item by setting its **State** to **Unpublished**. Once on the site, the content item can be edited by any publisher or editor.

Front-End User-Submitted Content

Mambo is not designed to allow general, registered users of the site to submit content items for approval and publication on the site. Mambo is designed for privileged groups of front-end users to do this instead. However, some components, like Web Links for example, do allow ordinary registered users to submit a web link. The Content component does not allow this.

Making Mambo work in a more "community-driven" way, so that anyone with a user account can submit a content item, is a more challenging problem, and is beyond the scope of this book.

Adding Links to Submit Content

Remember we had to look around a bit to find the **New** icon to create a content item as an author? It would make more sense if there was a menu link that took us directly to the page for submitting content. However, we don't want this link to be available to everyone, since most people will not be able to use it anyway.

Since you have to be at least logged on before you can even think of submitting content, the menu with the link should be visible at least to **Registered** users, which is exactly what the User menu is. Since not every registered user can submit content, the menu item itself will be for **Special** users. The **Special** users are authors, editors, or publishers.

For Zak Springs, we're going to add some menu entries to the User menu. We will make these menu entries visible only to the **Special** users (Authors, Editors, and Publishers). These menu entries will provide direct links to submit the **Club News** content items, and so on.

All we need is a URL for the menu to point to...

Remember the form of the URL for the content item submission page?

```
http://localhost/zaksprings/index.php?option=com_content&task=new&
sectionid=4&cid=1&Itemid=43
```

That's almost what we want. All we need to do is find the section ID and category ID of the section and category we want the content item to go into, and we're done. The Itemid will be added automatically by Mambo when we add this link as a menu item, so we don't have to worry about that.

First, let's check the section ID of the **Club News** section. You can see this in the **Section ID** column of the section in the **Section Manager**. The screenshot below shows the value of **2**:

Now we just need to add a **Link – Url** menu item to the **usermenu**.

Select **Menu | usermenu** from the administration drop-down menu to bring up the User menu screen, and click **New** in the toolbar to add a new menu item. Select a **Link – Url** type:

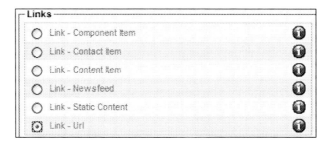

Click the **Next** button in the toolbar.

Add the information into this form as below. For the **Link**, we only add the section ID and not the category ID (`cid`), so that the front-end user can add a content item into any of the categories in this section. We also set the **Level** to **Special**, so that only the front-end authors, editors, and publishers will see this menu item:

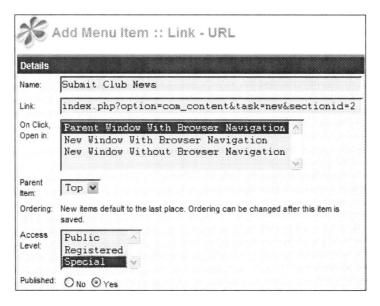

Click the **Save** button in the toolbar, and your menu entry is created.

Now when you log into the front end of the site with one of the author, editor or publisher accounts, you will see the **Submit Club News** link in the User menu. When you click it, you will find the link is now of the form `index.php?option=com_content&task=new&sectionid=2&`**`Itemid`**`=19`, with the `Itemid` added by Mambo.

Creating a Better Publishing Workflow

As we've seen, the notification system of the front-end publishing seems rather odd in these ways:

- Managers (content managers) can't get notifications, Administrators (who can't manage content) can.

- The notification is via a private message.

- Provided that an Administrator has setup their private message configuration to notify them by email when a new private message is received (and provided their private message inbox is not locked), they will receive an email notification advising of the private message.

- The Administrator needs to check the private message to be advised of the content item submission.

Of course, if they've gone to log in to check their private messages, they may as well look at the **Latest Items** tab in the Administrator front page, which will show them the most recently submitted content items.

In this section, we'll explore some other solutions for improving this workflow.

One solution is to create a virtual Administrator. This is an Administrator account that no one is actually able to access, and its sole purpose is to receive notifications of submitted content items. Of course, this account can have only one email address, so only one person can be mailed when an item is submitted.

However, the email address of this Administrator need not be a real email account, but can be an email alias. An email alias is an email address for which there is no corresponding email account. You could create, on your mail server, an email alias called contentmanagers for example, which could be configured to forward any mail received to each person responsible for approving and publishing content on the Mambo site; these would be Managers rather than Administrators.

In this way, you could have all people responsible for managing content notified when a new content item is submitted with only one email sent by Mambo.

However, the problem with that is that each person will receive a rather useless private message notification:

A new private message has arrived.

They still have no idea what the private message says. The exact notification of the content item submission is in the private message, which they would still need to check. So this isn't ideal.

There are two ways we could go above solving this:

- Modify the Content component to send email notifications directly
- Modify the Messages component to send a better email notification

The Messages component contains only two files, which together total only 4KB in size. The Content component has more files, and these are bigger. For the simplest solution, modifying the private message notification seems the easiest way to go.

Open the `com_messages` folder in the `components` folder of your Mambo installation, and open the file `messages.class.php` in a text editor. This file contains the `mosMessage` class, which is responsible for sending private messages.

If you're familiar with PHP, you'll have no difficulty in locating the `send()` function:

```
function send( $from_id=null, $to_id=null, $subject=null,
            $message=null ) {
    global $database;
    global $mosConfig_site_name;
```

This function sounds like just what we're after. If you look through this function, you'll see these lines:

```
$config = $database->loadObjectList( 'cfg_name' );
    $locked = @$config['lock']->cfg_value;
    $domail = @$config['mail_on_new']->cfg_value;

    if (!$locked) {

        $this->user_id_from = $from_id;
        $this->user_id_to = $to_id;
        $this->subject = $subject;
        $this->message = $message;
        $this->date_time = date( "Y-m-d H:i:s" );

        if ($this->store()) {
            if ($domail) {
                $database->setQuery( "SELECT email FROM #__users
                                    WHERE id='$to_id'" );
                $recipient = $database->loadResult();
                $subject = T_('A new private message has arrived');
                $msg = T_('A new private message has arrived');
                mosMail($mosConfig_mailfrom, $mosConfig_fromname,
                                    $recipient, $subject, $msg);
            }
            return true;
        }
    }
```

The first line here gets the private message configuration, and the next two lines store the configuration values in variables. If the inbox isn't locked, then the message is sent:

```
if (!$locked) {
    $this->user_id_from = $from_id;
    $this->user_id_to = $to_id;
    $this->subject = $subject;
    $this->message = $message;
    $this->date_time = date( "Y-m-d H:i:s" );

    if ($this->store()) {
```

The last line above "sends" the message, which actually just stores it in the database. We can see that the $message variable could be useful to us; it looks like it is the content of the private message.

If the message has been "sent" OK, in other words, there was no problem storing it in the database, then the email notification is sent (provided the user is receiving email notifications):

```
if ($this->store()) {
    if ($domail) {
        $database->setQuery( "SELECT email FROM #__users
                                WHERE id='$to_id'" );
        $recipient = $database->loadResult();
        $subject = T_('A new private message has arrived');
        $msg = T_('A new private message has arrived');
        mosMail($mosConfig_mailfrom, $mosConfig_fromname,
                            $recipient, $subject, $msg);
    }
    return true;
}
```

The email address of the recipient is got from the database, and the subject and body of the email are constructed. It seems reasonable that the $msg variable holds the body of the email message (it certainly matches the body of the emails that we receive). The T_() function allows the text to be returned in the current language. The mosMail() function sends the mail.

It would seem that all we have to do is modify $msg, and we will get a better email notification about a private message. Since we have the body of the private message in the $message variable, it seems pretty easy:

Modify the $msg line like this:

```
$msg = "A new private message has arrived\n\n----------
        ---\n\n$message";
```

The \n characters put line breaks into the message, (we've changed the ' to " to use these characters within the string), we have a sequence of dashes to break up the text, then we simply dump in the private message body with the $message variable.

There is one more thing we need to do before we test this. We need to add the highlighted line to the start of the function:

```
function send( $from_id=null, $to_id=null, $subject=null,
    $message=null ) {
        global $database;
        global $mosConfig_site_name;
        global $mosConfig_mailfrom, $mosConfig_fromname;
```

In the current version of Mambo, the line that sends the mail attempts to use the two variables $mosConfig_mailfrom and $mosConfig_fromname. However, these are global variables and the global statement is needed to allow them to have values within the function. By convention, we add the statement to the start of the function.

Now we're ready to go. Save the messages.class.php file, go to the administration area, and send yourself a private message, making sure you've set yourself up to receive email notifications.

Once that's working, make sure there is an Administrator account set to receive notifications when content is submitted, and that the email address of this account is one you can access (you may want to turn off the unique email address requirement in the Global Configuration first!).

After that, log into the front end of the site with one of the editor or author accounts, and add a new content item.

Now things are a bit more helpful. You'll get a message like:

A new private message has arrived

A new content item has been submitted by [author] titled [I added this myself] from section [Getting Started] and category [Getting Started]

If we wanted to go a step further, and actually add the link to view the content item in the administration area, we would need to make some (simple) modifications to the Content component. For now, we'll leave things here. Already, we've got a simple solution to notify any of the relevant Zak Springs staff when someone submits a new content item.

To fully implement this solution, we'll create an Administrator called `cmnotifier`, and set its email address to `contentmanagers@zaksprings.com`, and in fact, we'll deactivate that account (this does not affect the sending of notifications). We deactivate the account since it has no real purpose other than to receive notifications. We'll get the mail server setup to forward mails for that address to the relevant people who manage content. Of course this means that part of our solution has moved outside of Mambo, but it's much more straightforward than making even more alterations to the Mambo code.

Managing Comments

When looking round the Mambo site with the sample data, you may have seen the **Write Comments** link under some content items:

Write Comment (0 comments)

Last Updated (Nov 23, 2006 at 08:49 PM)

Read more...

The Comments feature of Mambo is powered by a component, but there is also a **mambot** for displaying the comments.

The **mambot** is called **MOS Comment** and is enabled by default. We haven't talked much about managing mambots so far, but they are managed in a familiar way from the **Mambots | Site Mambots** administrator drop-down menu:

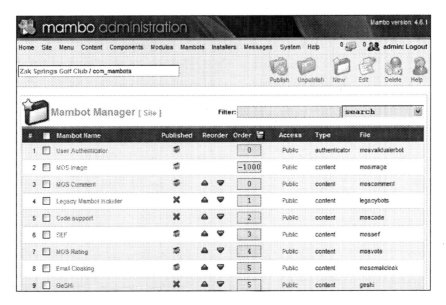

You can click the graphic in the **Published** column to enable or disable a mambot. In addition to the **MOS Comment** mambot, there is a mambot called **MOS Rating** that controls the rating feature for comment items, allowing items to be rated and displaying the rating.

If you want to turn off the Comments feature at any point, simply unpublish the **MOS Comment**'s mambot and people won't be able to see or post comments. (Similarly for the **MOS Rating** mambot to prevent people rating or seeing the rating for a content item). Currently there is no way to turn off the submission of comments but retain the display.

Comments can be added by an Administrator through the back end, or submitted by a user through the front end of the site from the form under a content item:

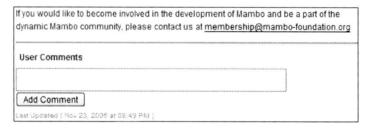

Exactly who can submit comments, what content items they can be submitted for and what happens after a comment is submitted can be configured from the **Components | Comment | Edit Settings** option of the administrator drop-down menu. There are three tabs for managing the comments settings (this is a view from sample data site):

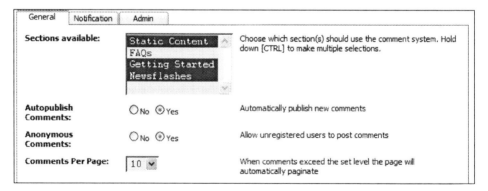

The first tab allows you to select which sections comments can be added to. Any content item in a category belonging to one of these sections can be commented on if they are selected in the **Sections available:** box. (Multiple section selections can be made here).

The **Autopublish Comments** option determines if comments should be published to the site as soon as they are submitted. The default value is **Yes**, and this means that any submitted comment is automatically published without any Administrator intervention. Selecting **No** means that an Administrator will need to "approve" a comment after it is submitted.

If you want to restrict comment posting only to registered users, set the **Anonymous Comments** option to **No**. The default value is **Yes**, which means anyone can post a comment to the site. A comment posted by a user who isn't logged in will be marked as submitted by **GUEST**.

The second tab, **Notification**, determines what should happen when a comment is submitted. If the **Notify Admin** option is set to **Yes**, then a mail will be sent to the Site Administrator. The email address for the Administrator here is specified in the **Mail From** option in the **Mail** tab of the Global Configuration.

 Note that unlike content item submissions, there is no private message sent to a set of Administrators advising of the submission of a comment.

Finally, the **Admin** tab allows you to specify the maximum number of characters in a submitted comment.

Preventing Comment Spam

The default values for the **Autopublish Comments** and **Anonymous Comments** options mean that you could be victim of "comment spam". Comment spam is the (automatic) posting of random comments to articles, blog posts, and so on, with a link to some target site somewhere. This is done to improve the search engine visibility of the target site (since it has more links pointing to it), but the type of sites that use comment spam are generally not the type of site you want to see featured on your site. Often, they sell products most of us would regard as "dubious".

You can prevent comment spam by either restricting comment submission to registered users, or, to make more work for yourself, setting **Autopublish Comments** to **No**, so an Administrator has to approve a comment before it goes on the site.

Another way to prevent comment spam is to set the **Use Captcha Authentication** option of the **Global Configuration** to **Yes**. Doing that makes some graphical text appears under the comment form, and the submitter needs to correctly identify the text displayed in the graphic before their submission is accepted:

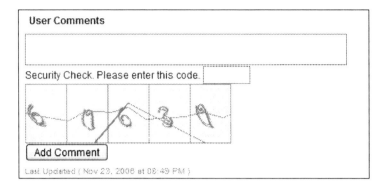

Sometimes, the graphical text is very difficult to make out. This graphical text-confirmation approach is a common technique for preventing automated comment posting.

Viewing and Approving Comments

You can view all the submitted comments from **Components | Comment | View Comments**. You are presented with a familiar-looking table listing the comments:

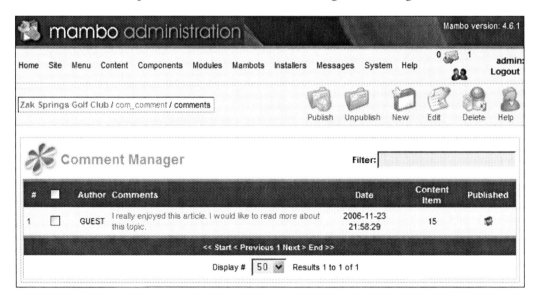

You should be used to this kind of table by now. You can delete comments, publish or unpublish them, or even create a new comment.

You can edit a comment by clicking its text in the comment in the table to take you to the **Edit Comments** screen:

Edit Comments

Name:	GUEST
Comments:	I really enjoyed this article. I would like to read more about this topic.
Published:	◯ No ⦿ Yes
Content Item:	Welcome to Mambo!

This gives you a chance to maybe "censor" or "tone down" the comment, another chance to publish or unpublish it, or even assign it to a different content item.

Summary

In this chapter we looked at how users that were members of the front-end author, editor, and publisher groups can add, edit, or even publish content to the site through the front end.

We had a look around to find the links that would allow the users to add or edit their content, and then had a look at the "workflow" involved in publishing these content items to the site, and the notification system that kicks in when one of these users submits some content. The notification system is based around private messages, and Administrators will only receive email notifications if they have correctly configured their private messaging to send emails when they receive private messages.

Finally, we had a look at the Comments feature in Mambo that allows users to add their own views on published content items.

10

Finishing the Site Off with Other Extensions

So far, we've spent a long time dwelling on the content management features of Mambo, and we also had a quick look at the Web Links component. There are a couple more useful components in Mambo, but there are also a number of other, third-party components and modules that can add extra functionality to our site.

In this chapter, we'll look at these third-party "extensions":

- The ExtCal Event component
- The MamboBoard forums component
- The zOOm Gallery picture gallery

We looked at installing components and modules using the Mambo Universal Installer in Chapter 5. You may want to refresh your memory of this for when we start installing the third-party extensions.

Standard Extensions

There are a number of "standard" extensions that ship with the complete version of Mambo. We'll cover a selection of them here.

Polls

A poll is a multiple-choice question for your visitors. You can view a list of the polls from **Components | Polls** in the administrator menu. Clicking on the poll question allows you to edit the question and the possible answers, and then attach the poll to any menu item (page). The poll itself is displayed with the Polls module, and once the user selects an answer and clicks on either **RESULTS** or **VOTE**, the results of the poll can be seen:

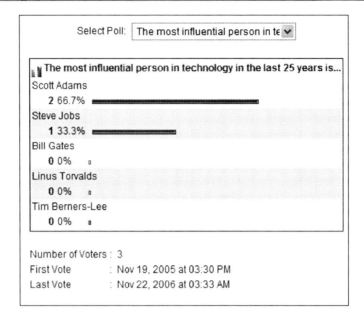

News Feeds

We had a quick look at the News Feeds component in Chapter 5 when we were experimenting with menu items. The News Feeds component grabs the RSS feed from a particular site and displays the stories. The sites themselves are defined from **Components | Newsfeeds | Manage Newsfeeds**, and the sites are organized into categories, which can be managed from **Components | Newsfeeds | Manage Categories**.

Syndicate

The Syndicate component does the opposite of the News Feed component; it sets up your site for syndicating your content. From **Components | Syndicate** you can control such things as the title of your news feed, its description, the number of items in the feed, and the ordering. The content items included in your news feed are the stories that would be displayed on the front page of the site, and it is also possible to control the order in which the content items are displayed in the feed.

People find your news feed with the **Syndicate** module:

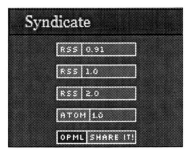

By clicking on one of these icons, or dragging it into an RSS news reader, a visitor can get your feed. The feed is available in a range of specifications; different versions of RSS, ATOM (see `http://www.atomenabled.org/` for more information), and OPML (`http://www.opml.org/`), which should suit almost anyone's taste.

Banners

With the Banners component you get facilities for creating and managing advertising clients, displaying banner adverts on your site, and managing the count of impressions. An impression is when the banner is displayed to a visitor, and when a visitor clicks on the banner to visit the advertiser site, a click-through is recorded.

First of all, you need some clients, and these are set up from **Banners | Manage Clients** in the administrator menu.

Once your client is set up, you can create their banner from **Banners | Manage Banners**. You upload the banner image by clicking the **Upload** icon in the toolbar, and after clicking **Browse** in the dialog that appears, you select your image from the file browser. The graphic is uploaded to the folder `images\banners` in your Mambo installation. Once you've uploaded the banner image, you can enter the banner details, selecting the client and the banner image from the drop-down box, and also the number of impressions that client's banner will be allowed before the banner is removed. Since the banner is actually a link to your client's site, a target URL will also be needed:

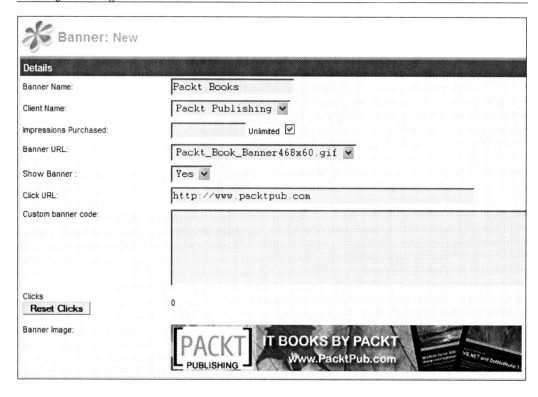

When the banner is displayed, it does not actually link to the target client site, it points to your site, where a click is recorded, and then the visitor is redirected to the target site. This is how the click count is updated.

Once you've entered the details of your banner and saved, then you can see the list of current banners, along with their remaining impressions and also the click-through count:

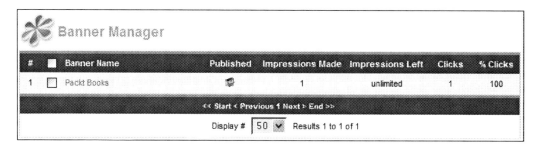

The banner is displayed on the front end of the site through the **Banners** module. This module will display all the published banners, but also allows you to specify a particular client so that only the banners from that client are shown. Once the banner has been viewed more times than its allowed number of impressions, the banner is not just removed from the front end of the site, it is actually deleted from the system!

ExtCal Event Component

This third-party component adds a calendar to the front end of your site, to which users and administrators can add events. At Zak Springs, this component will be used to provide a calendar of upcoming club events, such as tournaments.

We actually downloaded and installed the ExtCal Event component (and one of the modules) in Chapter 5. If you didn't do that then, you can download the component from its project page at the MamboXchange website:

```
http://mamboxchange.com/projects/extcalendar/
```

Events are categorized, and these categories are managed from the **Manage Event Categories** option of the **ExtCal Calendar** administrator menu entry. There is a **General** category added by default. We'll add a category called **Strokeplay Competitions** by clicking the **New** icon in the toolbar and adding the category information:

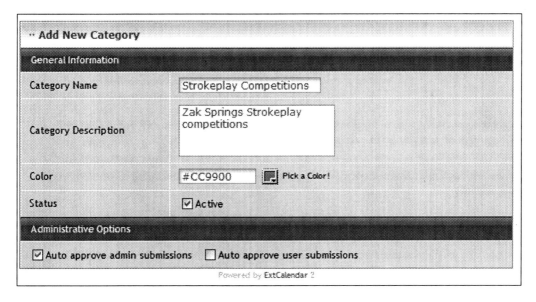

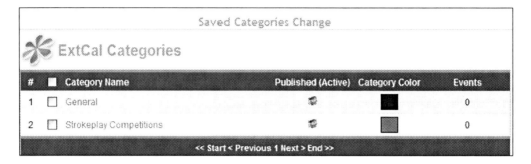

Before we add some events, we need to make some configuration changes. When you click the **ExtCal Settings** option in the **ExtCal Calendar** administration menu entry, you may be surprised to be confronted with a page of information rather than a page of settings. To get started on the settings, you need to click the **Edit Settings** icon in the toolbar:

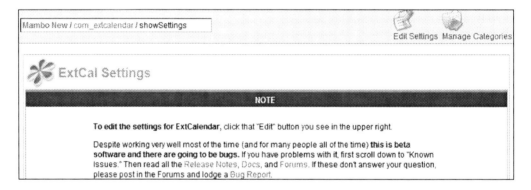

This brings you to a long page of configuration settings. You will have to duplicate some of the Mambo configuration settings here, for example, you will need to enter the details of your mail server again into the **Mail Settings** section of the **Calender Settings**; the component does not seem to take this information from the Mambo core.

In the **General Settings**, the **Calendar Administrator email** is worth setting to your email address. When new events are added to the calendar, a notification email can be sent to the account specified here, so that the events can be approved for publication. The people who can add events to the calendar are also controlled from the **General Settings** section:

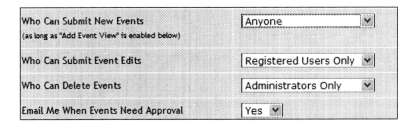

One thing you might have noticed is that there doesn't seem to be any way to add events in the back end of the site; we've seen a **Manage Event Categories** page, and a settings page, but no "Add an Event" page. That's because the events are added at the front end of the site. By default, anyone can submit events.

You can restrict this to allow only registered users or administrators to submit events from the **Who Can Submit New Events** option here. Who can edit or delete events can also be controlled. Events submitted by anyone other than administrators need to be approved by one of the administrators.

The word administrator here refers to a member of the back-end Administrator group (or Super Administrator group). A member of the Manager group will not be able to access the back-end ExtCal functionality.

What can be added for the details of an event is controlled by the **Add Event View** settings. First of all, you can turn off the feature to allow non-administrators to add events by setting **Enabled** to **No** in this section:

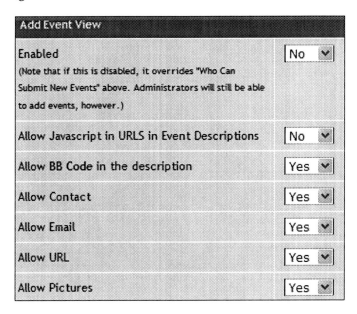

The section also contains options for controlling the type of content that can be added to the details of an event.

We're going to set **Enabled** to **No** (**Yes** is the default value), and click the **Save** icon in the toolbar to save our settings.

There are a number of settings for controlling the look and behavior of the calendar component that you can experiment with.

Now we've got our basic calendar set up, let's add a menu entry to link to the ExtCal component. We'll add a menu entry called **Events**, of type **Component** to the **mainmenu**. Enter **Events** for the **Name,** select the **ExtCal Calendar** component, click **Save**, and our calendar will become visible.

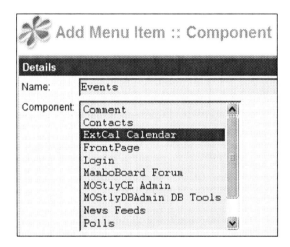

From the front end of the site, clicking the **Events** menu link brings up the calendar:

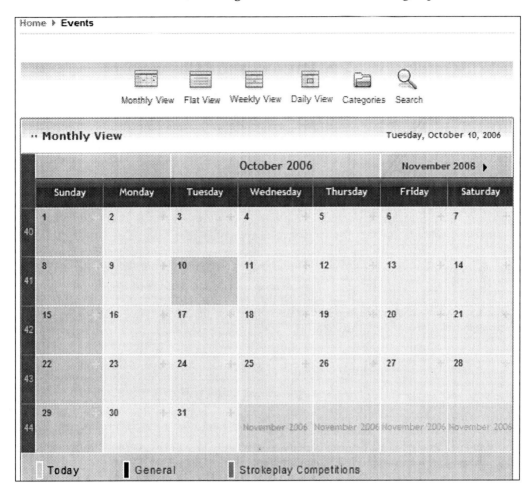

That's nice, but there's not an event in site! More than that, there seems to be no way of adding an event. Since only administrators can add an event, we'd better log into the front end of the site as one of our administrators (the Super Administrator will do), and after doing this and clicking the **Events** link again, you'll see the button for adding events:

Clicking the **Add Event** icon allows us to add an event. We'll enter details of the **Zak Springs Gold Medal** event, which will be an all day event, in the **Strokeplay Competition** category:

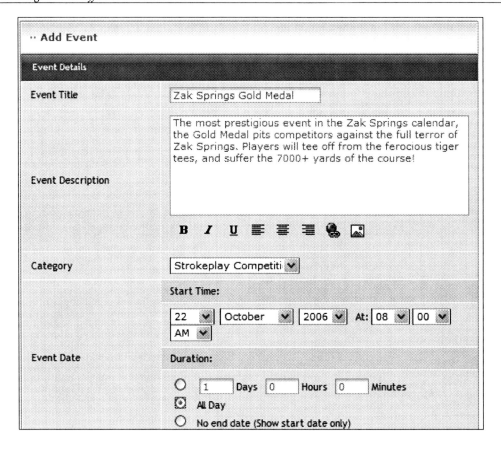

There are also options to make this event recur (which will be useful for the Monthly Medal event), and also an **Event Approved** option (checked by default) to have the event immediately published to the calendar

Here is a view of this event in the **Flat View**:

This has been a quick run-through of the ExtCal component. There are lots of options for controlling the look of the calendar further, and also, the ability to allow users to submit events adds even greater flexibility.

User-Submitted Events

If you decide to allow users to submit events, then one of the administrators will need to approve the event before it goes onto the calendar.

Once an event is submitted, an email notification is sent to the address specified previously:

```
The following event has just been posted on your Zak Springs
ExtCalendar and requires approval:

Title: "Zak Springs Unfair Medal"
Date: "2006-10-10 08:00:00"
Duration: "-2507 Day -7 Hour -60 Minute"

You can access this event by clicking the link below or copy and paste
it in your web browser.

http://www.zaksprings.com/index.php?option=com_extcalendar&amp;Itemid=
44&amp;extmode=event&amp;event_mode=view&amp;extid=2

(NOTE that you must be logged in as an Administrator for the link
to work.)
Regards,

The management of Zak Springs ExtCalendar
```

Note that unlike the rather clumsy content-submission notifications we saw in the previous chapter, this notification has a direct link for you to click to view the submitted event. If you follow the link, you will get straight to the submitted event.

When logged in as an administrator, newly submitted events are clearly indicated to you:

Clicking the link brings you to the list of pending events:

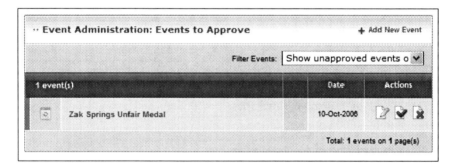

You can either click the checkmarked icon to approve the event immediately, or the crossed icon to delete it. Clicking the edit (pencil) icon allows you to edit it before approving it. Clicking the title of an event gives you a preview:

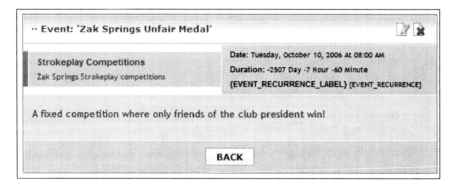

From here, you can click the edit icon to edit it and approve it, or the delete icon to remove it. (This view of the event is the page that the link in the email notification points to.)

Deleting Events

If you want to remove an event (for example, if you accidentally approved the rather libellous event above!), then click on it in one of the calendar views, and you will be presented with the preview we saw above. You can use the delete icon to remove all occurences of this event.

ExtCal Modules

There are two modules that can be downloaded from the ExtCal project page at the MamboXchange website: **MiniCal** and the **Latest Events module**.

The **MiniCal** module (identified as **ExtCal** in the list of modules) displays a miniature calendar, with the dates of events highlighted:

The **Latest Events** module is highly configurable, and provides a list of some of the upcoming events in the calendar. The number of events to show and the amount of information to show about each event are among the many things that can be controlled from this module's **Parameters**:

MamboBoard Forums Component

The MamboBoard discussion board component provides a threaded discussion environment. People can post topics in forums, other people can reply to the posts, and people can continue to reply to the replies, creating a nested stream of discussion. Or they can just make new posts!

This component can be downloaded from:

```
http://mamboxchange.com/projects/mamboboard/
```

Here you will find the main MamboBoard component, and also some modules for displaying the top posters.

The component can be downloaded and installed from your local hard drive, or else you can enter the URL directly into the **Install from HTTP URL** field in the **Installer | Universal**. The current URL for the MamboBoard component is:

```
http://mamboxchange.com/frs/download.php/8273/
Mamboboard1.4_Stable.zip
```

Once it is installed, you will see a **MamboBoard Forum** link added to the **Components** administrator menu:

Clicking this brings you to the main MamboBoard administration area:

With these icons you can configure your forum, manage moderators, set permissions and so on. MamboBoard integrates with the standard Mambo user accounts, so that any user registered with your site will be able to post to the forum.

Forum Organization

Rather than having a single discussion area, with topics intermingling with other topics, themes of conversation are organized into a number of different containers, rather like the folder and file structure of your hard disk.

The top level of organization is the **category**. Within categories, the next level of organization is into **forums**. Forums consist of **topics**, and finally, users are able to creating **postings** on these topics. Thus categories, forums, and topics act like folders, with postings being analogous to the files, to continue the file system analogy.

Only forum administrators can create categories and forums. Topics (and obviously postings, since they are the real body of a discussion area) can be added by users of the forum. A topic is essentially a 'first' posting, with subsequent postings on that topic being replies to the topic subject.

Here is a diagram of the forums hierarchy:

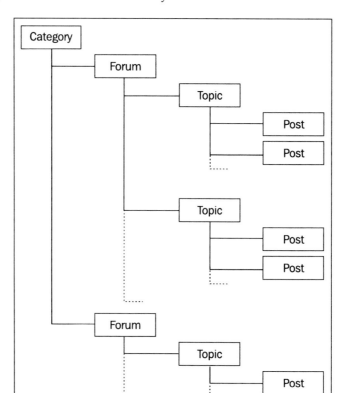

Although a forum is contained in a category, the term "forum" is generally used informally to refer to the whole discussion environment, covering categories, forums, topics, and postings. When you "post to a forum", you are actually posting to a topic in a particular forum of a certain category! The general term "board" or "discussion board" is usually used to refer to the whole forum experience.

Board Configuration

Before we create forums and topics for users to post to, we need to set up some basic board configuration first. This is done by clicking the **MamboBoard Configuration** icon.

This brings you to a tabbed form, similar to the **Global Site Configuration**.

The first thing to do is to set the email address of the forum administrator.

Creating Forums

Now we have our basic configuration out of the way, we will need to create some forums for people to post in.

Creating a forum is done by clicking the **Forum Administration** link. This brings you to the **MamboBoard Administration** page, which will display a list of the current categories and forums, but at the moment, it will be blank, since we have no forums. Let's not hang around, so click the **New** icon in the toolbar to begin creating a forum:

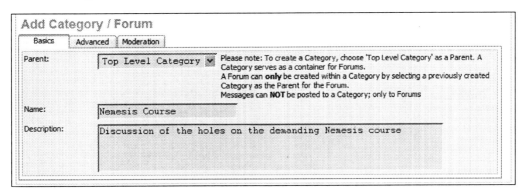

Before we can create a forum, we need to create a category to hold it. To create a category or a forum, simply enter its **Name** and **Description**, and click the **Save** button.

What you just created will be a forum or category depending on what you selected in the **Parent** drop-down box. If you left **Top Level Category** selected, you created a category. If you chose something else from the list, you created a forum. It won't take you long to work out that the elements in the **Parent** drop-down box are the categories, since you can't set a forum to be the parent of another forum.

We'll create a category called **Nemesis Course**, which will be used to hold forums about each hole on the course.

Now that we have a category, the list of categories looks a bit better:

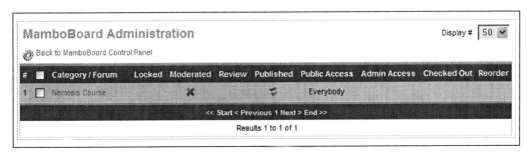

Note that your forum or category will not be published by default, you will need to click its graphic in the **Published** column to publish it. Without publishing your forum or category, it will not be visible to users.

Now we've got our category, we can create a forum (we'll call it **Hole 1**), and set **Nemesis Course** as its **Parent**:

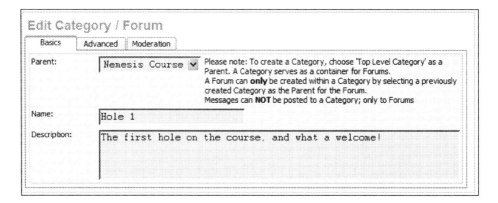

After entering the details, and clicking **Save**, we've got a forum structure for people to look at, so let's allow people to look at it (and hopefully post!).

Adding a Menu Link to the Forums

At the moment, you would have to guess the URL of the forum to view it, and this isn't a particularly good navigation strategy. Instead, we can add a menu item to point to the forums component, in the way that we have done over the last few chapters.

We'll add a link called **Forums**, of type **Component**. All we have to do is to select the **MamboBoard Forum** item from the **Component** box, click **Save**, and our forums are ready.

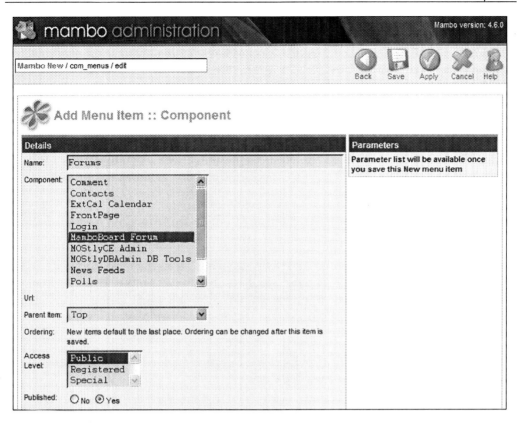

Now visitors will be able to view the forum. If you don't want to allow people to see the forums until they have logged in, you can do this in two ways:

- Set the **Access Level** of the menu item to **Registered**.
- Leave the **Access Level** of the menu item as **Public**, but set the **Registered Users Only** option on the **Security** tab of the **MamboBoard Configuration** to **Yes**.

The difference between these two approaches is that the first option will hide the menu item unless the user is logged in, whereas the second will leave the menu item visible (to indicate that you have forums on your site). You can choose whichever you prefer for your site. You can of course combine them both if you like!

Note that setting **Registered Users Only** on the **Security** tab to **No** will mean that not only can unregistered users see the forum, they can also post, which may not be what you want.

Now that our forum is set up, log in and start posting!

zOOm Media Gallery Component

The zOOm Media Gallery component allows you to create and organize galleries for holding images, and upload media to those galleries.

When an image from a zOOm gallery is displayed on the front end of the site, there is a rather nice surprise displayed along with it, which we will leave you to discover for yourself. There is a clue in the title of the component.

We'll only scratch the surface of this component here. There are many options to this component, and we'll cover the basics of getting your galleries set up, and media uploaded.

The zOOm Media Gallery component can be downloaded from the **Downloads** link of `www.zoomfactory.org`.

You will have to click the **Joomla! 1.x Downloads** link since the main support for the zOOm Media Manager module is now based around Joomla! rather than Mambo, although at this moment, the component is still compatible with Mambo. Once you have obtained and installed the current version of the zOOm Media Manager, you are ready to go.

The zOOm gallery is managed from the **Media Gallery Admin System**, reached from **Components | zOOm Media Gallery**:

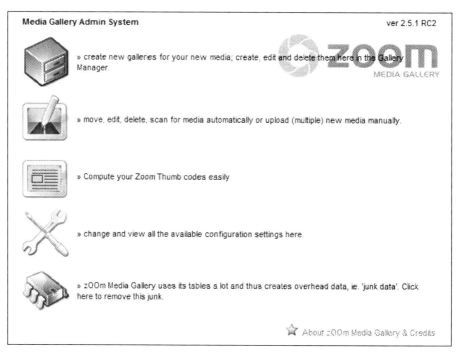

Here you will find options to create new galleries, manage your media, compute the code to use in a mambot that allows you to include images from your gallery in your content items, modify the configuration settings, and clean up the media gallery system.

First of all, we need to create some galleries to hold the media. We're going to create a gallery for the Nemesis Course, holding pictures of the holes on the course. This gallery will contain some subgalleries, Front Nine for pictures of the first nine holes, and Back Nine, for pictures of the last nine holes.

Click the **Gallery Manager** icon and let's begin. (If you hover your mouse cursor over the icons their names are displayed. The **Gallery Manager** icon is the one with the text that starts **create new galleries ...**)

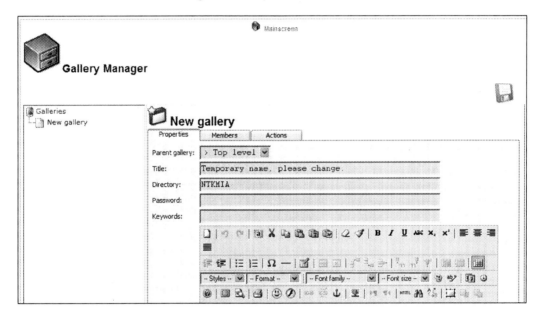

First of all, the **Mainscreen** link at the top takes you back to the zOOm gallery options. The left-hand panel shows a tree view of your galleries (when created). You'll be able to expand entries in the tree, and click on the galleries to edit their details from this screen.

Creating Galleries

To create our new gallery, we need to provide the **Title** of the gallery, which will be **The Nemesis Course**. The **Directory** is provided for you; it corresponds to a folder on the server created by zOOm that will hold the images you upload. Underneath is a **Description** field (not shown in the screenshot above), in which we'll enter a description for this gallery: **Holes from the Nemesis Course**. Once you've entered these details, click the **New Gallery** icon to save your changes (it's the one that looks like the familiar **Save** icon).

The tree view in the left-hand panel will update to show your new gallery:

Now we'll create another gallery, this time sitting inside **The Nemesis Course** gallery. This time, give it a title of **Front Nine**, and enter **The First Nine Holes on the Nemesis Course at Zak Springs** into the **Description** field. From the **Parent gallery** dropdown, select **The Nemesis Course**; selecting the **Parent gallery** in this way is how you nest galleries. Click the **New Gallery** icon and this gallery is created. You can repeat the process for the **Back Nine** gallery, or else you can move on to adding some images!

When you're done, click the **Mainscreen** link to return to the main options.

Adding Images

Images are added by clicking the **Media Manager** icon. First of all, you're asked to select one of the created galleries. We're going to add images to the **Front Nine** gallery, so select that from the dropdown.

This brings you to the (zOOm) **Media Manager**:

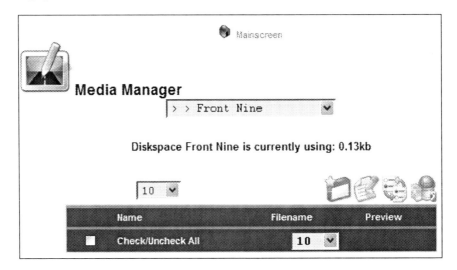

From here you can upload images, edit their details, move them into a new gallery, or delete them entirely. The graphic with a star allows you to upload images, so let's click that (note a window may pop up about the Java applet used by this part of the zOOm gallery; simply click to accept it). This brings you to the **Upload file** screen:

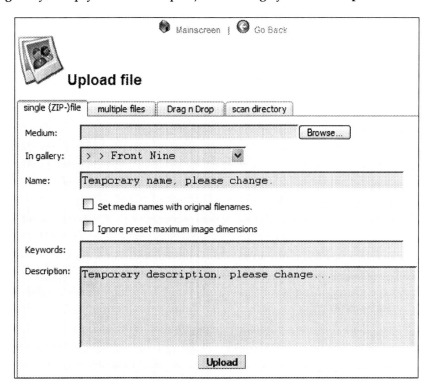

There are several ways you can upload images. You can upload a ZIP file containing your images from the first tab, or you can upload a collection of files from the second tab, or use a Java applet to select files directly from your file system, or scan a directory on the server (not your local machine!) for a set of images from the fourth tab.

In the code download for this chapter you'll find a ZIP file containing a few holes from Zak Springs. Grab that, click the **Browse** button on the **single (ZIP) file** tab, and select that ZIP file. Check the **Set media names with original filenames** option so the filenames are preserved, then click the **Upload** button.

When the page reloads, you are presented with the images contained in the ZIP file:

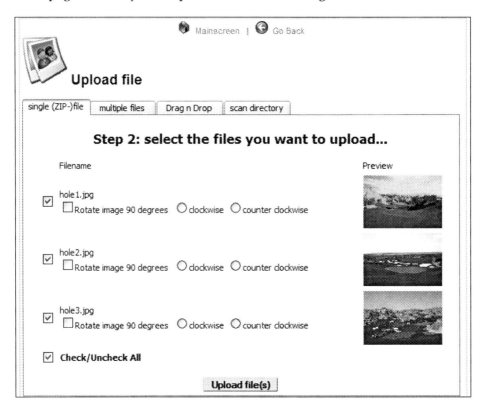

We don't want to rotate the images, and we want to use all these images, so let's just click **Upload file(s)**. You will return to the **Upload file** screen, and should see a message telling you **3 media uploaded succesfully!** Now click the **Go Back** link to see the images in the (zOOm) **Media Manager**:

From here, you can check the box next to one of the images and edit its details to provide a title and description, move the image to another gallery, etc. Our work here is done, for now, so let's get a menu item added so that we can see the gallery.

Let's add a menu item called **The Course** to the Main menu. The menu item type needs to be **Component – Component**, and we simply have to select the **zOOm Media Gallery** from the list of components:

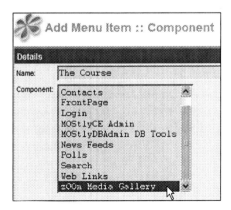

After saving the menu item, and clicking the **The Course** link from the front end of the site, we get a view of the gallery:

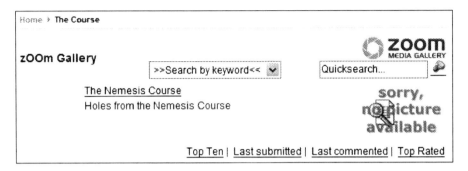

Not much to see here, so let's click the **The Nemesis Course** link. Once again, we don't see any pictures, we'll just see the subgalleries **Front Nine** and **Back Nine**. Click the **Front Nine** link, and hopefully our luck will change:

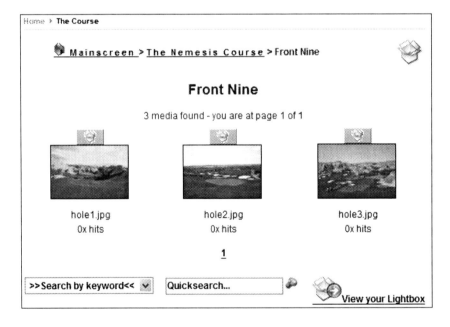

Now we're getting somewhere. Most of the things that you see here can be configured from the settings of the **zOOm Media Gallery Admin System**. Note that you are seeing real thumbnails of the images you uploaded; these thumbnails are created by zOOm and stored on the server. This means that until people click on your final image, they will only see smaller versions of the image, reducing the bandwidth used, and also speeding up the download. Clicking one of the images will display the image in its glory:

Under the image are a number of properties of the image, along with a panel for visitors to add comments. All of this is again configurable from the settings of the **zOOm Media Gallery Admin System**.

The **zOOm Media Gallery Admin System** has a massive number of options, spread across a number of tabs:

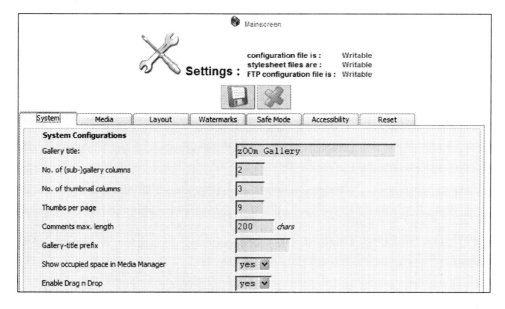

Incredibly, the number of thumbnails displayed per page is **9**, which is exactly the number we'd have in our galleries! The **Layout** tab contains a number of options for controlling the display of the galleries:

Data to display ON/ OFF			
Display Name	Display description	Display keywords	Display date
yes	yes	yes	yes
Display Username	Display filename	Display no. of hits	
yes	yes	yes	
Properties box visual state	Metadata box visual state	Comments box visual state	Animate boxes
visible	visible	visible	yes
Display "Top Ten" link on main page	Display "Last Submitted Media" link on main page	Display "Close" link in popup	Display Mainscreen link in navigation
yes	yes	yes	yes
Rating	Comments	Display Navigation buttons	Display Properties below medium
visible	yes	yes	yes
Display "Media Found" text in gallery	Allow anonymous comment		
yes	yes		

From here you can set whether the filename of the image should be displayed, whether the description should be displayed, whether comments can be submitted, and so on.

To round things off, we can use the `mod_zoom_pics` module (which can also be found at the `www.zoomfactory.org` site) to display thumbnails of the holes on the side of the page. Once you've installed this module, you will find that there a number of parameters for controlling how the images are displayed.

As you will have guessed as we worked through this example, there is much more to the zOOm Media Gallery than we can cover here, so have fun finding your way round the rest of it!

Summary

In this chapter we've covered a number of extensions, both components and modules, for Mambo. We looked first at some of the standard Mambo components, Polls, Newsfeeds, Syndicate, and Banners.

After that, we looked at the ExtCal Event Component. For Zak Springs, this component will be used to provide a calendar of upcoming club events, in particular, tournaments. We saw that users can submit their own events, and how to delete events. We also had a quick look at some of the modules that go with ExtCal, which display handy little views of the forthcoming events.

Next was the MamboBoard Forums component, which provides a threaded discussion environment. We saw the basics of organizing the forums and boards, and also adding a menu item so that users can actually use our forums.

Finally, we had a look at the awesome zOOm Media Gallery component, which we used to display images of some holes from Zak Springs. We saw how to create galleries, and how to upload images to those galleries. I tried hard not to tell you about the remarkable feature you see when the image is displayed on the front end of the site; I think you will enjoy it!

11
Customizing a Template

In this chapter we'll walk through making some basic customizations to one of the existing Mambo templates to produce a very different looking template for Zak Springs. We'll change the header graphic and the page background, customize the main content area, change the way modules and the menus are displayed, and so on.

We'll finish off with the steps required to turn your template into a unit that can be installed onto another Mambo site.

First, let's talk about what you will need to work with templates.

What You Need

We'll be working with three main things in our template activities; PHP code files, the CSS stylesheet, and graphics.

You don't need to know very much about PHP to work with the PHP code file in the template, partly because there isn't much PHP code in the file, it is mostly HTML markup. To edit the PHP code file you can use a standard text editor, like Notepad or one of the other free text editors like the excellent PSPad (available from www.pspad. com). The code file in question isn't that large or complex, and there isn't much to gain from editing this file in a more complex HTML editing application like Adobe's Dreamweaver or FrontPage.

The Cascading Style Sheet (CSS) is another plain text file, and can also be edited in a text editor. When doing further work on the stylesheet, you may find the extended features of a Dreamweaver-like application helpful, but for our work here, the text editor will suffice.

Editing the CSS file isn't particularly the problem here. The problem could be how comfortable you are working with CSS. As you'll see, most of the formatting for the template is governed by the CSS file. We'll take you through most of what you need to perform the tasks here, but to get serious with Mambo templates, growing your knowledge of CSS is a good idea.

You will find any number of CSS tutorials on the web, and if you want to read some more, *Head First HTML with CSS & XHTML* (O'Reilly, ISBN: 0-596-10197-X) and *CSS Web Site Design Hands on Training* (Peachpit Press, ISBN: 0-321-29391-6) by the legendary Eric Meyer are excellent introductions to CSS.

We'll be doing some work with graphics in the course of making our template as well. For this, you'll need some kind of image editing application, such as PhotoShop, PhotoShop Elements, or something like the open-source GIMP application. Any of these will be able to help you perform the kind of tasks we do in this chapter, and much more.

There is another set of tools that will be very helpful when working with templates, browser tools. There are a number of tools that you can plug into your browser that can help you work out what style is being applied to what part of the page, and also the overall structure of the page.

If you're using the Firefox browser, there are two particularly useful extensions that can be downloaded, installed, and used from within the browser. The first is the Web Developer extension, available from `https://addons.mozilla.org/firefox/60/`. The Web Developer toolbar allows you to outline various elements on the page, such as table or block-level elements, see what CSS classes are applied to particular elements, and also see the definition of those classes. The Firebug extension, available from `https://addons.mozilla.org/firefox/1843/`, offers even more power, including an inspector to reveal the structure of the page and a JavaScript debugger. Installing Firefox extensions is a straightforward operation.

For Internet Explorer 7, there is also a "Web Developer Toolbar", similar to both the Firefox Web Developer Toolbar and the Firebug extension. It can be downloaded from:

```
http://www.microsoft.com/downloads/details.aspx?familyid=e59c3964-
672d-4511-bb3e-2d5e1db91038&displaylang=en
```

There is also a similar toolbar for the Opera web browser, available from:

```
http://operawiki.info/WebDevToolbar
```

For the Safari web browser, you can try the Web Inspector available from:

```
http://webkit.org/blog/?p=41
```

One other thing to note: we'll be making changes to the files in our template, and then refreshing our browser pages to see the changes. If you find that refreshing the page in your browser isn't changing anything, you might want to perform a "hard" refresh (*Ctrl* + *F5* in many browsers), which will ignore any items your browser might have cached. Internet Explorer in particular often needs a hard refresh to take notice of a change in the stylesheet of your template.

Template File Structure

A "template" is a folder that contains a couple of files and two folders. First of all, the folders:

- `css`: This folder contains the CSS stylesheet for the template. The stylesheet file is called `template_css.css`.
- `images`: This folder contains the images that are used by the template. This can be background images, images for the site banner, and so on.

The files in the template folder are as follows:

- `templateDetails.xml`: This is an XML file that contains the metadata about the template; the name of the template, the author, date it was created, and also a full list of the files in the `css` and `images` folders.
- `template_thumbnail.png`: This image is a "thumbnail" of the final template as it would be seen on the screen. This is the image that pops up when you hover the cursor over a template in the **Template Manager**. Typically, this image is around 200 pixels wide.
- `index.php`: This is a PHP code file, and is actually the "template" itself. This file contains the HTML markup for the page, along with some inserts of PHP code that call Mambo functions to display modules and so on.

That doesn't seem so bad, just three files and some images in a template!

Creating a New Template

To get started, create a copy of the `waterandstone_green` folder and call it `zaksprings`. We're going to work with the green Water and Stone template, and gradually change it as we go.

Changing the Template Details

The first step is to change the name of the template, so open up the file `templateDetails.xml` in a text editor, and change the `name` element as highlighted below:

```
<?xml version="1.0" encoding="iso-8859-1"?>
<mosinstall type="template" version="4.5.3">
    <name>zaksprings</name>
```

After you've done this, save the file, and let's move on.

The `templateDetails.xml` file contains metadata for the template, which is used to identify it to the **Template Manager** in the Mambo administrator area, and also provide information that can be used by the Universal Installer when the template is installed. We'll talk more about this metadata at the end of the chapter when we've completed our new template.

Now if you browse to the **Template Manager**, you will see the `zaksprings` template in the list; select it, and set it is as the default template so that we'll be able to see how our changes look.

The Template File Itself

Although we are talking about "templates", the `index.php` file in our `template` folder can really by called the "template". You can open this file in your text editor to look at as we go further.

The file starts by preventing direct access to the template, and then declaring the document type of the page. The document type is XHTML, which is a "stricter and cleaner" flavor of HTML, intended to add a proper XML structure to HTML pages. You can read more about XHTML at: `http://www.w3schools.com/xhtml/xhtml_intro.asp`.

```
<?php
  defined( '_VALID_MOS' ) or
    die( 'Direct Access to this location is not allowed.' );
// needed to seperate the ISO number from the language
  file constant _ISO
  $iso = explode( '=', _ISO );
// xml prolog
  echo '<?xml version="1.0" encoding="'. $iso[1] .'"?' .'>';
?>
<!DOCTYPE html PUBLIC "-//W3C//DTD XHTML 1.0 Transitional//EN"
    "http://www.w3.org/TR/xhtml1/DTD/xhtml1-transitional.dtd">
<html xmlns="http://www.w3.org/1999/xhtml">
<head>
```

The next part of the template sets up the `<head>` element of the page, which includes such things as the `meta` tags that Mambo will generate (these are included by the `mosShowHead()` PHP function), and some references to include the JavaScript required for the HTML editor and also the CSS stylesheet for the template from the css folder of the template. If you wanted to add in references to other stylesheets or JavaScript libraries, you would do that in this part of the template:

```
<?php mosShowHead(); ?>
<?php
if ( $my->id ) {
    initEditor();
}
?>
<meta http-equiv="Content-Type"
      content="text/html; <?php echo _ISO; ?>" />
<link href="<?php echo $mosConfig_live_site;?>
            /templates/waterandstone_green/css/template_css.css"
      rel="stylesheet" type="text/css"/>
</head>
```

As you continue to look through the file, you'll notice the presence of the word waterandstone_green in links to images and also the stylesheet. For example:

```
<link href="<?php echo $mosConfig_live_site;?>
            /templates/waterandstone_green/css/template_css.css"
      rel="stylesheet" type="text/css"/>
...
<a href="index.php">
   <img src="<?php echo $mosConfig_live_site; ?>
             /templates/waterandstone_green/images/logo.gif"
        alt="logo image" border="0" align="top" />
</a>
```

These are references to our source template, so you will need to change this to point to your new template. If you don't, then you might wonder why nothing is happening when you start adding new graphics—it's because the wrong folder is being looked in for that new image!

Using the search and replace feature of your text editor replace all occurrences of waterandstone_green with zaksprings, and then save the file.

Quite a lot goes on in the index.php file, and display of the page only really starts with these lines:

```
<body class="waterbody">

<div align="center">
<div id="container">
   <div id="containerbg">
```

From then on, the file consists mostly of HTML container elements, and some PHP statements (as highlighted below):

```
<!-- start left column. -->
<div id="leftcol">
<?php mosLoadModules('left'); ?>
</div>
<div id="leftcolmenu">
<?php mosLoadModules('user1'); ?>
</div>
<!-- end left column. -->
```

The file also has a number of HTML comments (enclosed by `<!-- -->`), which help to give you an idea of what's going on. The snippet above displays the left-hand column. An HTML `div` element is created, with an `id` attribute of `leftcol`. This `id` attribute will be used to identify that particular page element by the CSS stylesheet. What goes into this `div` element? The output of the `mosLoadModules('left')` function will be the value of `div` element.

You can almost guess what `mosLoadModules('left')` does. It displays all the Mambo modules that have a position of `left`.

Further down the file, you can see some other functions:

```
<?php
            if (mosCountModules('user2') >= 1 OR
mosCountModules('user3') >= 1 ) {
            ?>
...
<?php mosPathWay(); ?>


...
<?php mosMainBody(); ?>
```

The name, of these functions gives a big clue to what they are expected to do. The `mosCountModules()` function returns the number of modules in a particular position. This function is used in case you wanted to enclose the modules in some kind of container element, but you only wanted the container element displayed if there were actually some modules to go in it.

The `mospathWay()` function displays the breadcrumbs:

The main part of the page is displayed by `mosMainBody()`.

No Logic Here

One thing you will notice is that once the display of the page starts after the `<body>` tag in `index.php`, there is very little "logic" in the `index.php` file. There are only two `if` statements in the entire file and both of these only check if a particular module position has some modules.

There is little point in putting logic into the template file. Through the module and menu management systems of Mambo's administration, you have already encoded a lot of logic on how your site will look and operate; displaying modules in certain positions on certain pages, restricting certain menu items to some types of user, and so on. Also, the ability to select a different template for different sets of pages adds another layer of logic, so there isn't that much left to put into the template. Also, you would need to have a very good knowledge of the inner workings of Mambo to introduce more complex logic into the page output.

Links to Images

Another thing to note is the links to images in the file. They look like this:

```
<img src="<?php echo $mosConfig_live_site; ?>
         /templates/zaksprings/images/img_header.jpg"
    alt="header image" />
```

The `$mosConfig_live_site` variable holds the path to your site (`http://www.zaksprings.com` for example), which is added to the path to an image. The images for a template are found in its `images` folder, so you might be wondering why you would need a long path to get to that image, why not simply `images/img_header.jpg`? That's because the browser is not requesting the file `index.php` in the templates folder. The page requests to Mambo always come through a few files in the root of the Mambo installation, `index.php`, `index2.php`, and so on. The `index.php` file of the template is "included" by Mambo for processing, so although the image looks like it's only one folder away from that `index.php` file, you need to write the full path to the image, which is `templates/<name of template>/images` for a visitor's web browser to get at an image.

No Layout Here

You may also be wondering where all the layout information in the template is. There doesn't really seem to be very much in the template in terms of HTML markup, just some `<div>` elements. That's because all the formatting is passed on to the CSS stylesheet. The tasks such as where these `<div>` elements go on the page, how big they are, what color they are, and what their text looks like are controlled by the CSS stylesheet.

To get a better picture of the importance of the stylesheet, this image shows the basic Water and Stone template without the stylesheet applied. As you can see, it's not particularly good!

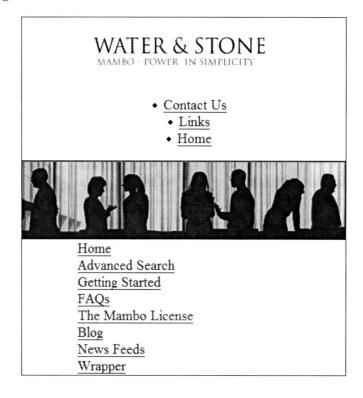

The stylesheet transforms this basic list of items into a web page.

XHTML Compliance

Before we go any further, it's worth reflecting on the idea that the page created by the template is XHTML rather than standard HTML, or put another way, the page is XHTML compliant. One of the obvious differences between XHTML and HTML is that tags need to be closed, in order to be valid XML. In HTML, you can get away with using tags like:

```
Time for a line break<br>
and now a picture: <img src="images/myimage.gif">
```

However, to be valid XHTML, the `<br>` tag would need to be closed. This is not done with a `</br>` tag, but with `/>` characters at the end of the tag instead of the `>` character. The same is true for the `<img>` tag. Thus, to produce valid XHTML, we would want:

```
    Time for a line break<br/>
    and now a picture: <img src="images/myimage.gif"/>
```

This might seem like a lot of work to produce XHTML. Every time you used tags like these, you would want to make sure the tags are closed. However, if you think about it for a moment, you really won't have to do this that often.

There are three main ways that text finds it way onto your pages in Mambo

- From the HTML editor
- From code in Mambo components, modules, and so on
- From the markup in the index.php file of the template

Whenever you add marked-up content in Mambo, you would generally find yourself using the HTML editor. When entering content through the HTML editor, if you've had a look at the HTML source as you're editing, you'll see that HTML editor itself ensures that the tags are XHTML compliant, <img> tags become <img/> and so on. If you work directly with the HTML source in the HTML editor, then you can try to introduce non-XHTML compliant markup, but even then, the HTML editor will do its best to make it XHTML compliant!

Mambo components produce their own output. It is up to the programmer of these components to make sure that the output is XHTML compliant, and generally, they do a good job of this.

The markup in the index.php file of the template looks like the only place you can really mess things up! This is one reason why the markup in the template looks simple; it basically consists of a number of <div> elements, and as we'll see, the formatting and layout of these elements is controlled by the CSS stylesheet. In addition to decoupling the layout of the page from the markup, this approach gives less opportunity for creating non XHTML-compliant markup as well.

So, keep an eye on the markup you add to the template, keep it XHTML compliant, and the rest of Mambo will keep things XHTML compliant as well. This is something to watch out for if you are editing the index.php file in some HTML editing application, such as FrontPage, which often has its own ideas about what kind of HTML it thinks you want to enter.

Customizing the Page Layout

We've seen the basics of what templateDetails.xml and index.php do. Now we're actually going to get started.

In this section we'll go through some basic changes to the page layout:

- Replacing the Header Graphic
- Moving the Top Menu
- Changing the Page Background
- Changing the Fonts
- Changing the Main Content Area
- Customizing the Read More Link
- Changing the Background Color of the Columns
- Adding the Bottom Menu

The first two will involve changes to `index.php`, after that, we're into the stylesheet!

Replacing the Header Graphic

We've got a rather nifty site banner for Zak Springs, and we want it to replace the existing two top images in the current template:

You'll find our new header graphic, `img_header.jpg`, in the code download for this chapter. Copy it to the `images` folder of our `zaksprings` template, and it will replace an existing file there.

You'll have noticed that there are two graphics in the current "header", the logo at the top (`logo.gif`) and the image header below (`img_header.jpg`), with the top menu in between them. If we look in `index.php`, this is what we see. The top menu is highlighted in the code below:

```
<!-- start logo -->
<div id="logo">
 <a href="index.php">
   <img src="<?php echo $mosConfig_live_site; ?>
             /templates/zaksprings/images/logo.gif"
```

```
        alt="logo image" border="0" align="top" />
   </a>
</div>
<!-- end logo -->
<!-- start top menu -->
<div id="topmenu">
<?php mosLoadModules('top',-1); ?>
</div>
<!-- end top menu.  -->
<!-- start image header -->
<div id="imgheader">
<img src="templates/zaksprings/images/img_header.jpg"
     alt="header image" />
</div>
<!-- end image header -->
```

We're going to do away with the logo part of the header, so we'll delete everything from `<!-- start logo -->` to `<!-- end logo -->`.

We don't need to change the link to the header image, since we replaced the existing graphic with one of the same name.

Save the file, and have a look at the front end of your site. You should see the new header graphic:

However, that doesn't look right; the main menu seems to have started too "high" on the page. There is no evidence for why this should have happened in the `index. php` file, so the culprit must be in the stylesheet, that's the only other thing involved in the template.

In your text editor, open the file `template_css.css` in the `css` folder. What are we looking for? Well, you may have noticed the `<div>` element containing the header graphic with an `id` of `imgheader`. In a CSS stylesheet, you can define a CSS class

to apply to an HTML element with a particular id attribute by using the syntax #
followed by the value of the id attribute. That means we're looking for something
called #imgheader in our file, so using the find feature of your text editor, hunt
down #imgheader. This is what you'll find:

```
/** div container for image header **/
#imgheader {
    position:relative;
    float:left;
    clear:left;
    width:100%;
    height:99px;
    background-color: #000000;
}
```

This is the style information—known as properties in CSS parlance—that we're
after. If you're not familiar with properties in CSS, they consist of the property name
followed by a colon, followed by the property definition, with a semi-colon denoting
the end of the definition.

Without being a master of CSS, you should suspect the height property could be the
problem. It's definition says 99px, which sets the height of the imgheader element
to 99 pixels. If you check out the img_header.jpg graphic, you'll find its 173 pixels
high. It's pretty clear what we've to do—set the height to 173 pixels like this:

```
/** div container for image header **/
#imgheader {
    position:relative;
    float:left;
    clear:left;
    width:100%;
    height:173px;
    background-color: #000000;
}
```

Save the file, and refresh the page of your site, and the main menu should now start
underneath the header graphic, rather than part way through it.

OK, we're off! Before we go any further, delete the file logo.gif from the images
folder of the template as we don't need it anymore.

Changing the Page Background and Fonts

The page background is our next stop. The Water and Stone template uses an odd gray, stripey background. We're going to replace that will a pure black background. In the `index.php` file, the body element looks like this:

```
<body class="waterbody">
```

There is no sign of a background setting there, so the answer lies again in the stylesheet. The definition for the CSS class `waterbody` looks like this. It is right at the top of the file:

```
.waterbody {
    background:#FFFFFF url(../images/bg_body.jpg) repeat-x left top;
    margin:0;
    color:#333333;
}
```

We don't want any background image, so delete everything on the background property line after #FFFFF, and then change #FFFFFF (which specifies white) to #000000 (black) to get this:

```
.waterbody {
    background:#000000 ;
    margin:0;
    color:#333333;
}
```

Make sure you've still got the semi-colon at the end of the line. The semi-colons denote the end of a CSS property definition.

Once you've done that, save the file and refresh your browser, and your page background will be black in color.

While we're here, let's change the body fonts. The definition at the top of the stylesheet handles the body fonts:

```
* {
    font-family: Arial, Helvetica, sans-serif;
}
```

This specifies a default font of `Arial`, followed by `Helvetica` if `Arial` isn't available, or some general sans-serif font if that one isn't available. We're going to change this to make `Verdana` the default font. If that isn't available, then this visitor will have to make do with `Arial`.

```
* {
    font-family: Verdana, Arial, Helvetica, sans-serif;
}
```

Changing the Main Content Area

We're going well now, so let's look at the main content area.

In `index.php`, you can find the main content area of the page, and see it is wrapped in a `div` element with an id of `content_main`:

```
<!-- start main body -->
        <div id="content_main">
...

                <?php mosMainBody(); ?>
...
        </div>
        <!-- end main body -->
```

This suggests our next target is the `content_main` class in the stylesheet. Search for it, and you'll find this:

```
/** div container for mainbody **/
#content_main {
   position:relative;
   float:left;
   width:520px;
   margin:15px 0 20px 20px;
   background-color:#FFFFFF;
}
```

The interesting things to note here are the `width` property, which specifies a width of 520 pixels. Also, the margin is set by the `margin` property. The margin is the spacing "outside" of an element, which means between an element and its parent. We're going to bring the main content area much closer to the header graphic, and put a gray border around it. We will also add some internal spacing with the padding property. We'll add eight pixels of padding on all sides. Change the definition for `content_main` to the following:

```
/** div container for mainbody **/
#content_main {
   position:relative;
   float:left;
   width:520px;
   margin: 0px 0px 8px 8px;
   background-color:#FFFFFF;
   padding:8px;
   border:2px #CCCCCC solid;
}
```

Note how we have set the margin. There are 4 numbers, and these correspond to the top, right, bottom, and left margins respectively. Thus we have moved the main content area closer up to the header graphic, and closer to the left-hand side.

Changing the Background Color of the Columns

Let's look at the background color of the left and right-hand columns of the page. We want to change the left-hand column to black, and the right-hand column to a gray color.

Looking in `index.php` gives us a clue where to start looking for the left-hand column:

```
<div id="container_inner">
  <!-- start left column. -->
    <div id="leftcol">
```

We need to look for the `leftcol` class in the stylesheet. Here we'll find something surprising. First of all, we'll find lots of definitions for `leftcol`. In fact, you will find lots of definitions for styles used "inside" `leftcol`.

If you keep looking, you'll not find a background for `leftcol`. The background actually belongs to a parent element, `containerbg`.

It is quite instructive to have a look at the page structure using the Inspector feature of the Firefox extension Firebug (this was one of the browser tools we discussed at the start of the chapter). If you don't have Firebug installed, you can still follow along the text. Open Firebug, click the **Inspector** tab and expand the `body` element, then expand the `container` element you find inside it. This is how the page structure looks in Firebug:

```
Clear  Inspect  Options ▾    Console    Debugger    Inspector

▼ <html xmlns="http://www.w3.org/1999/xhtml">
   ▶ <head>
   ▼ <body class="waterbody">
      ▼ <div align="center">
         ▼ <div id="container">
            ▶ <div id="containerbg">
            ▶ <div id="copyright">
            </div>
         </div>
      </body>
   </html>
```

In the container element there are two other elements, containerbg and copyright. If you expand the copyright element you will find it doesn't really have much in it, only the copyright message. Everything goes on in the containerbg element.

When you expand the **containerbg** element, you see this:

```
▼ <div id="containerbg">
    ▼ <div id="outerleft">
        ▶ <div id="topmenu">
        ▶ <div id="imgheader">
        ▼ <div id="container_inner">
            ▶ <div id="leftcol">
                <div id="leftcolmenu"> </div>
            ▶ <div id="content_main">
            </div>
        </div>
    ▶ <div id="outerright">
```

The outerleft element looks like it contains much of the page — the top menu, the image header, and the container_inner element, which has the left column and the content_main element.

Thus containerbg is our first stop to look for a background, after all, that could be what the bg stands for? This element does indeed have a background in the stylesheet:

```
#containerbg {
    position:relative;
    width: 900px;
    background:transparent url(../images/bg_inside.jpg) repeat-y left
      top;
    float:left;
    top:0;
    left:0;
```

The path to the background image is defined by this part of the background property:

```
url(../images/bg_inside.jpg)
```

This path is *relative to the stylesheet*, unlike the path to images used from index.php we saw earlier, which are relative to the root of our Mambo installation (like /templates/zaksprings/images/logo.gif for example).

To get away from the stylesheet (in zaksprings/css/template_css.css) you have to go up a folder (../) bringing you to the zaksprings folder, and then into the images folder. Specifying background images using CSS in this way means that you bypass the need for including the name of the template.

The `bg_inside.jpg` image itself is interesting. It has three parts, a green bit on the left, a white bit in the middle, and a darker green bit on the right-hand end.

Here is a representation of it:

This graphic defines the entire background for the `containerbg` element, including the right-hand column. The white bit in the middle defines a white background for the main content area, and the dark green on the right-hand side is for the right-hand column. One of the reasons to define the background for the columns in this way is that then the background will reach all the way to the bottom of the entire container element.

If you set a background for the right-hand column, it would only extend as far as the right-hand column reached. Sometimes the right-hand column may have less content in it than the left-hand column, and you would find that the background of your right-hand column just stopped part of the way down the page, because the element it was the background for had stopped.

We could change the background color of the left-hand column by simply changing the color of the left-hand part of the `bg_inside.jpg` in a graphics editor, using a flood fill or some careful brush work. What we'll do is to make the left-hand part of the image completely black, and then fill in the white middle part black as well. The right-hand side will be made a gray color (HTML code #363636).

You can find the changed version of `bg_inside.jpg` in the code download. Copy it to the `images` folder and when you refresh your page, you'll see how things have changed:

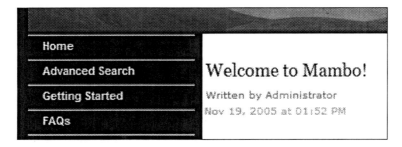

Customizing the Read More Link

The **Read More...** link displayed under the introduction of a content item is our next target. If you use the **Information | Display ID and Class Details** option of the Firefox developer toolbar, or just have a careful look at the HTML source of the page (search for **Read more**) you'll see the name of the CSS class we want is `readon`:

```
<a href="http://localhost/mambo/index.php?option=com_content&amp;
task=view&amp;id=15&amp;Itemid=9" class="readon">
                Read more...                </a>
```

The current format of this link is pretty basic. We're going to produce something a bit more impressive:

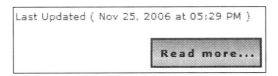

The **Read more...** link will "float" on the right, resemble a button with a nice gradient background, and when the user hovers their mouse cursor over the link, the background will change. This will not need any JavaScript.

Let's have a look at the `readon` class in the stylesheet:

```
/*** read more link ***/
.readon,
a.readon:link,
a.readon:active,
a.readon:visited {
    color:#666666;
    font-weight:bold;
    text-align:left;
    margin-top:10px;
    letter-spacing: 2px;
    font-size:10px;
    text-decoration:none;
}
```

We will add properties for the background image, some padding to keep some space between the text of the link and the border, and a gray border. Note that we use the `background-image` property to specify the background image rather than the `background` property as we have seen earlier. Using `background` allows you to specify a background color as well.

```
/*** read more link ***/
.readon,
a.readon:link,
a.readon:active,
a.readon:visited {
    color:#666666;
    font-weight:bold;
    text-align:left;
    margin-top:10px;
    letter-spacing: 2px;
    font-size:10px;
    text-decoration:none;
    float:right;
    background-image: url(../images/readon.png);
    padding:4px;
    border:2px #CCCCCC solid;
}
```

The float property allows the element to be shifted to either the left or right on its current line. Our element will float to the right of the current line. (Again you will find the readon.png image in the code download. Copy it to the images folder of zaksprings.)

The standard readon link is defined by a.readon:link, and a.readon:visited can be used to define the formatting for a link that has been visited. The behavior of a link as you click on it is determined by a.readon:active. There is another behavior whose formatting can be defined, the behavior when you hover your mouse cursor over an element. This is defined by <classname>:hover.

Looking through the rest of the file you find the extra a.readon:hover definition.

```
/** underline on hover **/
a.toclink:hover,
...
a.readon:hover,
...
a.latestnews:hover {
    text-decoration:underline;
    color:#0C362D;
    background-color:inherit;
}
```

This definition sets what happens when a user hovers their mouse cursor over these links. The color changes and the link is underlined. This is fine, but we want more, so let's add to the a.readon:hover definition:

```
/** underline on hover **/
a.toclink:hover,
...
a.readon:hover,
...
a.latestnews:hover {
    text-decoration:underline;
    color:#0C362D;
    background-color:inherit;
}
a.readon:hover { background-image: url(../images/readon_hover.png) }
```

We've left the first `a.readon:hover` defintion for the underlining. The second definition will add the `background-image` in addition to the properties from the first definition. This means that when the visitor hovers the cursor over the link, a new background image will be displayed.

Formatting the Content Items

Our customization of the **Read More...** link was our first encounter with CSS classes that do not come from the template itself. Things such as `waterbody`, `content_main`, and so on are mentioned in the `index.php` file of the template, they do not come from the Mambo "core" or the output of any component. The `readon` CSS class is produced from a Mambo component. We'll have a look at some more CSS classes that come straight from the Content component. For any template you want to create, you would have to define these styles.

This image shows a content item from the front page, and the classes that style various parts of it:

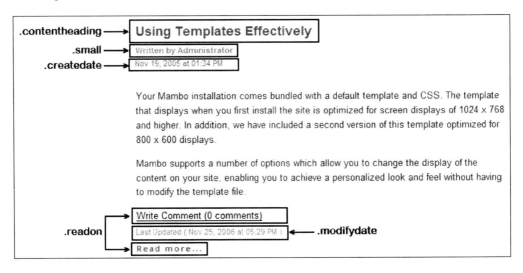

Whenever Mambo displays a content item, the Content component will spit out the same kind of output, with the different parts of the content item marked with various CSS classes. Whatever the content of the item, the classes will always be the same, and there is no real way to control this from the template, since these are "hardcoded" into the Content component.

First of all, this display is made up of two tables, both of class `contentpaneopen`. The title of the content item is in one table, and everything below **Written by Administrator** is in another table. The title of the content item is styled by the `contentheading` class.

The **Written By Administrator** text is in the `small` class, and the date is marked by the `createdate` class. The text of the item is in the default style of the page, and the **Write Comment** and **Read more...** links are both in the same style, `readon`.

For now, we're quite happy with the way the content items are formatted. In the following sections, we will point out which CSS classes come from the base template, and which are from the Mambo core or a component.

Adding the Bottom Menu

We began creating a menu to go at the bottom of the page in Chapter 6. At that time, we couldn't actually place it where we wanted, because of the template. We'll rectify that now by adding some code to the `index.php` file to display the modules in that position.

We set the position of the bottom menu to **bottom**, which conveniently existed. If we wanted to create a new module position, we can do that from **Site | Template Manager | Module Positions** of the administrator menu. All we would need to do is give our new module position a name and save it.

Adding the code to load the modules from the bottom position is easy. We add it near the end of the `index.php` file:

```
</div>
</div>
<div align="center">
   <div id="bottommenu" >
      <?php mosLoadModules('bottom'); ?>
   </div>
</div>
<?php mosLoadModules('debug', -1);?>
</body>
</html>
```

We wrap the `div` containing the bottom menu in another `div`, and align it to the center of the page. However, if you view the menu now it will look odd. That's because it will be styled like one of the side menus. To get a properly styled menu, we need to use the **Menu Class Suffix** property of the bottom menu's module parameters. This will add something onto the name of the class used by the bottom menu to produce a unique classname for the menu.

First of all, before we make any changes to the stylesheet, edit the **Bottom Menu** module from **Modules | Site Modules** on the administrator menu. In the module Parameters, set its **Menu Class Suffix** to **-navbot** and its **Menu Style** as **Horizontal**, and then click **Save**.

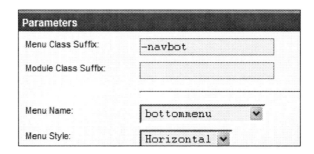

Now we add the definition for the bottommenu element to the stylesheet:

```
#bottommenu {

    width:350px;
    text-align:center;

    margin-bottom:32px;

}
```

Next we define the style for links in the bottom menu. The **Menu Class Suffix** of `-navbot` means that instead of `a.mainlevel` being the class for the link, the classname will be `a.mainlevel-navbot`.

```
#bottommenu a.mainlevel-navbot { margin:24px; color:#ffffff;}
```

You can get a little illustration of the difficulty of producing cross-browser templates here. If you omit the `#bottommenu` part of the definition for the link, Internet Explorer won't set the color of the link to white, while it looks OK in Firefox for example. One of the reasons for working with the Water and Stone templates from the start is that they display pretty well across different browsers, so we'll try to keep this up.

That completes the bottom menu.

Customizing the Modules

Now we turn our attention to the module output. We'll start by spacing out the modules; you'll have noticed that as soon as one finishes, the next module starts almost immediately. We'd like a bit of breathing room between them.

Spacing Out the Modules

Let's use Firebug's Inspector again to have a look at the `leftcol` element, which contains our left-hand modules:

```
▼ <div id="outerleft">
  ▶ <div id="topmenu">
  ▶ <div id="imgheader">
  ▼ <div id="container_inner">
    ▼ <div id="leftcol">
      ▶ <table cellspacing="0" cellpadding="0" class="moduletable">
      ▶ <table cellspacing="0" cellpadding="0" class="moduletable">
      ▶ <table cellspacing="0" cellpadding="0" class="moduletable">
      ▶ <table cellspacing="0" cellpadding="0" class="moduletable">
      ▶ <table cellspacing="0" cellpadding="0" class="moduletable">
      ▶ <table cellspacing="0" cellpadding="0" class="moduletable">
      </div>
      <div id="leftcolmenu"> </div>
    ▶ <div id="content_main">
```

Expanding the **leftcol** element shows a number of table elements, with CSS class `moduletable`. That sounds like what we're after. If we expand one of the **moduletable** elements:

```
▼ <table cellspacing="0" cellpadding="0" class="moduletable">
  ▼ <tbody>
    ▼ <tr>
        <th valign="top"> Holes at Zak Springs </th>
      </tr>
    ▼ <tr>
      ▶ <td>
      </tr>
    </tbody>
  </table>
```

You can see that the `th` element of the table holds the module title.

One thing to note is that there is no mention of `moduletable` in the `index.php` file of the template. This is another CSS class that comes from the Mambo core, and does not depend on the template.

A search through the stylesheet reveals no definition for `moduletable`. There are definitions for the `td` and `th` `moduletable` elements, but these only define part of the table. We'll modify the `th` definition in a moment.

We'll add a `moduletable` defintion into the stylesheet that will apply to modules in the left-hand column:

```
#leftcol table.moduletable {
    margin-bottom:8px;
    border-top:1px #CCCCCC solid;
    border-bottom:1px #CCCCCC solid;
    background:url(../images/bg_lhm_inside.jpg)
    repeat-y left top;
}
```

The `#leftcol` indicates that this definition will apply to the element with id `leftcol`, which is the container for the left-hand modules. (This is specified in the `index.php` file).

The `margin-bottom` property sets the spacing after the table. One reason to set the spacing after (rather than before using `margin-top`), is so that the top module can still be right under the header graphic. If we had `margin-top`, there would be a gap before the first module is displayed.

We set a border for the top and bottom (we will handle the side margin in a moment), and define a background image. (The image is again in the code download and needs to be copied to the `images` folder of `zaksprings`.)

The background image is 170px wide, which is the exact width of the left-hand column. The role of the background image is to provide the side border. The background-image looks like this:

The gray lines are the borders of the module. The `repeat-y` part of the property definition ensures that the image will repeat vertically rather than horizontally, since the image is really only a couple of pixels high.

This image is actually constructed from cropping the original `bg_inside.jpg` background image, and changing the colors, in the same way the current version of `bg_inside.jpg` was prepared.

Once you've made these changes, save the stylesheet and refresh your browser page. This is what the **Other Menu** looks like:

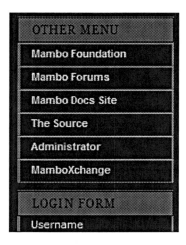

We're still not finished here, there is something not quite right with the module title.

Changing the Module Headers

To change the way the module titles look, we need to investigate the `moduletable` `th` definition.

In the stylesheet, you'll find the definition for the table headings:

```
#leftcol table.moduletable th {
    background-color: #8F8A2C;
    color: #000000;
    border: solid 1px #000000;
}

#rightcol table.moduletable th {
    background-color:#6EB28A;
    border: solid 1px #000000;
}
```

These define the table headings for left-hand and right-hand modules. The `#leftcol` refers to the left-hand column element and `#rightcol` refers to the right-hand column element.

Let's take a closer look at the current module title bar:

We would like to change the background color to a nice silvery gray, but it looks like we will also want to add a border above and below to match the gray of the side borders. This is our new definition:

```
#leftcol table.moduletable th {
   color: #000000;
   background: url(../images/moduletableth.jpg) repeat-y left top;
   border-top:1px #808080 solid;
   border-bottom:1px #808080 solid;
}
```

The top and bottom borders are easy enough. The color of the borders (#808080) matches up with the gray borders. It's our background image that's the interesting bit.

This image is similar to the background for the module table. Its 170 pixels wide, but it has a silvery gray background, with darker gray side borders to match the border with the rest of the module table:

However, if you look at your Mambo page now, there is still something not right about the module titles. Even with the new background image, it still doesn't look quite aligned properly. Something is interfering. The culprit is the general `moduletable th` definition:

```
/** general module title **/
table.moduletable th {
   border: solid 1px #000000;
   color:#FFFFFF;
```

It's that one pixel border that's throwing everything out. Let's comment out that line with the /* and */.characters:

```
/** general module title **/
table.moduletable th {
   /* border: solid 1px #000000; */
   color:#FFFFFF;
```

Now save the file. When you view your page, the module titles look pretty good.

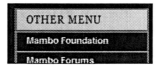

Customizing the Menus

We'll complete our customization by changing some of the properties of the menu entries. We'll first of all change the color of the menu entry when the mouse cursor is hovered over it, then we'll change the border of an menu entry to fit it in with our gray color scheme for the side borders, then we'll add a new definition to highlight the currently selected menu item.

All the CSS classes we encounter in this section come from the Mambo core. Their names do not depend on the choice of template, and for any new template you were creating, the class names you meet in this section will be ones you want to define in the template.

Changing the Menu Hover Color

Currently, when you hover the cursor over an entry in the main menu, the background color changes to green. We want to make this into a gray color, and also do something about the border between two menu entries. All we have to do is work out the name of the classes for the menu entries!

You can use the Firefox Web Developer Toolbar to display the ID and class information for a page (from **Information | Display Id and Class Details**). You would see something like this on your page:

This shows the class for a menu entry is called `mainlevel`. We're interested in setting what happens when a visitor hovers their mouse cursor over one of the menu entries, so we're looking for `mainlevel:hover` in the CSS file. If you search for this, you'll come upon its definition:

```
/** generic menu item link on mouseover **/
a.mainlevel:hover,
#leftcol a.mainlevel:hover,
#leftcolmenu a.mainlevel:hover {
    background-color:#B8B35C;
    color:#000000!important;
    text-decoration:none!important;
}
```

We'll change the `background-color` property to our new color, `#6e6e6e`, a gray color:

```
/** generic menu item link on mouseover **/
a.mainlevel:hover,
#leftcol a.mainlevel:hover,
#leftcolmenu a.mainlevel:hover {
    background-color:#6e6e6e;
    color:#000000!important;
    text-decoration:none!important;
}
```

Changing the Menu Item Borders

Let's look at the definition in the stylesheet for a typical menu entry, which is called `mainlevel`:

```
/** generic menu item **/

.mainlevel  {
    display:block;
    font: bold 11px/25px Arial, Helvetica, sans-serif !important;
    padding-left:15px;
    background:transparent url(../images/bg_mainlevel.gif)
               repeat-x center top;
    font-weight:bold;
    text-decoration:none;
}
```

From this, we see no mention of a border, so the border must be provided by the background image. The background image is only 10 pixels wide, and 2 pixels high, with the top row of pixels in the image a dark green color, the bottom a lighter green. We will replace this background image with a simple dotted, gray border (#808080):

```
/** generic menu item **/

.mainlevel  {
   display:block;
   font: bold 11px/25px Arial, Helvetica, sans-serif !important;
   padding-left:15px;
   border-top:2px #808080 dotted;
   font-weight:bold;
   text-decoration:none;
}
```

Highlighting the Current Menu Item

When you view a page in Mambo, the Itemid in the query string of the URL indicates the menu item corresponding to this page. That means you should be able to highlight the currently chosen menu entry. The currently selected menu entry is marked with an id of active_menu in the page. If you click the **Home** link on the main menu for example, and have a look in the HTML source of the page, you will see this markup:

```
<a href="http://.../index.php?option=com_frontpage&amp;Itemid=1"
   class="mainlevel"
   id="active_menu">
Home</a>
```

However, the CSS class for this is missing from the base Water and Stone templates, so we will need to add it ourselves.

We'll set the background for the currently selected menu item to a dark greeny color. We will also add some margin on the left and right, so that this background color does not overwrite the side border of the menu item, which is provided by the background image for containerbg if you recall. This is our definition for active_menu that we add into the CSS file:

```
#active_menu {
   background: #527428;
   margin-left:2px;
   margin-right:2px;
}
```

The use of the # character is because the class is applied to the element with `id` attribute of `active_menu`.

A good place to add this definition is just before this part of the file, to keep it with the other menu definitions:

```
/* --------------------
mambo module layout
-------------------- */
```

Finishing Off

There are two more steps before we have a "packageable" template. We need to create the template thumbnail, and then complete the metadata in `templateDetails.xml`.

The template thumbnail is easy enough. View the page in your browser, take a screenshot (*Ctrl + Alt + Print Screen* on Windows copies the current screen to your clipboard), and you can paste it into your graphics editor. Crop the image to make sure that it's only got the output of the web page, and not the entire browser window, then resize the image to 200 pixels wide. In most graphics editors, when you resize an image by specifying the width, the height is automatically calculated based on the original ratio of the width to the height. Once the image is resized, save it as a PNG file called `template_thumbnail.png` in the `zaksprings` folder. The next time you hover your mouse cursor over the template in the **Template Manager**, this new thumbnail should pop up.

We also need to complete the rest of the metadata in the `templateDetails.xml` file. First of all, there is the general information about the template, its description, and its authoring:

```
<?xml version="1.0" encoding="iso-8859-1"?>
<mosinstall type="template" version="4.5.3">
    <name>zaksprings</name>
    <creationDate>20/11/06</creationDate>
    <author>packtpublishing</author>
    <copyright>GNU/GPL</copyright>
    <authorEmail>doug@packtpub.com</authorEmail>
    <authorUrl>http://www.packtpub.com</authorUrl>
    <version>1.0</version>
    <description>The Template for Zak Springs Golf Club</description>
```

Underneath this is part of the metadata where you need to list all the files that would be included in the template, all the CSS files (we've used only one), and all the images, or any other files that go in the `images` folder:

```
<files>
  <filename>index.php</filename>
  <filename>template_thumbnail.png</filename>
</files>
<images>
  <filename>images/bg_body.jpg</filename>
  <filename>images/bg_header.jpg</filename>
  <filename>images/bg_inside.jpg</filename>
  <filename>images/bg_leftcol.jpg</filename>
  <filename>images/bg_leftcol_module_th.gif</filename>
  <filename>images/bg_lhm_inside.jpg</filename>
  <filename>images/bg_mainlevel.gif</filename>
  <filename>images/bg_mainlevel_checked.gif</filename>
  <filename>images/bg_mainlevel_right.gif</filename>
  <filename>images/bg_module.jpg</filename>
  <filename>images/bg_module_contenttop.jpg</filename>
  <filename>images/bg_pagenav.jpg</filename>
  <filename>images/bg_spacer.gif</filename>
  <filename>images/bg_topright.jpg</filename>
  <filename>images/file.html</filename>
  <filename>images/img_header.jpg</filename>
  <filename>images/img_header_old.jpg</filename>
  <filename>images/indent1.png</filename>
  <filename>images/indent2.png</filename>
  <filename>images/indent3.png</filename>
  <filename>images/indent4.png</filename>
  <filename>images/indent5.png</filename>
  <filename>images/indent6.png</filename>
  <filename>images/moduletableth.jpg</filename>
  <filename>images/readon.png</filename>
  <filename>images/readon_hover.png</filename>
</images>
<css>
  <filename>css/template_css.css</filename>
</css>
```

It is important that you list of all the files in the folders; the reason for doing so is explained in the following part.

Creating a Template Package

We've currently got two Mambo installations on our local development machines (the one with the sample data and the Zak Springs site), so let's test out the template on the other installation. Rather than simply copying the zaksprings folder from one installation to the other, let's create an installable template, which can then be installed on the other site from its Universal Installer.

To create the installable template, simply ZIP up the `zaksprings` folder in to a ZIP archive. Make sure you ZIP up the folder, not just the contents of the folder. (For example, on Windows, right-click on the folder, select **Send To** from the pop-up context menu, then choose **Compressed (zipped) folder**.)

Now you can log in to the administration area of your other installation, go to the Universal Installer, and install the new template in the same way you have installed components and modules earlier in the book.

The importance of specifying all the files in the `templateDetails.xml` file may reveal itself when you attempt to install the new template. During installation, only the files listed in the `<files>` or `<images>` section of the `templateDetails.xml` file will copied from the ZIP file and placed into the template folder on the destination server. Although you might have all the images in the ZIP file, if they're not listed in the `<images>` section of the `templateDetails.xml` file, you won't find them in your newly installed template.

Summary

In this chapter we walked through some basic customizations to one of the standard Water and Stone templates that ship with Mambo.

We began with a discussion of the template file structure, the `templateDetails.xml` file that contains the metadata for the template, and had a look at the `index.php` file in the `template` folder. We saw that Mambo produces XHTML-compliant pages.

We began our customization by first changing the header graphic for the page, then the page background, and then the main content area. This introduced us to the template stylesheet file.

We also made some customization to module display, increasing the spacing between modules, and creating a new title bar for them. We made some further changes to the menus on the page, including highlighting the currently selected menu item.

We finished off by creating the template thumbnail, and completing the `templateDetails.xml` file to allow the template to be installed onto another Mambo site.

12
Deploying and Running Your Site

In this chapter, we will walk through the steps to deploy a Mambo installation onto a remote web server, and set the permissions to allow it function properly.

We will begin by talking about how to upload the standard Mambo installation, and then supplement this with a site that you may have developed locally. After that, we'll see about uploading the local database to your remote site, and finally updating the remote configuration so that all the tweaking to your local site is preserved on the remote server.

Overview of the Process

Our process will be this:

- Upload the files for our local Mambo installation via FTP
- Upload the `installation` folder from the original set of Mambo files via FTP
- Get an empty database ready for Mambo
- Use the web installer to get a basic Mambo site working
- Restore the database from our local installation onto the remote server

The reason for this process, which would seem to involve an extra step of creating a fresh installation and "not using it", is that the fresh installation of Mambo on the remote server allows us to access the administration area, from where we can easily restore the local database, which has all our site data. If we didn't have this fresh Mambo installation, we'd have no Mambo database, and we've have to start poking around on our remote server to restore the database using a tool like phpMyAdmin.

Checking Server Requirements

In this chapter, we are assuming that your remote server supports Apache, MySQL, and PHP. The main difference to look for between your local machine and the remote server is the PHP configuration settings and available extensions. To run properly, Mambo does not require any particular PHP configuration settings to be made, but this could be one area to look into if things aren't behaving as expected.

Mambo makes use of the ZLIB PHP extension, which allows PHP to handle ZIP archives. This is used by Mambo during its Universal Installer process, and you will have to check that the server is configured for this. If your server does not support the ZLIB library, then you can still install extensions; we'll tackle this later in the chapter. The first page of the web installer will tell you if the server is able to support this.

The "captcha" feature for displaying graphical text to prevent automatic comment posting makes use of some PHP graphic functions that require the GD extension. You can check for both these extensions by using the `phpinfo()` function. Create a file called `phpinfo.php` on your remote server, and add these lines:

```php
<?php
phpinfo();
?>
```

When you view this page on your browser, scroll down the long list of information, and you should see both the details of the GD extension, and further down, the ZLIB extension. If you see something like this for the GD extension, it will work fine:

gd	
GD Support	enabled
GD Version	bundled (2.0.28 compatible)
FreeType Support	enabled
FreeType Linkage	with freetype
GIF Read Support	enabled
GIF Create Support	enabled
JPG Support	enabled
PNG Support	enabled
WBMP Support	enabled
XBM Support	enabled

In this chapter, we are assuming that your remote server is running one of the various UNIX operating systems: Linux, or FreeBSD for example. These operating systems for the server, along with Apache, MySQL, and PHP, are probably the most popular setups for web-hosting services.

File System Permissions

File system permissions determine what can be done to a filer or folder, and by whom. "Whom" does not mean a person here, it means a machine user account. File system permissions are a typical stumbling block for many people working with Linux — if something isn't working, it's probably a permission problem!

The reason we are talking about them now is that Mambo often needs to write things to files within its installation. For example, the configuration data is written to the file `configuration.php` when changes are made. When an extension is installed, folders are created, and new files are copied into those folders. The problem is that you don't really want to allow Mambo to be able write to any file in its installation all the time. When we say "Mambo writing to a file", this actually means "any PHP script on the server writing to a file".

The problem isn't the normal operation of Mambo. The problem is that some security vulnerability could arise that could allow some unknown script to be written to your installation. This script could act in a completely malicious way; corrupting files in your installation (since everything would be writable) or grabbing user data and sending it off to some other location on the Internet for some unspeakable purpose.

In other words, we need to allow Mambo write access to certain folders from time to time, but we want to be careful with this. Fortunately, most of the file writing is done only for certain administrative operations that do not take place that often. Mambo can attempt to modify the file system permissions itself, but depending on the configuration of your web-hosting account, the server may not permit these operations, so you will need to make permission changes yourself.

A full discussion of Linux file permissions is beyond the scope of this chapter; but in essence the permissions for a file or folder will be represented by three digits:

- The first digit specifies what the owner of the file or directory can do.
- The second digit specifies what the owner's group can do.
- The third digit specifies what everyone who isn't in the group can do.

For a detailed explanation of the Linux file permissions, you can have a look at the following URL:

`http://en.wikipedia.org/wiki/File_Permissions#Octal_notation`

To allow Mambo to write to files within a particular folder, the permissions for that folder need to be set to `777`. If there is no need to write to the files in the folder, then the folder permissions should be set to `755`. This will allow PHP scripts to be run within the folder.

On your remote server, you will have some form of "control panel" (similar to Mambo's administration area), that allows you to configure various things on your server, including the file and folder permissions. There are a number of such "control panel" tools, (cPanel is one of the most popular ones), and you will be able to see the file and folder permissions something like this:

In this image, the right-hand column shows the file or folder permissions. Here we see that the `administrator` and `cache` folders can be written to (777), but the `components` folder cannot, although PHP scripts can be run from it (755). From your control panel, you will be able to set new values for the permissions.

If you have the ability to connect to the remote server via a secure shell, then setting the permissions can be done with the `chmod` command.

For example, to set the permissions of the `configuration.php` file to allow everyone to read, write, and execute, you would do this:

```
$ chmod 777 configuration.php
```

Or you can set the permissions of folders, and everything within by using the recursive flag, `-r`. The next command sets the permissions of the `images` and `components` folders, and their contents, to 777:

```
$ chmod -r 777 images components
```

Uploading the Mambo Code via FTP

Deploying your site begins by uploading the Mambo files with an FTP client to your web server. You will of course need an FTP account on your remote server for this, which you will likely be able to set up from your server "control panel".

There are lot of files in the standard Mambo installation, over 600 in the `administrator` folder, 130 in the `includes` folder, and close to 200 in the `templates` folder. Unless you want to choose from all the templates included with the standard installation, you do not have to upload these to the web server.

If you don't have an FTP client, you can download the excellent CoreFTP from `www.coreftp.com`, or FileZilla from `http://filezilla.sourceforge.net/`.

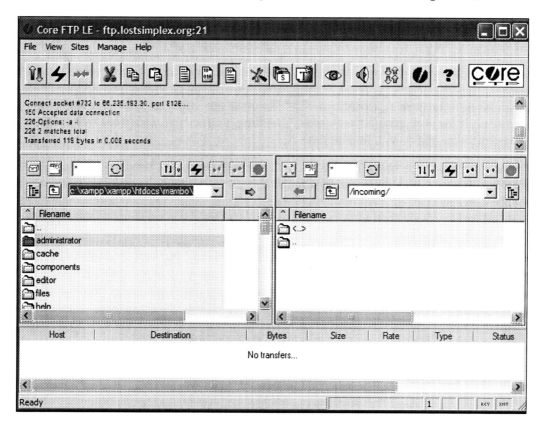

On our local machine, our Mambo installations were of the form `http://localhost/mambo`, the files living in a folder called `mambo` in the document root of our local web server installation.

If you upload the `mambo` folder to your remote server, then your site will have a URL of the form `http://<yoursite.com>/mambo`, which may not be what you want; you may want the site to simply be of the form `http://<yoursite.com>/`. This means that you will have to upload the contents of the `mambo` folder on the local machine into the document root of your remote server, which will be called something like `public_html` or `htdocs`.

To begin our deployment process, upload the files from our local Mambo installation onto your remote server.

If you still have a copy of the `installation` folder in your local Mambo installation (if you do, you must have renamed it!), then make sure that is uploaded as well, and once its uploaded, rename it back to `installation`. If you deleted the `installation` folder from your local Mambo installation, then grab a copy of that folder from your original download of the Mambo files, and upload it to your remote server.

Once everything is uploaded, and the files are copied to your web root (on some servers the location of uploaded FTP files and the document root of the web server are often different), you can enter the URL of your site into your browser, and you'll be met with the web installer welcome. This time, you will probably see that all the file permissions show as **Unwriteable**.

For now, this isn't too much of a problem. You don't have to worry about these folders being unwriteable to install Mambo. It will install quite happily with these folders unwriteable.

Setting Permissions for configuration.php

The problem here is setting the permissions of the `configuration.php` file into which the configuration settings will be written. It's a problem because the file doesn't exist!

There are two ways to solve this problem. The first is to create a file called `configuration.php` in your remote Mambo installation, and set its permissions to `777`. You don't need to put anything in this file at the moment; its about to be replaced during the installation process.

If your remote Mambo installation is inside a folder in your document root, rather than sitting directly in the document root, you can set the permissions for this containing folder to `777` before beginning the installation process. After the installation process, remember to reset the permissions of the containing folder to `755`.

Creating the Database

On our local installation, we used a MySQL account that had permssions to create databases, the `root` MySQL account. On your server, you may not be quite so fortunate, and may not have direct access to an account with such power.

Instead, you may have to work with your web server's control panel to create the database. Possibly your web hosting account can't actually create databases, and instead, your account comes set up with a number of databases that you will have to choose from for your Mambo database.

Once you have a blank database for Mambo selected, and have chosen a database user that has permissions to create tables in this database, you are ready to begin the installation process. Don't forget to make a note the details of the database and the database user, since you will need them in the web installer.

Running the Web Installer

Once you've set the permissions for the folder containing your Mambo installation, and created (or chosen) the database and the MySQL user account to go with it, you are ready to run the web installer. Step through the pages, filling in the details, making sure that you pick a password different from **admin** for the admin account! You don't need to worry about the sample data on this site, we're about to replace the database completely.

Once the web installer has finished, remove the `installation` folder from your Mambo installation, and the front end of the site can be seen, and also, you can log into the administration area.

Migrating the Locally Created Database

Our next step is to move the data from your local site onto your Mambo server installation.

We begin by making a backup of the local database we want to migrate.

Backing Up the Database

Backing up your database can be done from the **Backup Database** option of the **Components | MOStlyDBAdmin DB Tools** menu. This component comes with the standard Mambo installation, but not Mambo Lite, and it would need to installed separately if you are using Mambo Lite.

You select what you want done with the backup; whether it should be displayed on the screen, downloaded to your browser so you can save it locally, or saved directly onto the server. You can also choose the format of the backup, a ZIP file or a text file for example, and even choose to back up only certain tables. The default choice is to back up all the tables in the Mambo database.

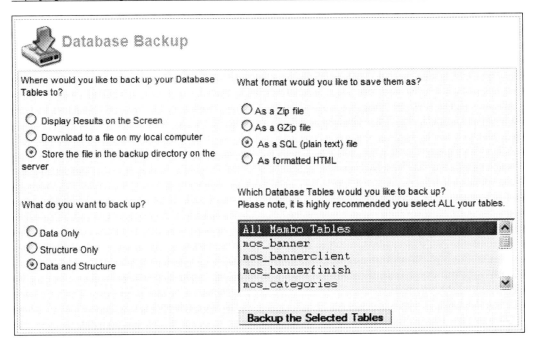

Click the **Backup the Selected Tables** option, and your backup will be created. A message like the following will greet you, which shows the filename of the backup file just created:

```
Database backup successful!Your file was saved on the server in
directory :
.../administrator/backups/mambo466rc2_20082006184554.sql
```

Restoring the Database to the Remote Server

Grab a copy of the database you just backed up (you'll find it in the `backups` folder in the `administration` folder of your local testing machine). Before restoring a database to the remote server, it is probably worth switching the site off (from the **Site** tab of the **Global Configuration**), just in case there is some problem.

Restoring a copy of your database can be done from the **Restore Database** option of the **Components | MOStlyDB Admin DB Tools** menu. You will be presented with a list of any backups stored in the `backups` folder on the remote server.

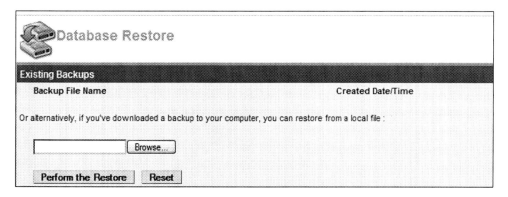

There is no need to upload a backup to your remote site by FTP; you can upload from this screen by clicking the **Browse** button and selecting the database backup file.

Before we can get this all to work, we need to make another file system permission change. When the database backup is uploaded to the remove server, Mambo copies it into the `uploadfiles` folder in the root of your Mambo installation, so that folder will need its permissions set to 777 before you attempt to restore the database. Once you've restored the database, you can change the permissions back to 644 to secure it from writing.

Once the file has uploaded, click **Perform the Restore**, and the information in the database backup is processed and the database restored. Success will bring a message like this:

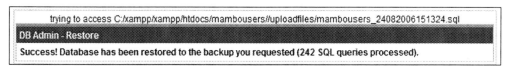

Replacing the Site Configuration

If you spent a long time configuring your local site, and want your remote site to be configured in the same way, you can simply replace `configuration.php` on the remote server with `configuration.php` from your local machine.

However, there are a couple of things that will probably need to be changed from the local `configuration.php` file. For your remote configuration file, you will want to make sure you've got the correct database settings from your remote configuration, and also the path to the installation and the URL of the live site. These are the main lines in the `configuration.php file` that need attention:

```
$mosConfig_host = 'localhost';
$mosConfig_user = 'mamboer';
$mosConfig_password = 'mamb071Passv0rd';
$mosConfig_db = 'mambo';
$mosConfig_dbprefix = 'mos_';
$mosConfig_absolute_path = 'C:/apachefriends/xampp/htdocs/mambo/';
$mosConfig_live_site = 'http://<YOURSITE>/mambo';
```

After that, you will want to make sure anything that refers to a "path" or a URL is pointing to the remote server rather than your machine. For example, the cache path will need to be updated before you upload the local configuration.php file:

```
$mosConfig_cachepath = 'C:/apachefriends/xampp/htdocs/mambo/cache';
```

It's easiest to make these changes to a copy of the local configuration.php file before you upload it to the remote server, because you can copy the information directly from the remote file and include it in the local copy. This is another benefit of following the process of creating a fresh installation on the remote server; we don't have to look around for the details to connect to the database, or work out the paths on the remote server, we can just take the details straight from the remote configuration.php file!

Once you've made your changes, upload the modified local configuration file to your remote server, and your new site is ready for action!

Resetting the Permissions of Your Installation

At this point, its probably worth resetting the permissions of the folder containing your Mambo installation on the remote server back to 755, but then setting the permissions of the configuration.php file itself to 777 (since changing the permissions on the folder will likely change the permissions of the files in the folder). This means that you will be able to write configuration changes. Rather than leaving the entire Mambo installation with the 777 permissions, we'll just set the permissions of this single file. In general, you do not want all of the files in your installation to be writeable by anyone, since this opens a possible security hole.

Although Mambo makes an attempt to change the permissions of various files and folders, it is likely that your server will not permit these operations (except possibly to lower the permissions — 777 to 755 for example, but then it can't change it back!), and you will have to work with your server control panel to change permissions yourself.

During its normal running Mambo does not perform a lot of writing to the files and folders in the installation. It is only really when installing new extensions, or making configuration changes, that Mambo needs access to the file system. We'll talk about these permission settings in a moment.

Rename the Super Administrator Account

Since anyone attempting to infiltrate your site only has to put /administrator onto the end of the site URL and they've got to the login page of your administration area, you had better make sure that the Super Administrator account cannot be cracked very easily. By default, it's called **admin**, so that would be the first guess of any villain.

You can change the username of the Super Administrator account from the User Manager, so make sure you do this before going any further. And make sure the password is not **admin** either!!!

Setting Permissions for Mambo Operations

We've talked about the file system permissions, and their importance for allowing Mambo to go about its business. During its normal running Mambo does not perform a lot of writing to the files and folders in the installation. It is only really when installing new extensions, or making configuration changes, that Mambo needs access to the file system. Here we'll look at some of the common Mambo tasks, and the permission settings needed to get them working.

Configuration Settings

Whenever you need to make configuration changes, you will need to reset the privileges of the configuration.php file to 777. After the changes have been saved, it is wise to restore these to their original values. Although Mambo can attempt to change the permissions itself, this operation could fail on your web host depending on the way your server has been configured for you.

Media Uploading

One folder that will definitely need to be writeable is the images/stories folder. This is where resources are uploaded to by the Media Manager. To allow the Media Manager to operate properly, you will need to set the permissions for images/stories to 777.

Caching

For caching to work properly, you will need to set the `cache` folder in your Mambo installation to writeable. If you have chosen another folder to cache to (this can be done from the **Cache** tab of the **Global Configuration** page) then obviously that folder needs to be writeable.

Modules that display RSS feeds can use caching as we saw in Chapter 5. This cache is stored in a different place, in `includes\magpie_cache`. You will need to make this folder writeable to cache RSS feeds for your modules.

Database Backup Permissions

If you use Mambo's tool for backing up your database, and attempt to store the database backups on the server along with your Mambo installation, they will be stored in the `administrator/backups` folder. Again, you will want to make this folder writeable before you attempt to create a backup of your site's database, or writing the backup will fail.

When attempting to restore a database backup, the `uploadfiles` folder in the root of your installation needs to be writeable as we mentioned earlier.

Installing Extensions or Templates

To install extensions, the folder into which they will be installed needs to be writeable. However, since an extension may have a front-end and a back-end part, you will need to make sure that both folders are made writeable.

For example, to install a component, you will need to set the permissions of the `components` folder to `777`. You will also need to set the permissions of the `administrator/components` folder to `777`.

As you install an extension with the Universal Installer, it should report errors. Sometimes, however, it may not do, and it might appear that your extension has been installed, since it's on the list of components, for example. However, when you look in the `components` folder, you don't see any code for it. You can detect this kind of thing from looking at, say, the list of Installed Components:

You will see the zOOm Media Gallery component has no information, suggesting that not everything is as it seems with that component, and it should be deinstalled straightaway before attempting to reconfigure and reinstall. When uninstalling a "phantom" extension (namely one that Mambo says is installed, of which you can't find any evidence), Mambo may report some errors, but the overall procedure should be successful.

A module is generally either a Site module or an Administrator Module. A Site module only needs permissions to the `modules` folder in the root of the Mambo installation; it does not need access to the `administrator` folder. Although the module has an administrative aspect, this is taken care of by the XML file that accompanies the module PHP file in the `modules` folder. Administrator modules, namely modules that work only on the back end of the site, need permissions to the `administrator/modules` folder.

If you want to install new templates, you will need to set the `templates` folder to be writeable while you install the new template.

After installing your extension, you can reset the permissions of any of the folders involved in the installation back to 755 for security.

Installing Extensions without ZLIB

The ZLIB PHP extension allows PHP to work with ZIP archives, and extract files from (or add files to) the archive. Your server may not support this extension, and uploading extensions to your Mambo site may fail because of this.

If this is the case, you will first need to extract the files locally, and then upload them to a folder on your remote server. You can install them from the **Install from Directory** option of the Universal Installer. To do this, you will need either to know the full path (on the server) of the folder where you uploaded the extension files, or if you can't work that out, to create a folder inside the `administration` folder, and copy the folder with the extension files into that folder.

The screenshot overleaf shows attempting to install a component copied to a folder called `tobeuploaded` in the `administrator` folder. Mambo will look for the folder relative to the `administrator` folder if you don't specify the full path to the folder.

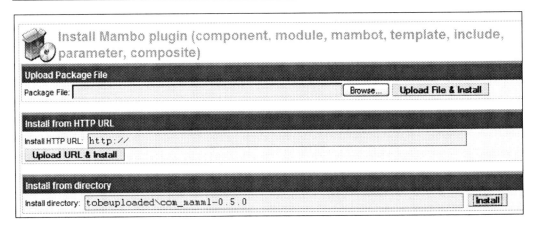

Click the **Install** button on the **Install from Directory** panel and (provided you've set the permissions properly for the folders into which the various parts of the extensions need to go, as discussed above) the files will be distributed where they are supposed to go, and the extension will be installed.

Restricting Access to Folders

Although there are an awful lot of PHP scripts in the Mambo installation, only a handful of these are actually accessed by a browser. The different variables in the querystring are used by Mambo to decide which other files to include and process. What this means is that you can restrict browser access to a number of folders in the Mambo installation without affecting your site. This effectively increases the security of your site, since visitors are not able to go to places where they shouldn't.

In general, pages do not need to be requested from folders like `components`, `modules`, `language`, and `cache`. These folders contain mostly PHP or XML files that are used directly by Mambo. There is nothing in here that a visitor should be requesting directly.

The `includes` folder is another folder that feels like it shouldn't contain any directly requested files, but there are some JavaScript files in there that will be needed by browsers.

The `templates` folder and the `images` folder contain files that browsers will need to access: images, CSS files, JavaScript files, and so on. The `mambots` folder should not really allow access, except that the `editors` folder contains the HTML editors, which have a number of resources that web browsers need to use them (JavaScripts, images, and so on).

The easiest way to restrict browser access is through the use of `.htaccess` files. Your Mambo installation has an `.htaccess` file supplied with it, (its called `htaccess.txt` by default). This is the file you need if you want to turn on the search-engine friendly URLs. You can restrict access to the folders we mentioned above by adding the highlighted lines below to the end of the file:

```
RewriteCond %{REQUEST_FILENAME} !-f
RewriteCond %{REQUEST_FILENAME} !-d
RewriteRule ^content/(.*) index3.php
RewriteRule ^component/(.*) index3.php
RewriteRule ^mos/(.*) index3.php
RewriteRule ^modules/(.*) index3.php
RewriteRule ^language/(.*) index3.php
RewriteRule ^cache/(.*) index3.php
```

These lines simply add some extra rewriting rules. For example, any request that begins with `modules` will be sent to `index3.php`, and any thing in the request after the initial `modules/` part will be discarded.

These rules need to be added to the end of the file because there are some rewrite rules used by Mambo's search-engine friendly URL mechanism earlier in the file. These need to be dealt with before we restrict access to the folders, since some of these rules actually involve the folders in question.

If you want to use the `.htaccess` file for restricting access, but don't want to turn on the search-engine friendly URLs, that's fine. Turning on the search-engine friendly URLs is a two-stage process: first of all, Mambo processes any URL pointing to part of the site into the friendlier form, and then the `.htaccess` file processes these friendly URLs back into a form understood by Mambo internally.

Restricting Access to the Administrator Area

The administrator area of any Mambo installation will be in the `administrator` folder. Renaming or moving the administrator area is problematic in the current version of Mambo. This means that any visitor to your site can easily locate the administrator area and start trying username and password combinations to gain access to your most precious place. One way to add an extra layer of security is to use HTTP Authentication. HTTP Authentication requires a visitor to enter a username and password into a dialog box before they can continue:

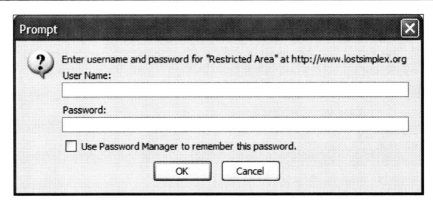

If your server supports SSL, then you can access the administrator area under HTTPS, which adds another layer of security to all of this.

On your remote server, your control panel may allow you to protect certain folders with passwords, which would take care of this process for us. If you don't have that feature on your remote server, you can set up HTTP Authentication with an .htaccess file in the administrator folder. Create a file called .htaccess, and add this text:

```
AuthName "Restricted Area"
AuthType Basic
AuthUserFile /home/.htpasswds
Require valid-user
```

The important line is AuthUserFile, which specifies the location of the password file. You can create the password file using the htpasswd utility supplied with Apache in your local XAMPP installation. This file is located in the bin folder of the apache folder in your XAMPP installation, and is used like this, from the command-line:

```
htpasswd -c "c:\passwords\mypasswords" secretuser
```

This command creates a file for holding usernames and passwords (called mypasswords) in a folder called passwords. The first user to be added is secretuser. After entering this command, you will be prompted for the password for secretuser, and then asked to confirm it:

```
C:\apachefriends\xampp\apache\bin>htpasswd -c
                          "c:\passwords\mypasswords" secretuser
Automatically using MD5 format.
New password: *******
Re-type new password: *******
Adding password for user secretuser
```

The password file is simply a text file, with the username followed by an encrypted version of the password:

```
secretuser:$apr1$UQ1.....$A0wq13rxrbSNFKADay.qi
```

You can add another username and password to the file by using the `htpasswd` command again:

```
C:\apachefriends\xampp\apache\bin>htpasswd -c
                        "c:\passwords\mypasswords" anotheruser
```

You will be prompted for the password for this user, and the details will be saved to your passwords file.

Once you've created your password file, you can upload it to your remote server, and ensure that the `AuthUserFile` line of the `.htaccess` file points to the uploaded file. Since this is a text file with usernames, you want to make sure that this file is not in the document root of your web server, so that it can't be requested by a browser. If the path to the password file is wrong, you will be asked for the username and password over and over again when you browse to the folder, since the server can't find a file to check the passwords against!

If you are having problems with the exact path to your password file on the remote server, have a look in the Mambo configuration file for some of the paths in there:

```
$mosConfig_absolute_path = '/home/zaksprings/public_html/..';
```

If you have put your passwords file off the web root, so it's in the folder above `public_html`, then the path to the folder containing the passwords file would be `/home/zaksprings/` in this case.

Summary

In this chapter, we walked through the steps to deploy a Mambo installation onto a remote web server, and set the permissions to allow it function properly. Creating a new installation of Mambo on the remote server isn't too big a problem, the twist here was to take all the data from the local installation and migrate it to the remote site.

We began with an overview of the process to follow:

- Upload the files for our local Mambo installation via FTP
- Upload the `installation` folder from the original set of files Mambo via FTP
- Get an empty database ready for Mambo
- Use the web installer to get a basic Mambo site working
- Restore the database from our local installation onto the remote server

We discussed file system permissions, since Mambo needs to write files into various folders during parts of its operation, and it is important to set these properly to avoid failure of various activities.

We saw how to back up and restore the Mambo database from the administration area of Mambo, and then had a look at a number of common Mambo administrative tasks and the permission settings needed to get them working.

A
Installing XAMPP

In this appendix we will walk through downloading, installing, and setting up the XAMPP package. XAMPP is a free package that has a collection of free applications assembled to provide you with an easy-to-set up web server (Apache), database server (MySQL), and server-side scripting language (PHP). XAMPP lets you experiment with these technologies and develop your own web applications.

Setting up an AMP (Apache, MySQL, PHP) environment has typically required configuring the different applications to work on their own, and then to work with each other. With XAMPP this interplay has already been set up for you, and the system comes ready configured and ready to go. In addition to being easy to get started, XAMPP includes a number of useful extensions, code libraries, and other applications, all already configured so you don't need to spend a long time trying to get them working together.

Note that we are installing XAMPP here as a 'development' or 'testing' environment only. We will only be using XAMPP for testing and exploring the technologies, and not as a 'production' environment for serving our website to the outside world. Setting up a production web server and a database server, and securing and optimizing them is a topic beyond the scope of this text.

There are versions of the XAMPP package available for Windows, Linux, Mac OS X, and the Solaris operating system. XAMPP is free to download, and the package contains the following:

- The AMP environment of Apache 2, MySQL 5, and PHP versions 4 and 5.
- Lots of PHP extensions, which add extra functionality. In particular, the extensions required by Mambo are all in the XAMPP installation.

- phpMyAdmin, the leading web-based interface to MySQL.

- The PEAR library. PEAR (PHP Extension and Application Repository) is a framework for reusable PHP components, and is a favorite among professional PHP developers. You can find out more about PEAR at `pear.php.net`.

- An implementation of OpenSSL for running your site under HTTPS.

The advantage of the XAMPP package is that everything you need is collected together for you, tested, and ready to go. The downside is that you will have a very large file to download. On the brighter side, you only have to download one file rather than downloading lots of files, and then trying to get them working.

The home of the XAMPP package is the site `www.apachefriends.org/en/`. The installation walkthrough in this chapter may not solve all your problems, and only covers Windows. If you find yourself in need of further help, check out the XAMPP documentation page at:

```
http://www.apachefriends.org/en/faq-xampp.html
```

Details of the XAMPP package itself can be found at:

```
http://www.apachefriends.org/en/xampp.html
```

On that page, you will find a link to the XAMPP version for your particular operating system. We will be choosing XAMPP for Windows. Clicking the **XAMPP for Windows** link on this page brings you to:

```
http://www.apachefriends.org/en/xampp-windows.html
```

You will find that there are several options for downloading XAMPP. First, you can choose one of three types of package:

- XAMPP

- XAMPP add-ons

- XAMPP Lite

Each of these packages is available in different download formats, a Windows installer file, a ZIP file, or a self-extracting 7-ZIP archive:

XAMPP for Windows 1.5.5, November 26th 2006		
Version	**Size**	**Content**
XAMPP Windows 1.5.5 [Basic package]		Apache HTTPD 2.2.3, MySQL 5.0.27, PHP 5.2.0 + 4.4.4 + PEAR + Switch, MiniPerl 5.8.7, Openssl 0.9.8d, phpMyAdmin 2.9.1.1, XAMPP Control Panel 2.3, Webalizer 2.01-10, Mercury Mail Transport System für Win32 und NetWare Systems v4.01a, FileZilla FTP Server 0.9.20, SQLite 2.8.15, ADODB 4.93, Zend Optimizer 3.0.2, XAMPP Security. For Windows 98, 2000, XP. See also ⊠ README
⊠ Installer [MD5]	33 MB	Installer
⊠ ZIP [MD5]	86 MB	ZIP archive
⊠ EXE (7-zip) [MD5]	28 MB	Selfextracting 7-ZIP archive

We will be choosing the **Installer** version of the Basic XAMPP package. This is some 33MB to download.

There is also a XAMPP Lite package that is about half the size of the full XAMPP package, but it does contain everything that you will need to run the code in this book. However, the Lite package does not come as a Windows installer.

Clicking the **Installer** link takes you to a page where you select the 'nearest' SourceForge mirror site from which to download the file. You can download the file from any of the sites listed, so you might want to pick the one nearest to you. The downloaded file will have a filename of the form:

```
xampp-win32-1.5.5-installer.exe
```

The 1.5.5 part is the current XAMPP version.

We will install the XAMP package into a folder called c:\apachefriends\. Before we begin, create that folder.

We begin by double-clicking on the file, and we will be presented with a dropdown to choose the language of our installation. Select **English** and click **OK** to move on to the welcome page, which displays a simple message, and you can click **Next** to move to the start of the process.

You will be presented with a dialog asking you to choose the location for XAMPP to install its files into. XAMPP will create a folder called xampp in the **Destination Folder** specified, and add its files in there. Clicking the **Browse** button allows you to choose our apachefriends folder.

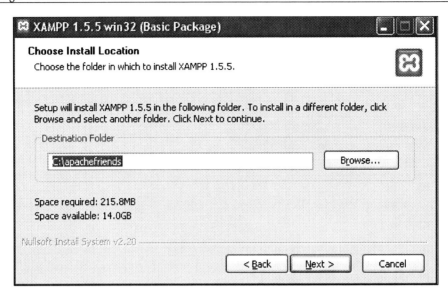

Click **Next**, which will allow you to choose XAMPP install options:

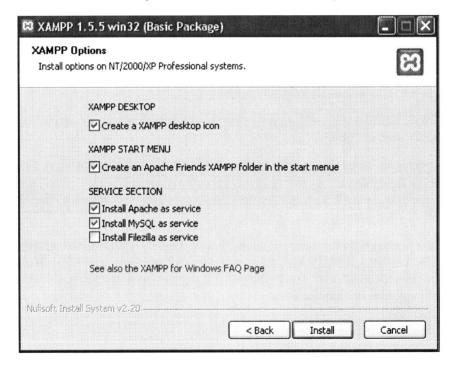

In the **SERVICE SECTION** choose the **Install Apache as service** and **Install MySQL as service** options. You can keep the the last option to install Filezilla as a service unchecked since we don't have any need to run an FTP server in this book.

 If you are running the IIS server or Skype VOIP application, then exit them before attempting to install Apache as a Windows Service. Otherwise, the Apache service will fail to install as a Windows Service, with XAMPP reporting a problem with port 443 (for Skype) or port 80 (for IIS).

Click **Install** to continue and the installation begins. The files are extracted and copied to the specified folder. A command-line window will open at one point, right before the end; do not be disturbed by that. After the command-line window closes, the installation is complete, and you are presented with the end screen. Click **Finish** to complete the installation.

After this, you are presented with a congratulatory message, and an option to view the **Control Panel**:

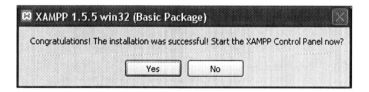

The XAMPP Control Panel is used to control and monitor the status of the services that XAMPP has installed. When the Control Panel is running, you will see an icon like:

in your System Tray, and you can double-click it to get the XAMPP Control Panel back on your screen. If you have closed the Control Panel, you can open it again from **Start | Programs | apachefriends | XAMPP | XAMPP Control Panel**. Alternatively, you can control and monitor these services in the usual way from the Windows Control Panel (**Start | Settings | Control Panel**) by using the **Services** area found in **Administrative Tools**.

With our servers installed as services, we are ready to go. Open up your browser, and enter `http://localhost/` into the navigation bar. You should see the following splash screen, inviting you to select a language. We will select **English**:

Now you will be taken to your XAMPP homepage. In future you will be taken directly to this page when you enter `http://localhost/` into your browser, bypassing the language splash screen.

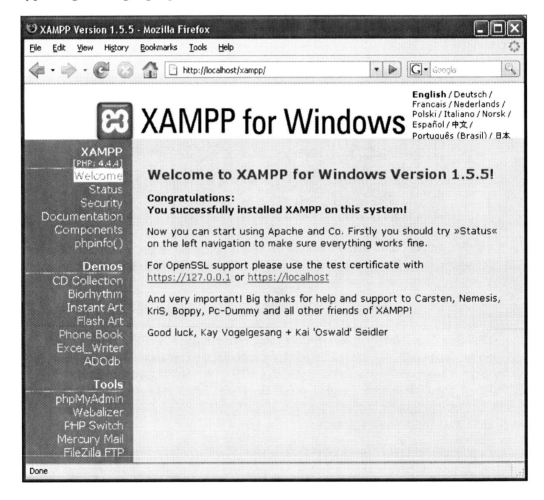

You will find a range of options in the left-hand panel for you to test out what comes with XAMPP. Of particular interest is **phpMyAdmin**, which we will be making use of in many parts of the book, and which is likely to become a very important tool as you work more with PHP and MySQL. You can click the link in the left-hand panel, or enter its URL (`http://localhost/phpMyAdmin/`) directly into the browser to get started with it.

By default, XAMPP is configured to run PHP 5. If you want to switch to PHP 4, then you will find a file called `php-switch.bat` in the `apachefriends\xampp\` folder that allows you to make the switch between PHP 5 and PHP 4 (and back again). However, before you can use it you need to stop the Apache Service.

Open up the XAMPP Control Panel, and click the **Stop** button next to the Apache service. You should see a message reporting the service has been stopped:

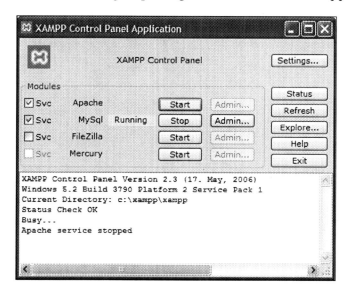

Now double-click the file `php-switch.bat` in the `apachefriends\xampp` folder, and a command-line window will open, and you will be prompted to choose the version of PHP.

Simply press 4 followed by *Enter*, and XAMPP will switch over to PHP 4 for you. Once it has completed, you will see a message containing this report:

```
OKAY ... PHP SWITCHING WAS SUCCESSFUL
```

Press any key to close the window. You will now have to restart Apache from the Control Panel by clicking the **Start** button, and then you can return to your browser and visit your XAMPP home page. Once you are finished with the Control Panel, click **Exit** to shut it down.

You can use `php-switch.bat` to switch back to PHP 5 again if you want to continue working with PHP 5, but remember to stop the Apache service before using it.

Before we finish off, it's worth noting two important folders in your XAMPP installation.

- `C:\Program Files\apachefriends\xampp\htdocs`: This folder is your 'document root'. A file placed in this folder will be made available by the web server. We will be copying our installation of Mambo into this folder to get it working properly.

- `apache`: This folder contains a file called `apache_installservice.bat`. If Apache failed to install as a service during the installation process, then you can run this file to try again.

Your XAMPP installation is now set up and working, and you are ready to begin installing Mambo.

Index

S

sections
  copying 187
  creating 158-160
  deleting 187
  for Zak Spring 159
  managing 187
  section manager 159, 160
site modules
  custom HTML module, adding 95-97
  managing 85-87
  module copy, creating 97-100
  module details 89
  module instances, deleting 101
  module parameters 90-92
  module position 87
  module properties, editing 88-92
  new module instance, adding 92-101
  pages/items 89, 90
  RSS feed module, adding 92-94
spams
  from comments, preventing 207
standard extensions, Mambo
  banners 213, 214
  news feeds 212
  polls 211
  syndicate 212, 213
  uploading image, banners 213
static content
  about 156
  for Zak Springs 184-186
  views 183

T

templates
  creating 243-249
  customizing 241
  customizing, prerequisites for 241, 242
  details, changing 243
  file structure 243
  folder structure 243
  index.php 244
  links to images, template file 247
  managing 131-133
  menus, customizing 267
  modules, customizing 263

no layout information, template file 247
  page layout, customizing 249
  pages, assigning to 133
  structure, template file 244-246
  template file 244
  template file, no logic used 247
  template package, creating 271
  template thumbnail, creating 270, 271
  XHTML compliance 248, 249
testing environment, XAMPP 297
troubleshooting, installation
  XAMPP Apache service problem 295

U

user managment
  accessing 141-143
  login module, configuring 144
  logout link, adding 145, 146
  new user at back end, creating 147, 148
  registration process 148, 149
  registratrion options, registration process 148
  super administrator details 146, 147
  user details 143, 144
users, Mambo
  administrators, managing 149-151
  back-end groups, user groups 136
  front-end groups, user groups 136
  front-end user goodies 140, 141
  managing 135
  registering as 136-140
  required information 136
  special category, user groups 136
  types, user groups 136
  user groups 135, 136
  user management, user manager used 141-149

V

views, content
  about 176
  blog views 182
  content category view, table views 177-179
  content section view, table views 179-181
  single item view 177
  table views 177

table views, assigning templates 181
types 177

W

Web Links
about 109
categories, creating 109
creating 111

X

XAMPP
about 291
advantage 292
configuring 296, 297
documentation website 292
folder structure 298
installing 291-295
operating system, compatibility 291
package, types 292
package contents 291, 292
port 443 problem 295
port 80 problem 295
version, choosing 293
website, for downloading 292
XAMPP package
about 291
apache folder 298
configuration 296
contents 291
control panel 295
download options 292
htdocs folder 298
installation 293

Installer version 293
php-switch.bat file 297

Z

Zak Spring Golf Club
about 13
administration area, visiting 65, 66
content structure, planning 157, 158
files, putting into web server root 20
functionality, general 15
functionality, specific 15
future developments 16
global configuration 67
installing 64
key objectives, site 15
logo, uploading 83
menus 113
menu structure, planning 125-131
permissions, required 16
president, staff 14
private messages 78, 79
privileges, required 16
site requirements 14
staff 14
staff, administrative 14
staff, golf 14
staff, hospitality 14
user groups 152, 153
users 152, 153
zOOm Media Gallery component
about 230
galleries, creating 231, 232
images, adding 232-238
managing 230, 231

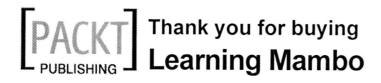

Thank you for buying
Learning Mambo

Packt Open Source Project Royalties

When we sell a book written on an Open Source project, we pay a royalty directly to that project. Therefore by purchasing Learning Mambo, Packt will have given some of the money received to the Mambo project.

In the long term, we see ourselves and you—customers and readers of our books—as part of the Open Source ecosystem, providing sustainable revenue for the projects we publish on. Our aim at Packt is to establish publishing royalties as an essential part of the service and support a business model that sustains Open Source.

If you're working with an Open Source project that you would like us to publish on, and subsequently pay royalties to, please get in touch with us.

Writing for Packt

We welcome all inquiries from people who are interested in authoring. Book proposals should be sent to authors@packtpub.com. If your book idea is still at an early stage and you would like to discuss it first before writing a formal book proposal, contact us; one of our commissioning editors will get in touch with you.

We're not just looking for published authors; if you have strong technical skills but no writing experience, our experienced editors can help you develop a writing career, or simply get some additional reward for your expertise.

About Packt Publishing

Packt, pronounced 'packed', published its first book "Mastering phpMyAdmin for Effective MySQL Management" in April 2004 and subsequently continued to specialize in publishing highly focused books on specific technologies and solutions.

Our books and publications share the experiences of your fellow IT professionals in adapting and customizing today's systems, applications, and frameworks. Our solution-based books give you the knowledge and power to customize the software and technologies you're using to get the job done. Packt books are more specific and less general than the IT books you have seen in the past. Our unique business model allows us to bring you more focused information, giving you more of what you need to know, and less of what you don't.

Packt is a modern, yet unique publishing company, which focuses on producing quality, cutting-edge books for communities of developers, administrators, and newbies alike. For more information, please visit our website: www.PacktPub.com.

Mastering Mambo : E-Commerce, Templates, Module Development, SEO, Security, and Performance

ISBN: 1-904811-51-5   Paperback: 270 pages

An advanced level guide to customizing and extending.

1. Create custom layouts, modules, Mambots, set up an e-commerce store, and more

2. Make your site multilingual, accessible, and optimized for speed and search engines

3. Master DOCMAN, the document manager for Mambo, to turn your Mambo site into a dynamic repository of shared documents and files

4. Avoid common security traps and pitfalls and learn how attackers think

Drupal: Creating Blogs, Forums, Portals, and Community Websites

ISBN: 1-904811-80-9   Paperback: 267 pages

How to setup, configure and customise this powerful PHP/MySQL based Open Source CMS.

1. Install, configure, administer, maintain and extend Drupal

2. Control access with users, roles and permissions

3. Structure your content using Drupal's powerful CMS features

Please check **www.PacktPub.com** for information on our titles

Printed in the United Kingdom
by Lightning Source UK Ltd.
122790UK00001BB/141-144/A